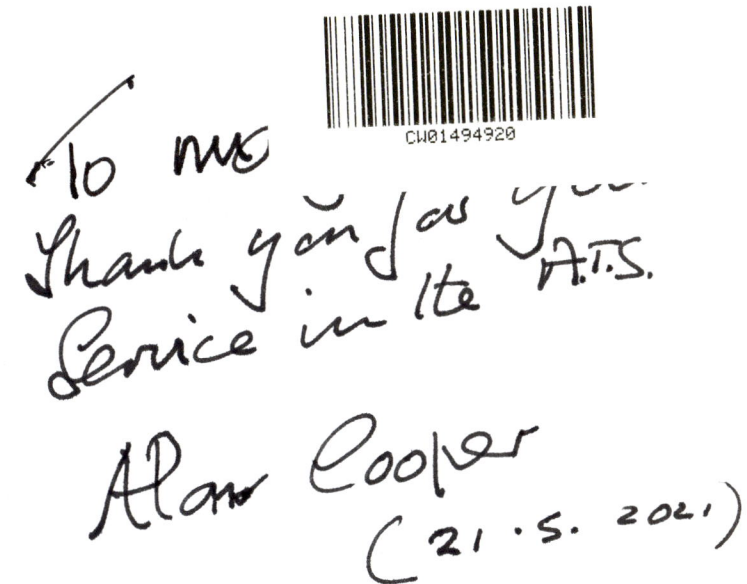

To me

Thanks you as you

Service in the A.T.S.

Alan Cooper

(21 . 5 . 2021)

Soldiers in Petticoats

Soldiers in Petticoats

Britain's Women in the Second World War

Alan Cooper

MENTION
THE WAR
PUBLICATIONS

First published in the United Kingdom in 2018 by Mention the War Ltd. Leeds LS28 5HA, England.

Previously published as *The Gentle Sex* by J & KH Publishing (Aug. 1999) and since re-edited.

Cover design: Topics – The Creative Partnership www.topicdesign.co.uk
Cover image: *Sgt. Joan Turner MM at RAF Biggin Hill, 1940* (Author).

A CIP catalogue reference for this book is available from the British Library

ISBN 978-1-911255-32-1

Contents

Dedication 6

Sources and Acknowledgements 7

Foreword.. 9

Chapter 1 Women's Role in War 11

Chapter 2 WRNS.. 13

Chapter 3 The ATS.. 38

Chapter 4 WAAF.. 78

Chapter 5 Air Transport Auxiliary 133

Chapter 6 Military / Civilian Nurses 144

Chapter 7 The Home Defences 169

Chapter 8 Industrial Work... 202

Chapter 9 FANY 220

Chapter 10 Entertainment 227

Chapter 11 Women's Land Army / Timber Corps....... 240

Chapter 12 The Civilian Services 253

Chapter 13 Prisoners of War....................................... 265

Chapter 14 Casualties and Awards 280

Chapter 15 They Were Also There............................... 305

Dedication

To Dad, whose brainchild this book was, but which sadly he did not live to see come to fruition.

A special thanks to Hilda, my wife, for continued support, encouragement and help whenever it was required.

Alan Cooper

Sources and Acknowledgements

Air Historical Branch – Graham Day
Association of Wrens
ATA Association, especially Commodore Diana Barnato-Walker MBE
Ivy Benson
Eric Braun
The British Red Cross Society
Commonwealth War Graves Commission
Drury Lane Museum / Archives
FANY Association
Girl Guide Association
The Goon Show Association
Graham Hallowes
Dame Joan Hammond DBE CMG
Lincolnshire Bomber Airfield Society
Ministry of Defence, the Admiralty and Director of the WRNS
MOD Library
Lady Mountbatten (who gave her invaluable time to see me)
NAAFI
Newspapers all around the UK
Michael Ockenden
Public Records Office (now The National Archives)
Star & Garter Home
Sheila Tracey
WAAF Association
WRVS

Third Officer Patricia Mountbatten in 1946 (Countess Mountbatten of Burma).

FOREWORD

by

The Countess Mountbatten of Burma

After three very eventful years in the Womens Royal Naval Service, from 1943 to 1946, I am particularly pleased that Alan Cooper has produced a book recording the whole range of war work undertaken by women. I am sure readers will be amazed by the variety of work undertaken by women in order to free the men for the actual fighting, and by the magnitude of the contribution towards winning the last war which was made by women.

This ability, when called upon, to do a man's job as well as any man could, came as a surprise to many people who, in the 1940s, still thought of women basically as only occupying themselves with their families and homes.

Their endurance, ability and fortitude shines through the pages of this book, which is a valuable record of many surprising first-hand accounts, and answers to the question "What did you do in the war — Mother?"

Patricia Mountbatten of Burma

Chapter 1 Women's Role in War

Until April 1941, the only method of employing women was by an appeal for volunteers. The change came after a concentration of production in certain industries was announced and supplementary measures taken in Parliament which released the work of women. The London Clothing Trade, for example, was asked to release 50% of its employees. Between March and December 1941, 250,000 women were transferred from non-essential to essential work. In April 1941, women were compelled under the Registration for Employment Order to register for employment and were registered in age groups. Any unreasonable refusal to register led to prosecution. On 18 December 1941, came the National Service Act which applied to unmarried women between the ages of 20 and 30 years of age. The women who were eligible were interviewed and conscripted for the women's services, civil defence, and essential industries. 50,000 interviews took place per week and vacancies, at a rate of 35,000 a week, were filled.

The population of the UK was 46,750,000 of which 33,250,000 were between the ages of fourteen and 64; of this 33 million, 11 million were married and had about nine million children to care for. Between the ages of 18 and 64 there were 15,800,000 women of which only five million were single.

The women with husbands in the forces, or Merchant Navy, were not compelled to take employment away from home or in the Services. However, if they did not have any domestic responsibilities they were directed into war industry, many had indeed already volunteered.

The 11 million married women in the country were described as "Our largest reserve for industries and home defence for the future." Part-time employment was considered for expansion. The Essential Work Order of 7th January 1942 covered 33,000 undertakings, employing six million men and women. These workers could not leave or be dismissed from their occupation without the authorisation of the Local National Service Officer. Before the end of 1941 women of the same age group were withdrawn from the woollen and worsted industries to transfer to mills engaged to 75% capacity on Government work, or in utility clothing. In November 1941, Post Office women in some classes aged between 20 and 25 were released for transfer to the Services, or munitions. By December 1941, 250,000 women had been transferred from non-essential to essential work. At the end of 1941, under the National Service Act, industrial registration, aliens registration for employment, women's registration for employment and fire watching was 17 million; this rose to 20 million later on. On 23rd July 1942, Mr. Eden said in Nottingham "At home we have good reason to believe our factories are turning out more munitions, in proportion to our population, than those of any other nation."

Over 2,000 women were employed in 625 hostels for evacuated school children, 6,300 were employed in wartime nurseries of which 7,000 were in the open, and 3,000 wartime resident nurseries. Over 11 divisions and 75 local welfare officers were appointed to supervise this work. A number of women were employed as salvage officers, in charge of salvage depots where waste paper could be left, also cotton rags which could be used on gun sites. Such things as saucepans to make aircraft, and iron railings surrounding parks were collected by council lorries. The people were encouraged not to waste anything but to save. Their badge of office was red and made of plastic. Some 16,000 women were employed as post women by the GPO, over 4,000 were Post Office engineers, 26,000 telephonists, 29,000 telegraphists, and others were counter clerks. On the dock quays at the River Tees there were women stevedores earning the same as the men. On the railways there were 41,000 women employed as clerks, porters, cleaners, truck drivers and ticket collectors. In the hospitals 63,000 were employed as domestics, working at least 96 hours a month, many giving unpaid service for shorter periods.

On London Passenger Transport Board, 10,000 women had replaced the men on the buses, trams and on the underground. The Women's Land Army had in 1941 some 40,500 members, and a special WLA Auxiliary force was recruited to do short term seasonal work for a minimum period of four weeks at a time, including forest work. In many counties rural women who were unable to join the WLA were organised into an Emergency Land Corps to give help on farms in the immediate vicinity during the busy seasons.

In the NAAFI service, some 36,500 women were employed all over the UK. In the civilian organisations, such as the St John's Ambulance and the Red Cross Service. In local defences there were 29,000 women fully employed, and 199,000 in part-time employment.

By the time March 1942 came some one million women were working in munitions, vital war industries, or the three services. At the beginning of 1942 more than twice as many guns were being produced as at the peak of production in the 1914/18 war. The supplies to the Army were three times as great as after Dunkirk, and ten times as great as at the outbreak of war in 1939. In June 1942, ammunition for the big guns was being produced at the rate of 25 million rounds per year. Over the period between January 1941 and June 1942, production had nearly trebled.

Chapter 2 WRNS

In 1938, moves were made to form a women's service ancillary to the Navy. It was to be called the Women's Royal Naval Service, its title in WW1, as it seemed impossible to improve upon it and was the only one of the three female services which kept its previous First World War title in the second conflict, having been disbanded in 1919.

The Times reported "Women for the Navy: New Shore Service to be Formed". The new Director to be appointed to the WRNS was Mrs. Vera Laughton Matthews, who had served in the First World War.

At first there was a limited number required, and then only in the Portsmouth, Plymouth and Chatham areas. They signed up for four years and received ten shillings a year to cover expenses. In April 1939, came an official announcement: "About 1,500 women between the ages of 19 and 45 are required for service in the WRNS and enrolment and registration will start immediately. Volunteers had to be British subjects and the daughters of British born parents. In the first instance the corps was raised at the naval ports on an immobile basis, i.e. officers and ratings will only be accepted who will undertake to serve from their own homes in the Portsmouth, Plymouth, Chatham and Rosyth areas."

At the end of September 1939, there were 126 officers and exactly 1,475 ratings, which, by the end of 1940, had risen to 561 officers and 9,439 ratings, pay starting at 1/8d a day.

There was one major difference between the WRNS, the ATS and the WAAF concerning military law; the Army wanted the question of the status of women in uniform under international law to make desertion and other serious offences punishable by civil courts. The Admiralty however decided that, as the WRNS and other serving women were fully covered by The Hague Rules of 1907 and the Geneva Convention of 1929, no action to define their status, whether by Defence Regulations or otherwise, was necessary to secure their protection under International Law, even the Hitler version of it, and even if they undertook full combat duties.

They were, in other simpler words, content with the state of discipline which existed, and the women were put on their honour to obey the rules. The Director, Mrs. Laughton Matthews, wanted the WRNS to come under the Naval Discipline Act and WRNS treated in the same way as ratings; maybe her thinking was that the women would be better accepted by the men if they were on equal ground as far as discipline went. She was, however, overruled and the WRNS never did not come under the Naval Discipline Act as they did in WWI, until 1977. It is interesting to note that, in the present day, the WRNS are to be trained in the use of weapons, whereas the other two services, the WRAC and the WRAF, have been for some five years.

In July 1942, enlistment had reached 30,000 and all ratings, including WRNS, had to pay 5d a week towards the National Health and Pensions Insurance.

The title Wren was adopted as the title of individual members, the ranks being Wren, Leading Wren, Chief Wren and just after the war had started, Petty Officer Wren.

The categories of jobs were divided into specialised and unspecialised, one was cook which at first was unspecialised but soon became specialised. At the outbreak of war there were 384 cooks in the WRNS, by the end of 1940 this had risen to 1,082. Also, in 1940 came courses for WRNS ratings at the RN Cookery School.

In July 1940, Peggy Davies began her WRNS service as a cook in the Painted Hall, at the RN College, Greenwich, replacing the civilian prewar cooks who had been called up for military service. Here she was based for the next two years, but not before she had passed her audition which entailed coping with 34-gallon copper saucepans which were used to cook for an officers' mess of 300 officers, plus a staff of about 50 cooks and stewards. She began as an assistant in the pastry larder but when her boss, whose age was between 38 to 40, was called up to serve as a cook on the Port of London Trawler, she was promoted to Petty Officer Wren and appointed pastry chef, one of four sub chefs, the other three being aged between 40 and 50 and unfit for military service. During the Blitz period of 1940/41 nights were mainly spent in the wine cellars under the college.

Another vital branch was also expanding. Telephonists and Teleprinter Operators went from 247 in 1939, to 500 by the middle of 1940, at first, they were mainly ex-GPO operators. In 1939, the shortage of men in the signals branch became acute and it was decided that women should be trained for this work. At this time Priscilla Fuller was at Drama School and hoping to join ENSA, but with the London Bombing and more theatres closing, it became more and more difficult for actresses to find work. She then saw an advertisement for women to join the forces and applied to be a teleprinter operator, the requirement for which was the ability to type 30 words per minute. She was sent to Greenwich College for a probationary period of two weeks, one to see if she was suitable for the work and the other to see if the Navy suited her. After this period, she was accepted as a HO (Hostilities Only) and was on her way to her first posting at St Martyn's, followed by relief work at Falmouth and Plymouth. In Plymouth work was carried out in converted beer cellars, without beer one hastens to add! A day watch consisted of 8am to 8pm one day, and 8pm to 8am on other days, no less than nine watches were worked straight off in order that the free time or "Off Watch" was extra-long. During these watches a rest period consisted of sleeping on a shelf in a cupboard with one blanket and a pillow, the blanket was always warm from the previous "Rester", snacks were made on an upturned electric fire.

The pioneers of the WRNS serving overseas ended up in Singapore in 1941. They were a party of Chief Wren Telegraphists, in charge of which was second officer Betty Archdale, who, pre-war had been in the All-England women's cricket team which toured Australia. When they arrived in Singapore they found the swimming club only admitted officers, this was later changed when an approach was made by the Navy on behalf of the 20 CPOs. When the Japanese invaded the Far Eastern Fleet, the 20 CPOs were moved to Ceylon and when this was bombed they moved to Mombasa. At one time it looked like they would arrive in Chatham but still be attached to the Far Eastern Fleet. After further service in the Persian Gulf she was sent home by troopship to the UK for a long rest. When she arrived in the UK she heard that Wrens were being sent out to Australia, but as there were so many Australians serving in the WRNS and were themselves trying to get back out there she felt she had little hope. Then one day while playing cricket for the WRNS against ATS at Mill Hill she was called to the phone

15

and told to be ready to sail the following week. And it was here that she spent the rest of the War, and indeed since the War.

In the case of Priscilla Fuller her father was reluctant to give his permission for her to go abroad, which was necessary for women under 21; he wanted her to become an officer on the basis that officers were treated better by the enemy if taken prisoner. When her posting came it was to East Africa on the SS *Amcroa*. There were 100 Wrens in the draft, all of whom had been issued with tropical kit which included two pairs of white woollen knickers, three ill-fitting white dresses, white shoes and a white skull cap to be worn over the "Pudding Basin" hat used in the tropics. The journey at times was eventful, dodging U-boats and often sleeping in life jackets fully clothed clutching a small waterproof bag containing pay books and other personal belongings. Their journey continued on another ship which was crawling with mice and beetles. When they arrived at Basara they found Betty Archdale waiting for them and an Iraq Army band playing 'Rose Marie'. After a year, which was the normal tour in the Gulf with its temperatures of 120 in the shade, she and two others were told to report to an OTC in Colombo, the transport was a US tanker fully loaded. The Captain decided one night they should all play strip poker, the Wrens played so well, however, they only lost their shoes.

For Nora Peacock the trip overseas was to be a sad one. She had volunteered for the WRNS in 1940 but her papers were lost, and it was January 1941 before she got in and became a wireless operator. In January 1943, she was sent to Egypt and eventually arrived at HMS *Nile* in Alexandria. In June 1944, while coming off watch her transport, a lorry, was hit by a tram and she was knocked out and under the wheels of the tram. The outcome was that she had her right leg amputated, and, in her own words, "1 have spent most of my time since trying to find a comfortable leg". In 1946, she became a member of BLESMA and later served on the Executive Council. In 1981, for her work with BLESMA and the Girl Guides she was awarded the MBE.

Another Wren posted to Cairo was Joyce Buhagia, who had also volunteered for overseas duty. Her transport was the Combined Operations HQ Ship HMS *Bulolo*. They set sail from Gourock, but she had no idea where they were bound. The day they arrived on the ship it was cold, wet and windy and they were taken out to the ship by small ship's boat and then had to climb up the gangway with the ship heaving and swinging about in the large waves. Once they got out to sea the sea sickness started. She, however, was not affected and with another non-seasick Wren spent the next few days cleaning up after people who were being sick and became known as 'Chars'. The food was hauled along ropes in between the waves, if one mistimed it, the whole breakfast would land on the deck. The first landfall was Freetown, Sierra Leone. She can still, today, see jungle clad hills and ships lying at anchor as the rest of the convoy arrived. Here at Freetown they stopped off and went ashore in their white uniforms and topees to be met by West African women carrying bananas. From here they continued their journey to Durban and then Aden, no stopping here but straight on to the Red Sea and the Suez Canal. It was here that they left the ship and went by train to Cairo, and then to Alexandria. Their job was dealing with the Fleet mail, working from Rasel-El-Tue and living in a former convent at Stanley Bay. From here she was posted to Port Tewfick, HMS *Stag* (Suez). It was here that she met her husband to be and they married in 1945. She later saw a letter written by a sailor to his wife and he was telling her about the wedding and said, "He's a local chap with a funny name (Buhagiar); she's not much to look at but she's got a nice disposition".

There were several Wrens who served in both wars, such as Beatrice Brown (nee McRae), who today is probably the oldest living Wren. She joined in 1918 and served until the WRNS were disbanded in 1919. During WWII she joined as immobile and travelled back and forth to her home in Hornchurch. In 1945, she was awarded the BEM and it was 1947 before she finally left the WRNS. Since then she has been an active member of the WRNS Association, and on one occasion was selected to place a wreath on behalf of the WRNS at the Cenotaph. Today she is her 90's and still attending most of the WRNS Association meetings. When Jean Tremayne was called up as a writer in the signals district office at the RN Barracks, Portsmouth, her quarters turned out to be a former orphanage which had been condemned and was due to be knocked down. It had a hot water system that sounded as if it would blow up at any minute. In the length of the building were 20 mattresses, 20 chests and nothing else except a hanging cupboard for uniforms and storing coal. The Wrens got an extra ration of sugar to cope with the loss of sleep caused by the bombing at night. Their food consisted of Canadian butter and eggs. Jean worked shifts at the SDO and often the day shift Wrens would play tricks on the night time ones, such as sewing up the sleeves of pyjamas, but the night time Wrens usually got their own back by leaving revolting things in their beds. The tea breaks were known as tea boat, and it was served in a large urn. During the bombing in 1941/42 hammocks were slung in the air raid shelters, but it was a case of first come first served. If you turned up late your bed for the night would be a concrete floor and cuddling up to your neighbour for warmth. The Wrens came from all walks of life, and from far and wide.

The uniform for a rating in the WRNS was navy blue and made from serge, the buttons were black as were the stockings and shoes, white shirts were worn, not blouses, with a black tie and a round sailor's hat with the Naval depot or ship on a band around the top, although in some of the early films and pictures Wrens are shown as wearing a soft hat with a brim. The Wrens of course were shore based and did not go to sea. One station for an example was HMS *Victory* in Portsmouth. The Petty Officers wore a velour tricorne hat with a blue Naval crest and brass buttons instead of the black worn by the ratings. The officers uniform was made of doeskin, a tricorne hat. Ranks were light blue rings and worn on the lower part of the sleeve, the more rings, the higher the rank. A Wren could not be considered for a commission under the age of 21.

Many a Wren began smoking at an early age. For Jean it began a period of 27 years smoking, despite there being a shortage of food and many people being hungry, there never seemed to be a shortage of tobacco. In 1944, she was offered a commission but was returned to her base at Chatham as not having enough confidence. However, when she returned a month later she was told that she had too much! On becoming an officer, it was a case of looking after young 17-year olds who came into the Wrens as trainees, some of the NCOs were like dragons. As a draft officer (Admin) it was her job to post women all over the UK to jobs which would release men for sea going duties. If possible, they would be posted with their friends.

Her demob seemed to take an age, her age group and demob number 37 seemed to take forever to emerge. The women who were married were given 50 clothing coupons and a small gratuity on demob. The single women were worried about employment and being told by older women, who had not been in the services, that civilian life was not a bed of roses, and Britain was not, in fact, the land fit for heroes, which was what servicemen and women were led to believe at the end of the war.

In 1942, a Government Committee was set up to enquire into the welfare conditions of the women's services, the Chairwoman was Miss Violet Marham. In 1946, at a meeting of the Wrens' Association she referred to the women's services as "…a bright lifeline through the dark war years."

In 1942, a new U-boat hunter sloop was launched, and it was called HMS *Wren*. The Wrens were given permission to contribute towards its construction and £14,000 was subscribed. One method of collecting money by the Wrens was to raffle a pair of French silk stockings, which somehow had got back from the beaches of Dunkirk, fetching the handsome sum of £14. The ship was launched on 11th August 1942, at Dunbartonshire. A number of Wrens were present and the launch itself was made by the Director of the WRNS. The ship was commissioned in February 1943 and became part of the 2nd Escort (Hunting Killing) Group under Captain Walker DSO DSC who was to die later in 1944 on the bridge of his ship. The ship survived the war and was scrapped in 1956. In Plymouth, for the first time in the history of the Navy, Wrens were manning boats, albeit small ones used for taking to and from the ships while they were in harbour, mail and stores, VIPs and crews going on shore leave. In the case of Leading Wren Margaret Jefferies, she was at the wheel of the first RN vessel entirely manned by women, and to fly the Royal Standard. This came about when, in April 1942, the King and Queen paid a visit to Plymouth to see the air raid damage on the city. They were taken around the dockyard in a small boat manned by Wren Jefferies and her crew. A portrait was later painted of this to mark the occasion. The Wren crews often cooked, ate and slept aboard for a week at a time. At its peak there were 575 Wrens manning such vessels, the largest contingent being in Plymouth. In 1944, Petty Officer Wren Pat Furner became the first woman river pilot, to claim ten shillings pilotage fee for navigating a ship in tricky waters. Before she joined the WRNS, she had never even been on a boat or ship. Her first role as a pilot was to deliver a flotilla of landing craft to their destination. The boat crews worked 24 hours on and 24 hours off duty. Jean Douglas was 19 when she was sent to Plymouth for boat crew training, the job most Wrens wanted. The two-week course consisted of Morse, signals and knots and general boat training. From there she was sent on attachment to the US Navy running their liberty or shore boats back and forth from the ships. She soon discovered that being a boat helmsman was a more interesting job and more money, so another course, this time for a month. But at the end of it her money rose from 32 shillings to 48 shillings a fortnight.

On one occasion she had to take over a boat from a Wren going on leave. It was a 50-footer, a bigger boat than her own 38-footer, with two huge Perkins diesel engines which had to be primed with petrol before starting. On Christmas Eve she was ordered to take a carol singing party around the fleet which was at anchor. On another occasion she had to take five officers to Plymouth Sound, the five sat with the three Wren crew, their arms around each other and singing their heads off. On one misty morning she was given an order to go to the Breakwater, when, in the thick fog, she followed a ship leaving harbor. Suddenly through the gloom came a red searchlight, and the noise of a Sunderland flying boat of Coastal Command. Both ships stopped and the crew of the ship they were following took off their hats and put them on their chests. Jean called up from below the engineer and they waited as the aircraft got nearer and nearer. Suddenly the tone of the engine stopped and they realised the aircraft had climbed and cleared them, a tense moment was had by all. On 4/5th June 1944, she was ordered to report to the operations room at Naval HQ. Here she found the officers in their pyjamas under their uniforms. She was told to deliver a pile of letters to the landing craft moored in the Sound and then return for more. As she drew alongside the craft she saw American soldiers asleep on the decks. However, when they heard the voice of a female, sleep was forgotten, although perhaps thinking they were still dreaming. She became the first Petty Officer Coxswain of a Naval diesel harbour launch, and never failed to get a look of amazement when the officer in charge saw his pilot was a Wren.

Other jobs consisted of bringing ashore wounded and mentally ill sailors and taking parties alongside damaged ships. On one occasion her duty was to scatter the ashes of a dead sailor on the sea.

After boat crews the most sought-after job in the Wrens was despatch rider. The first four Wren despatch riders were based at the Admiralty. One of these was Petty Officer Fraser, who at the age of 48 began her despatch riding in 1939. She went on to serve for another eight years in the WRNS. The C-in-C Portsmouth despatch riders did not start until 1941, but later grew to no fewer than 18 riders. Wren Pamela Betty McGeorge was decorated in 1941 by the C-in-C Plymouth Command. On 2 April 1941, she had brought an urgent despatch to the C-in-C during a heavy air raid on Devonport, in so doing she was badly shaken and thrown off her motor cycle by a nearby bomb explosion. Her motor cycle being damaged she then carried on on foot and delivered the despatch, then volunteered to go out again. For her bravery and devotion, she was awarded the BEM. It was this sort of effort that made sure the UK did not lose the war. She was later commissioned and by the time the war had ended was a second officer.

Over a period of two weeks, ten despatch riders completed 10,000 miles and delivered 700 messages and despatches without a hitch. On the night of 19th August 1942 Leading Wren Tustin led convoys in thick mist and over strange territory to their destination. Petty Officer Wren Harris carried out valuable work in carrying a staff officer over dark and difficult routes. They were both on duty for 21 hours without a break, Harris previously completed 250 miles in seven hours, 100 miles of which were in the dark and, apart from two hours sleep, she was on duty for no less than 26 hours. Leading Wren Ferguson completed 300 miles to Dover and back in nine hours and Wren Steel went from London to Plymouth, a 200-mile journey in five hours. Wren Marsden completed the same journey in ten hours despite a puncture and her lights failing and having to use a torch for the last 20 miles. To both Wrens the road was strange and included crossing Dartmoor.

Left: Kathleen Wainwright, HMS Arthur, 1941 (K Wainwright). Right: An unnamed Wren (Author). Below: Queen Elizabeth inspects some of the early Wrens (Author).

Above: The first Wrens into Singapore, 1941 (Betty Archdale). Below left: PO Pat Turner at the helm and (right) her claim to fame (P. Turner).

Above: Wren Marjorie Pringle (now Williams) left, with Wren Celia Moran (M. Williams). Below: The Wrenery, HMS Watchful. Pamela Grace's cabin is nearest the camera (P. Grace).

Captured German U-boats, Londonderry, 1945 (Author)

WRNS display at the Redoubt Fortress, Eastbourne (Beckett Newspapers Ltd., Eastbourne)

Above left: Molly Crisford (Mrs Millot). Above right: 3rd Officer Pamela Grace (P. Grace)

By the time the war had ended the WRNS had 234 transport drivers, having begun the war with 88. At first the Admiralty lorries that Wrens were allowed to drive were limited to one ton; by the middle of the war this had gone up to three tons, carrying a heavy cargo and being driven hundreds of miles in the blackout. One of the roles was to take bomb disposal experts to the site of an unexploded bomb or mine.

Although Mollie Crisford joined the WRNS in 1941, her Radar Training was done with the RAF at Yatesbury. She was among the first batch of Wrens sent to an RAF Station on this course. To undertake the radiolocation side of plotting and for discipline they came under the WAAF, this of course did not go down well as she and the other Wrens had joined to serve with the Navy, not the RAF.

At Barrow-in-Furness there were four Wrens attached to the radar station. It was their job to report shipping to the Liverpool Naval Plot. When she was posted to Portland she was back with the Navy and on home territory. The radar station there was run by the Navy, but even then, although manned by Wrens, the man in charge was a Sgt in the Royal Artillery. Any shipping seen was reported giving its bearing and gunnery range etc. In 1945, she developed symptoms of a cold, which gradually got worse and she was found to have a shadow on the lung. This of course meant her Wren days were over and the wheels were soon in motion for a medical discharge. She sent her mother a telegram 'Bowler Hat Received Arriving Liverpool Station 12.30 Tuesday February 9'. As she made her last walk along the sea front her hat blew off and into the sea; it seemed to be the last word in her Naval career, as it went sailing away with her cap.

In 1943, Sheila Melville was serving at HMS *Dipper* which was the Royal Naval Air Station, Henstridge, Dorset. It was here that she met a woman named Prudence, one of those types that always seemed to get into all manner of trouble. She was assigned as a trainee cine gun assessor, but her bike always seemed to break down and she was late for duty, she never seemed to hear the tannoy system correctly or knew what the bugle calls meant her to do. Her hat would never stay on and she always marched out of step, always appearing blissfully unaware. On commissioning day at HMS *Dipper*, the Wrens were formed up and marched off the parade to the tune of 'Hearts of Oak' played by a marine band. As they got near the reviewing dais Prudence suddenly said, "My knickers are coming down," and began to hobble in her stride. As Sheila glanced to her left she saw 'Black Woollen Official Issue, Wrens for The Use Of,' around Prudence's knees. It was time for instant action, which came from Sheila. She shouted, 'Fall out, Fall out!' This Prudence did, rolling over and over on to the side of the parade ground and near the dais pulling off the offending garment, in doing so giving a glimpse of white thigh. There she stood with cap, hair and everything else askew. Later she thanked Sheila for giving her the order to fall out. The story soon got around the area, but Prudence seemed to think by complying with the order to the letter she had done well.

On the tannoy on one occasion came the instruction, "Hands to Dinner, Hands to Dinner", and then, in deference to the women, "Wrens to Lunch, Wrens to Lunch".

After a sortie on 15th June 1944, by a Spitfire pilot over France, Sheila was assessing the cine film when she saw a German Staff car being chased along a road in France by an aircraft. The pilot was getting bursts in with his 20mm cannons and pursued the Mercedes type staff car into a courtyard of a small French Chateau. The film was of the greatest interest and sent by despatch rider to Churchill. She is sure to this day that the attack was on Rommel's car, in which he was badly wounded. Joyce Weyshay was an officers' steward at Bognor Regis and one of her duties was to take tea to the middies, or midshipmen, at the end of the pier who were practising gunnery. The journey along the pier meant carrying a tea urn, cups and saucers in all manner of weather conditions.

The combined Operations HQ for D-Day was at Fort Southwick which was 100 feet below ground at the end of a steel lined corridor. It was here that the Invasion at Normandy was controlled. In the long narrow tunnels were switchboards, teleprinters, coding rooms, plotting rooms and the signals office from which messages were passed. Jean McCormack was the radio/telephone officer on the staff of the C-in-C and had a staff of 100 telephonists, Wrens, ATS and WAAFs all working with her as a single unit. From 18 switchboards for general circuits, special personnel were trained on radio monitoring for home and overseas duties. This was a new idea for linking land lines and radios. The only test route available until the very moment they were needed was to the IOW. Suddenly there were soldiers everywhere, but as quickly as they came they had gone and radio silence was imposed. A red lamp, signalled on one switchboard when the landings had been made at Normandy.

On 15th August 1944, the first Wrens landed at Normandy for duties with the flag officer in the British Assault area at Courselles. One of these was Margaret Boothroyd, a teleprinter operator. She landed at Arromanches via the Mulberry Harbour, and from there to Granville on the Cherbourg Peninsula. Her dress for this journey across the Channel was a duffle coat, naval trimmer and square rig. In a green canvas bag, she carried a washbag and other basic requirements. She later moved to Paris after it had been liberated serving with the Allied Naval Command Expeditionary Force. By the end of August 1945 officers and 146 ratings had moved to a new base at Granville, coming from Portsmouth Combined Ops HQ. The WRNS by this time had grown to 74,620. By the end of the occupation Wrens were based at Kiel, Wilhelmshaven, Cuxhaven, Bremen and most of the former German Naval Bases at Hamburg. Wren Phylis Horsey had joined the Wrens in 1942, at the age of 17. At the time she was earning 30 shillings a week as a shorthand typist. However, when she became a Wren this dropped to 26 shillings a fortnight, the price of serving one's country! After a period of initial training she was posted to HMS *Vernon*. This was the first course of torpedo training Wrens and she was the youngest of the 24 being trained. Her job after training was towing the torpedo or 'Fish' as it was known, to the waiting submarine. It was carried on a vehicle called a 'Lister' which would travel at about five to ten mph. Because the job was so dirty they were issued with a double ration of soap and could bath every day. The hardest job was keeping finger nails clean as they were stuck in thick oil all day. This however had its advantages in that the oil seemed to keep the hands very soft. Every fourth night they were required for searchlight duties covering the narrow part of Portsmouth Harbour. The main searchlight was manned by the Royal Marines,

Later she was drafted to Grail in Scotland, working with the Fleet Air Arm who were training pilots to fly Swordfish aircraft. A dance one Saturday night was attended by no less than Lawrence Olivier, a pilot in the FAA himself and Vivien Leigh, at the time famous for the film 'Gone with the Wind'. The village pub in Crail would not allow females in unescorted. From HMS *Crail* she was posted to HMS *Dolphin* in Portsmouth. It was here that she was photographed helping to push a 'Fish' to the submarine alongside the quay, on that day she felt ill and had been a little reluctant to be included. Today she remembers the Navy taking three of her teeth out and giving her four fillings, which she still has today. She is grateful for the character it built and instilled in her.

In 1943, Margaret (Betty) Ash was serving at HMS *Haig* in Dover. While there she was given permission to marry a Canadian soldier. However, when on leave for her wedding a message came to say that he was stuck in the Mediterranean picking up survivors from a torpedoed ship. One can imagine the ribbing she got when she arrived back off leave and was still unmarried, 'Left at the Altar Betty' as she became known, the marriage was postponed until 1945. To keep them occupied while underground, watchkeeper Wrens were allowed sewing classes; she asked if she could make her own wedding dress and to this effect a signal was sent to the Admiralty requesting permission to purchase six yards of bridal satin. To her great surprise permission was granted, and with the help of an instructress, a petty officer, she made a beautiful wedding dress entirely by hand. In 1987, when her daughter was to be married the dress was once again, after 43 years, resurrected for the occasion. However, it had in that time acquired brown spots all over it and nothing the cleaners could do would remove them. However, Betty's husband was not to be deterred and decided to bleach it based on nothing lost nothing gained. This did the trick and the dress came up like new. So there in 1987 was a very proud mother at her daughter's wedding wearing a dress made from pre-war material which she had made and worn all those years before.

When she married in 1945 a signal was sent by the 9th Canadian Infantry Brigade "Greetings from the Brigade and may your pint of beer and stroll on the front, be in peace from now on. We have all of Jerry's Big Berthas."

Another who also joined the WRNS at the age of 17 was Irene Rubens who became a wireless telegraphist trainee, but later remustered to become a writer G. Her first posting was to Liverpool, and then to the Fleet Air Arm Base at HMS *Landrail*, Machrihanish in Scotland. With this posting she also inherited a 90 miles an hour gale and was obliged to wear her cap strap under her chin to keep it on. The only cinema was in Campbeltown where it had 'Golden Divans' (double seats). The entertainments officer was Richard Baker, later of BBC Radio and TV fame. Each morning he would broadcast on the tannoy all the social events taking place on the station, much in the way he would subsequently broadcast each Sunday morning.

Irene recently spent some time in the Star & Garter Home in Richmond, Surrey. The home was for ex-servicemen who may be in constant need of care and attention or, in the case of Irene, getting over an illness or operation. Although founded by women after WWI it is only recently that ex-servicewomen have been admitted. On the Isle of Scilly, the total Wren strength was 2, one in 1943, Marjorie Pringle, and the other Celia Moran. Their job was working the radio but they also helped with airmen who had been rescued from the sea having ditched as the base was an Air Sea Rescue base, and an emergency base for Sunderland flying boats. When the rescued crews were brought ashore they walked up through the streets of St Mary's to the hotel where they were looked after. On one occasion the Coastguard rang to say a body had been washed ashore. The CO of the base went in a cutter and picked the body up from one of the islands. When it was brought back to the base, Marjorie had the job of packing his belongings, his money belt and ID discs and sending them to the mainland. His funeral took place the next day and the coffin was given an escort by the crews from the rescue launches. The romantic side of her story is that she married her CO's son, himself a pilot on Sunderlands.

In 1945, the WRNS strength in Australia was 564, mainly being based in Melbourne, Sydney and Brisbane. The first Wrens had moved there from Ceylon in October 1944 when the British Pacific Fleet was formed. One was Joyce Weyshay who found the conditions on board the ship Dominion Monarch were superb, having white and brown sugar, jam, marmalade and several types of cereal including porridge with cream for breakfast, followed by eggs, bacon, sausages, kidneys and tomatoes. The lunch and dinner consisted of four courses, and, at night, they were brought in ship crew mugs of thick cocoa laced with condensed milk. When they arrived in Sydney, for the first time for many a year they saw bananas, oranges, pineapples and every other form of fruit which in the UK many children had never even seen, let alone tasted. Before leaving the UK, they had been issued with hot water bottles, which proved to be very useful in the Australian winter. Hazel Andrus went to Australia in 1945, she also found the ship's food to her liking but the conditions aboard were a little cramped. In Melbourne the sign post said 'London 13,325 miles'. They could send home four parcels a month, none over five pounds and not more than two pounds of any one commodity. While in Melbourne, Hazel took part in the Victory parade, over 20,000 took part, in pouring rain, the milelong parade taking two hours to pass. In 1942, Joan Hansford joined the WRNS and joined a Special Duties section operating huge machines called 'bombes' which helped to defeat the German Enigma codes. To become part of this unit she had to sign the Official Secrets Act and was not able to tell her family what she was doing. The HQ for this work was at Bletchley Park, in Bucks. It was known as the Code and Cypher School, all the stations connected with it were either in London or the Bucks area. By the time the end of the war came no less than 2,000 Wrens were involved in this work. The work of breaking the codes was done in blacked out rooms lit only by strip lighting. They were told not to think about the work they were doing, unless of course they were doing it, then the highest concentration was required. The memory of this work stayed in Joan's subconscious mind for over 30 years. It was when she saw an ex Wren on television talking about her secret work and reading a few books written on the subject that it came back to her. In 1944, she was posted to SEAC (South East Asia Command) and to Ceylon. Here, the Japanese decoding work was quite different, and less demanding. The quarters were called Wrenneries and guarded by marines.

When they became redundant after the war had ended they were given a new role, greeting released POWs and drafted to troop ships in small numbers to travel back with them to the UK. She tried to travel back with her brother, an Army Captain who she had not seen for four years. She got a message to say that he was coming ashore that day and when they met they went to see her commanding officer to ask permission to sail together. This was refused, and he was set to sail on the Boissevain and she on the Worcestershire. But at the last moment he was able to transfer ships and they travelled home together.

The Wren nursing sisters who had been prisoners of the Japanese only had the rags they stood up in and their footwear was old tyres, a collection was made for them amongst the Wrens, the look on their faces when presented with these gifts was as if they had been given the crown jewels. In March 1946, Joyce Weyshay travelled home on the SS *Stirling Castle*. En-route Australian POWs were taken to Western Australia. During the night a shark followed the ship through the Australian Bight, which was said to be a sign of death. During the night one chap who had been a POW for some four years died, the doctor said his heart gave out at the excitement of getting home, it was too much for him to cope with.

In July 1945, a small cadre of hand-picked ratings were appointed for duty with the staff of the flag officer, Malaya and it was a Wren who typed up the terms of surrender by the Japanese. The Wren officer in charge of the Colombo Censor Office was 2nd Officer Peggy Fearnley. When she went on leave on one occasion she was asked where she was going. Her reply "Oh. I shan't be going away; I shall retire to bed with 400 French letters to catch up on". The remark went all over the fleet in no time. She spent a lot of time meeting ex-POWs who, of course, wanted information of their relatives and from whom they had been separated for some time. On one occasion the news was not good, a wife had been raped by a Japanese guard while a prisoner and had a child as a result. Peggy hoped the woman's husband was kind and understanding when she told him. When she was demobbed after six years' service she was given a gratuity of £80. One Wren officer, Jean Sutherland, from Aberdeen was one of the first Wrens to enter Germany after it had surrendered in 1945. She flew from Brussels to Hamburg in a Dakota aircraft, accompanied by armed guards. In Hamburg they stayed in the Hindenburg Barracks, the city itself was devastated, much worse than anything she had been in London from the bombing. As with the other two services there were many Wrens who were decorated. PO Mary Lunnon, later a 3rd Officer was stationed at HMS *Alfred* when, on 1st September 1941, a Hampden bomber crashed in the area and caught fire. Despite this, she went to the aircraft and tried to release the pilot, but because of the flames etc it was impossible, and she had to be ordered from the area but was still there when the fire party arrived, only then did she retire to safety. For her efforts she was awarded the BEM.

Leading Wren Steward Nina Marsh was at Ford in Sussex in August 1940 when it was bombed, and the sick bay hit and badly damaged. Despite this she continued to urge people to the sick bay shelter. She herself had been hit by bomb splinters in her back and elbow. Irene Marriott was a Wren cook and was also hurt by bomb splinters when the galley near where she was working was hit. She however went back in and put out the fire. Both women were awarded the BEM. 3rd Officer Audrey Coningham was on board HMS *Medway*, a sub depot ship bound for Haifa when it was torpedoed. She took to the water with the remainder of the ship's company wearing the regulation service lifebelt. she swam towards HMS *Hero* she saw it was being swamped by survivors, so she turned and swam towards HMS *Zulu*. As she did she saw Lt C J Bennett Ds, in trouble and without a belt, so she swam to him and gave him her belt, which undoubtedly saved his life. For her actions she was recommended for the Albert Medal by the C-in-C Mediterranean, but her efforts were only rewarded with Mention in Despatches. Recently Audrey once again met Lt Bennett. She was delighted to hear that he had led a very full life and was now a grandfather.

On 23/24th July 1942, HMS *Watchful* at Gt Yarmouth was bombed. In peacetime it had been an asylum, in wartime it was the Wren quarters. The main targets were the night fighter bases in the Norfolk area. A German bomber, for one reason or another, decided to jettison his bomb load and a stick of bombs was dropped near the quarters damaging it badly by blast. The quarters' officer, 3rd Officer Pamela Grace, was awakened by the east wall of her room being blown inwards. Although not hurt she was covered in debris. She remembers going down into the basement accompanied by a naval rating. "I thought I could smell gas and the rating said, 'Strike a match and see if I can see anyone.'

I remember knocking the match box out of his hand. I ran around throughout the night wearing a monkey jacket over a transparent nightdress. When I put my claim in for a new uniform to replace the one that I had lost, my claim was halved as they were used to people putting in for more than they should". In the recommendation for her MBE it mentioned that all that was left of her uniform which had been on the chair by her bed was her jacket; the rest had vanished in the blast. Her cabin in the asylum days had been a padded cell and would only lock from the outside. She had joined the WRNS in 1939 and was commissioned two years later.

Third Officer Anne Jago Brown was also awarded the MBE when the Wren quarters of HMS *Midge*, where 82 Wrens were accommodated. She personally inspected every room in the pitch black as all the lights were out to make sure no one was trapped; she had only that day returned from a week in the sick quarters.

One Wren became an agent in France, Mademoiselle Madeleine Bayard who was given a code name *Barclay* by Navy Intelligence. She had left France when it fell and joined the WRNS where she gained rapid promotion, one day she was a cadet officer and the next a 1st officer. She served on HMS *Fidelity* which was formerly a French ship, Le Rhine. The ship was detailed for work with the SOE, landing agents in France and bringing out resistance workers. The captain was a Frenchman with the code name Commander Jack Langley. On board also was Dr Albert Marie Guerisse who had the pseudonym Lt Cdr Pat O'Leary.

In 1942 the ship was used for carrying out experiments. This included highspeed launches armed with depth charges released from built-in stern chutes. In 1942, the ship sailed with a convoy to the French Guinea as a decoy ship and was on station at the rear of the convoy. When one of the ships in the convoy was torpedoed she dropped back to deploy the highspeed launches and attacked the offending submarine No one knows what happened to the Fidelity as she was never seen again. With her went the petite Madeleine, who must have been one of the very few Wrens who saw action at sea.

Wren Peggy Heenan was at HMS *Tormentor*, the base for Combined Operations, Hamble, for four years. During this time, she saw General De Gaulle's son and Douglas Fairbanks Jnr, as they passed through.

On one occasion she was asked by a First Lieutenant if she could rustle up some tea and perhaps a sandwich or two. This she did and took it along on a tray to the wardroom where she was confronted with no less than Admiral Mountbatten, the head of Combined Ops, Lord Reith and General Eisenhower, the Supreme Commander. It was only a week before D-Day, the invasion date set for the invasion of Normandy, but of course she did know that then.

Another Wren there at the time was Admiral Mountbatten's daughter, Patricia, who had joined the WRNS in 1943 at the age of 19. This came just about the time she was to become a debutante, something she did not want and was dreading. She spent two years in the ranks as a rating despite a certain amount of pressure for her to take a commission. Her greatest ambition was to become a Petty Officer and have the hooked rank badge on her sleeve. She remembers those days being so nice and innocent. At a dance she learned to drink shandies because sherry was too expensive for the sailors to buy. Her experiences then, she now feels, stood her in good stead for the years ahead, especially now that she has taken on so many of her father's commitments, as well as being the Colonel-in-Chief of a Canadian Regiment. Eventually she did take a commission as she wanted to travel abroad and at this time they were only posting cypher officers overseas.

She was posted to the Far East where, of course, her father was then. She was described by the Signal Officer in Chief as 'the most efficient young Wren cypher officer in the headquarters'. She also met her future husband Lord Brabourne, who at the time was a Coldstream Guards Officer and ADC to her father. When her father became the Viceroy, she went with him on a visit to Siam and to visit the Ghurkhas in Nepal. Aircraft were barred from flying over the area of Nepal on the grounds that it would interfere with the souls going to heaven. This meant going as far as possible by car and making the remainder of the journey on ponies, which required two days' travel but, of course, it was a great honour to be invited.

When based at HMS *Gannet* in Londonderry, Wren Beryl Minot went aboard a captured U-boat that had surrendered to Admiral Max Horton of the Western Approaches. It had surrendered at Lisahally, Co Londonderry. The crew stood on deck looking very glum and scruffy, whilst a soldier was posted with a fixed bayonet in the conning tower. When Beryl went aboard it was still armed with torpedoes. As an aside, she was told by other Wrens who had already been aboard to wear regulation 'Blackouts', the Navy issue knickers which were closed at the knee, as the sailors had a nasty habit of standing at the bottom of the ladder which led down into the boat.

In June 1946 the WRNS had been reduced from 74,620 from its peak in December 1945 to 15,000. The Commonwealth countries also had their own equivalents of the WRNS. In Australia there was the WRANS, the Women's Royal Australian Naval Service, which was formed in April 1941. Its leading role was in the signals section but as with the other services it grew and covered many additional trades. In Canada there was the WRCNS, the Women's Royal Canadian Naval Service formed in May 1942. Three senior WRNS officers were sent to assist in its creation; by August 1943 the ranks had swelled to 3,000.

Chapter 3 The ATS

On the 27th September 1938, the Auxiliary Territorial Service (ATS) was formed. The companies in the ATS were formed on the county basis, each under the direction of county commandants. In August 1939, with war looming, the ATS were called to 'Action Stations' and, on 3rd September 1939, when war was declared, it was an ATS operator who transmitted the declaration. The basic induction, or 'Square Bashing' period as it was known, took five weeks, each day starting at six am when a bugler sounded reveille. After breakfast came kit cleaning followed by drill lectures and PT, ending with supper at 6.15 pm after an intensely tiring 12-hour day. On the 28th September, the Army Council issued a directive as to how the ATS could be best used. At that time the jobs and trades were very restricted, and consisted of clerks, orderlies, stores, and so on. The uniform consisted of a drab serge, the stockings were in heavy lisle of a sealed pattern sade, but not transparent, and the brass cap badge had ATS inscribed in the middle to distinguish it from the ATS worn by the Army Technical School. The ranks were, for officers, 2nd/Subaltern, Subaltern, Junior Commander, Senior Commander, Controller, Senior Controller and finally Controller which was equal to the ranks given to men, from Second Lieutenant to Major General. The other ranks were two stripes for Junior Leader, three stripes for Leader, and CSM, with the addition of a crown for Senior Leader.

Soon after the outbreak of war the Queen accepted the position of Commander-in-chief with the rank of Lieutenant General. The Princess Royal had already enlisted in the ATS and accepted the appointment of Controller in Yorkshire. In February, she became Chief Controller and was formally enrolled, and on the 8th August 1941, Her Royal Highness was gazetted as Controller Commandant.

On the 10th April 1941, the ATS was given full status as part of the Forces of the Crown. The age limit was 43 but, as with the WRNS, ex-servicewomen were accepted up to the age of 50. The starting pay, also as with the WRNS was 1/8d a day, which rose with each year of service. There were by now over 50 trades, they even had their own Military Police, and under the full status, the officers held a full King's Commission.

At the same time came the formation of mixed anti-aircraft batteries, this causing more discussion and speculation than any of the other ATS activities. In 1941, experiments were carried out in secret to test the possibilities of employing ATS personnel on searchlight units, the outcome was that in July 1942, the first ATS Searchlight Troop was formed, although not actually firing the anti-aircraft guns, they served as rangefinders, and predictors. Their role to locate the target and direct the gunfire on to it, or, as a plotter, to plot the course of enemy aircraft. The telephonist would then pass the information down to the gun site.

The rangefinder was an optical instrument which computed the height and range of the enemy aircraft. This was passed on to the gun post officer who then ordered the correct amount of fusing for the shells to be fired. The predictor, the most complicated of all the instruments, was also a computing machine. The data received from the height and range finder, the 'Spotter', at the identification telescope, plus the information on wind speed and direction, were set into the predictor by the movement of dials. The target could be moving at about 300 mph and the predictor would keep pace with it, producing a constant flow of accurate advance information which was passed on to the guns. This, in turn, enabled them to keep the guns pointing in the right direction, where the enemy aircraft was calculated to be when the shell burst.

The women worked on a four-day 24-hour basis, and lived at the gun park complete with bedding, books, and knitting. Out of those 24 hours each woman would be on duty for six-hour spells, varying from half an hour to two hours. The remaining time was spent on the gun park in readiness for an alert. At meal times a relief team was sent in to take over. The meals were taken on bare tables in a hut which served about 150 men and women, each carrying a knife, fork and spoon, and a large thick china mug, which was twice as thick as today's coffee mugs. Throughout the day time was spent training, maintaining the guns and other equipment. An evening pass-out would apply from 4pm to 11pm and would be spent in the local town, or YMCA.

Margaret Lampard began her ATS service as a radar operator on a Mixed Heavy Anti-aircraft Battery. In those days of 1942 radar was never mentioned as it was still secret. When she underwent her training at Oswestry as an Operator Fire Control the radar sets were guarded night and day by military police with very fierce dogs, she remembers today. The heavy batteries were usually isolated on the edge of a big town. The men were usually older or not A1 fit. A1 men were usually posted to light ack-ack units which were mobile.

Her first posting was to a battery at Rhoose near Cardiff, in a camp perched up high overlooking the Bristol Channel. It was winter, and very bleak with no comforts at all. The only recreation was the NAAFI. The men looked after them like brothers or even fathers.

In 1943, Margaret was commissioned and became a plotting officer, which was the only operational job open to ATS officers in Ack-ack batteries. The plotting room was underground with a thick concrete roof. Here the predictor, height finder, and spotter were all women, but the gun position officer was a man. The plotting officer and the three women stood around a square table with a glass top. When an enemy aircraft was picked up by the radar it came through to the plotting table in the form of a tiny light which travelled across a map of the area which they were protecting and was within the range of their guns.

The plotting officer would follow the pinpoint light with a pencil and make geometric calculations with a set square and other instruments as he then assessed the exact moment when to open fire. She had a telephone strapped on earphones and speaking phone so that her hands were free. Their calculations had to be mighty accurate. The order to fire was sent to the Gun Position Officer and the gun crew. When the order 'fire' was given there was a second or so time lag and then all hell broke loose as all the guns fired, it was then on to the next plot. On one occasion the guns got so hot from firing that they had to be shut down, the vibration became so great that all the blackouts wooden screens in slots came away from the windows in the plotting room and Margaret had to send for two women who were off duty to come and hold them up. At this time the battery was stationed near Clacton-on-Sea and right in the flight path of the bombers who came to bomb London. With a shortage of Ack-ack officers at the time it meant working night after night, in eight weeks she only undressed to have a bath. It was not safe to undress at night as they had to be operational and on the gun park within three minutes of the balloon going up. The theme was 'No time to dress only time to run'. Margaret's husband Geoff was in Bomber Command flying Lancasters and she had become pregnant, mad, she now feels, to try for a baby in the wartime circumstances. The ATS did not discharge pregnant women for at least three months and after being blown down the plotting room steps by a stray stick of German bombs she lost the baby. Every night they got a plastering from the Germans knowing they were there from the flash of the guns. The one thing she remembers most was the emotional stress and strain of 'keeping faithful to your man', who in her case was flying bombers from a distant airfield. Although they had boyfriends, fiancés or husbands who were in the Forces, and rarely saw, and yet were working very closely with other men day after day, they tried very hard as it seemed desperately important to preserve something that might be permanent and a hope for the future. There were affairs and a lot of heartbreaking, but for many the 'code of honour' was something to aim at day by day.

Despite losing her first child Margaret later had two healthy children, although one eminent gynecologist said that he had more trouble with ex-former Ack-ack women than anyone else. What he meant by this is not known. Her battery was confirmed by Fighter Command to have shot down three German aircraft in ten days.

In August 1938, Vera Faulkner, who at the time was working in an office in the City of London saw an advert in the Daily Mirror "Join the Auxiliary Territorial Service: report to your nearest Territorial Hall." This she did the very next evening at a hall in Hounslow. She had to produce two references from professional people who knew her, and a letter from her doctor pronouncing her fit.

She was accepted in the 41st Middlesex Coy ATS and enlisted on the 12th October. Once a week from then on, she attended for drill and training, including first aid and gas attack drills. A quick whiff of the gas without a gas mask on was not a blissful experience, but one that made you remember to have your gas mask with you at all times. Her uniform consisted of a blue arm band with (WATS), later ATS in black lettering and a silver ATS brooch. For a visit to the Aldershot Tattoo they managed to get some form of uniform, she now today thinks they must have been the first to wear the ATS uniform. In March 1939, she took part in a parade which was reviewed by the then Foreign Secretary Mr. (later Sir) Anthony Eden. A young child watching said to his mother "Look mummy a lady soldier." Although within a year it was to be a common sight, the child ran up to her and asked for her autograph.

At midnight on the 23rd August 1939, a policeman called at her door with a calling up notice, she was to report to Hounslow Barracks the next day with full kit, and a day's rations. Before leaving she phoned her office and said, "I have been called up and will not be back until further notice." That would turn out to be in 1946. The quarters for the ATS at Hounslow was the old condemned married quarters. quarters, the bedding was the old biscuit type mattress, 3 army blankets and a pillow, but no sheets. Girls brought their civvies and went out on an evening pass. Nothing at that time could be done to prevent them doing so, as they were not under military law, which was to come later. She and others who survived the first year of the war were presented with bracelets which were inscribed on the back '41st. Middlesex Coy ATS' and dated 26th August 1939. A table was booked at a restaurant, Frascati's, in Oxford Street for a dinner on the 24th August 1940. In 1941, she was posted to Guildford the training centre for the ATS, this today is the training centre for the Women's Royal Army Corps (WRAC) which the ATS became after the war. In 1943, she transferred to the Ack-Ack Heavy Batteries at Hastings during the time of the flying bombs. In 1946, and by then a CSM, she returned to her office, in London, but continued to serve in the City of London Coy WRAC TA.

One woman was serving as a predictor on a gun site at Dartford Heath in 1941/42, the site was equipped with 8 x 4.5 guns. From there she was posted to the Isle of Sheppey where she found herself under canvas, and up to her neck in mud, a bucket of water had to serve four girls. They were told their boots were dirty, but as she said, "We couldn't even see our boots because of the mud let alone clean them."

Diana Chipling joined the ATS in 1942 at the age of 18. After training at Guildford and Arborfield she moved to a mixed battery where cooking was done on a field kitchen, and the quarters were nissen huts with one bucket of coal for heating every 24 hours. The battery was based at Oylette Lane, near Liverpool. They had got hold of a pig which they called Oylette, the idea was that at Christmas they would kill the pig and roast it for dinner. However, the women had other ideas and refused to eat it, as they regarded the pig as a pet. Diana was later posted to Southampton for a so-called rest period, but the Germans changed that idea by setting their sights on Southampton as a target, so there was no rest. She later learned that the pig was killed for the next Christmas dinner.

Private, later Corporal, Betty Kriel's site was on the cliff tops in Norfolk where the huts were often peppered by German machine guns from low flying aircraft.

Pauline Leslie was with 342 Searchlight Battery manned entirely by women, at the time it was the only all women battery in Europe. There were no fewer than four weddings for ATS girls serving in Belgium, the traditional white dresses were provided by courtesy of the YMCA.

For Ernie Davidson her site was Greenock, covering the Clyde. A sergeant would come along each morning and run his stick all along the nissen hut wall, which she remembers as making a row. When she moved to Weston-Super-Mare she saw a lot of action, when the stand down finally came the batter machine-gunner fired a round from his Lewis gun into the sanatorium windows, which was the battery barracks at the time. At Spurn Head in the winter they were marooned up to the nissen hut door, the water tanks were frozen, and the toilet cisterns a block of ice, hot water was a bucket of water boiled on the stove in the barrack room, this gave two inches of water for 22 girls to wash. When the first doodle bugs came over London she was on duty in Bristol. When they heard on the telephone messages saying, "Diver, Diver, is down" they thought the guns were doing very well, only to discover they were flying bombs.

The only all-ATS Battery was the notorious '93rd' as they were known, a searchlight battery. At one time they were at Hever Castle, the home of Lady Astor. Somehow the CO of the Battery Major Peter Kenyon got hold of a train to move the battery then obtained permission to invade the castle. A photograph was taken of the whole battery with Lady Astor. At her feet sat a Private Lindsay, whose husband was a pilot in the RAF.

The battery was formed on the 25th October 1942, mainly to release the men who were needed overseas. It was at the beginning though the women would not be able to cope with the isolation of the sites and the manual labour required in operating and maintaining the searchlights. But, by 1943 it was evident that they could, and more women were recruited. Each site was manned by twelve women, consisting of a sergeant, corporal, leading corporal and nine privates. The searchlights were powered by a diesel generator and equipped with radar. On VE Day it was the searchlights of the 93rd which lit up St Paul's Cathedral and other public buildings in London.

Joan Beckett was given three types of jobs to choose from, but she chose to be a Radar Director (RDF). After training she was posted to Coventry, in 1942, with 488 Heavy Anti-aircraft Battery. The area had been very heavily attacked, but this became less then she arrived, to be a Range Direction Finder[1](RDF), Operator one needed good eyes and a steady hand. The RDF sites were away from the gun sites as, at the time, the equipment was on the secret list. A beam from a transmitter manned by a team of six homed on the aircraft and reflected to a receiver. Her ambition was to get on the site at Hyde Park, a site which had Mary Churchill, the Prime Minister's daughter, as the officer in charge of the ATS. Obtaining a posting here was not easy as, being in London, it was very popular. In the meantime, she was sent to War Officers Selection Board (WOSB), the course was held at a large house in Hampstead. Out of 40 sent only four were accepted. They were commissioned in the FANYs, but she was not one of them.

However, one day she was asked to make up a party being posted to the Hyde Park site, which she accepted without any reservations. In a taxi on the way to the site the driver said "Hyde Park Site? Mary Churchill is the ATS Officer there." The Battery stationed at Hyde Park was No 481, and often Winston Churchill would come over to watch his daughter and her women working. The dress at night on the sites was a sweater under battle dress with slacks over pyjama trousers and a steel helmet over curlers.

---

[1] Later renamed Radar – Radio Direction and Ranging.

Being in London the Battery was a show case and many VIPs were brought to see them perform. Mary Churchill was also the entertainments officer and managed to get a lot of free tickets for shows in London. The Battery hockey team was often watched by the American troops, while training and keeping fit was done by running around the Serpentine. On one occasion Joan and a friend put their names down to go to a concert at the Albert Hall, the day before the concert they were told their bid to go had been successful, but to make sure they were all spruced up and well turned out. The reason they found out was they were to have tea with Mrs. Churchill at No 10 Downing Street, Mary brought six ATS women and her sister, six NAAFI women from RAF Medmenham. They were all given a tour of the Cabinet Rooms by Mary, and then went into the gardens of No 10 for soft drinks, the occasion being recorded with photographs.

Their day was made by the appearance of Winston who shook hands with them all. Later at the concert in the Albert Hall they were sitting in a box, the programmes were being sold by women from the WRNS. From London she was posted to Hastings and billeted in the Queens Hotel. The guns were set up on Fanlight Cove to try and combat the V-1 flying bomb attacks that came over the Channel. In January 1945, she set sail from Tilburg for Ostend, in Belgium. The journey which today takes a couple of hours then took three days, requiring zigzag routes and avoiding minefields which meant a much longer journey. The weather on the journey was freezing so they were given the new type of blanket, probably on the lines of the thermal blanket today to keep them warm. The three days were spent in exercise, and dancing to the music of an old piano. When they arrived in Ostend it was frosty, and it was difficult to remain standing, because of the icy conditions under foot. They still had Mary Churchill with them, but now she was a camerawoman! Her husband was an officer in the infantry and was the first officer in his battalion to be decorated at Caen, the scene of some very bloody fighting, where he was awarded the MC. When the batteries were disbanded she was in Antwerp, her job to check the radar equipment being shipped back to the USA as it was on a 'Lend Lease' scheme. She later arrived in Hamburg, which was flattened so much their accommodation was under canvas. Her war ended working for the Lubeck HQ Control Commission.

Jean Petrie joined the ATS in 1941, and soon became an instructor with 'B' Battery 205 Heavy Anti-aircraft (Mixed) Anti-aircraft Regiment at Arborfield. She now readily admits she had no sense of humour when she joined but soon learned how to laugh, and on occasions at herself. On the 6 June, D-Day, she was with 601 (M) HAA at Gilkicken Camp, Alverstoke, Gosport, and remembers seeing the invasion troops in convoys go past the camp, and inwardly praying for them. On the 7th the first wounded began to return, and she and others went to the local hospital to help in any way they could. When she was at a training depot in Oswestry her CO was the actor Leo Genn, then Major Genn. On inspections he would poke his swagger stick into the women's bed rolls to see if a nightie, instead of the regulation issue pyjamas, would drop out.

The memories of Eunice Lewis who also joined the ATS in 1941, was the powers to be having to cope with her Welsh name Eunice; she soon became instead known as Helen. Prior to joining she had been a Civil Servant in Cardiff, although she lived in Newport. After training she was posted to 531 (M) HAA at Erskine in Glasgow, the battery was protecting the John Brown Shipyard at Clydebank. The city itself had been devastated by German bombers. In August 1941, she was posted to Raynes Park in London; the firing of the 3.7inch guns there was deafening. In December 1944, she was at Leigh-on-Sea preparing to be shipped to the continent on a ship called the McRae which was crawling with cockroaches. On board they had a New Year's Eve party, and dancing to Victor Sylvester 78 records. Their destination was Ostend, and their role to guard 20 miles of docks from V2 rocket attacks. For the first two to three months it snowed, and they were billeted in a farm at Wilbok, near Antwerp. As soon as VE Day came, the field used for the gun site was returned to the farmer and soon nothing remained to say they had ever been there. She met and married her husband Gunner Albert Meachen at this time, he was in the same battery as her. When she was demobbed in 1946, she returned to her job in Cardiff with the Civil Service, and soon she was thinking back and wondering, "Did that really happen to me?"

A similar experience came to Flo Pooley who served in 523 (M) HAA Battery whose claim to fame was having shot down the fastest recorded German aircraft with anti-aircraft fire. At the time it was flying over the Isle of Wight, a new method of tracking and destroying it by remote control had been brought in to combat the faster German aircraft. She ended her service on the Continent being posted out there at the end of 1944 and billeted near Antwerp.

She remembers that whenever the women went out for a meal the tab was picked up by one soldier or another. In the UK they were often considered to be 'a soldier's groundsheet', but on the continent and perhaps being in a combat zone it was different. When Anti-Aircraft guns were no longer required as the advancing armies over ran the V1 and two sites, she went to work for the Graves Registration, in Brussels, whose job was to identify and locate every grave. The Pioneer Corps would then exhume the bodies for re-interment at a properly designated cemetery, this later was taken over by the Commonwealth War Graves Commission, as we know them today. She was once asked what ATS stood for, 'Are They Smart?' was suggested, but the Battalion Officer, a man, replied "Yes, but also 'Admirably They Served.'" On one occasion when she was with a battery at Raynes Park a sergeant had his head blown off by a shell which exploded prematurely at the gun site. He was tended to by a ATS woman who had only two weeks before volunteered to be a medical orderly, for her efficiency on this occasion she was rewarded with her first stripe.

For Jean Holloway her prewar service had been spent in a baby food and pharmaceutical factory, but she felt she wanted a more active occupation during wartime and joined the ATS in 1942. With a packed lunch she set off from Euston on a train for Warrington. Her so-called first hot meal at the barracks consisted of a pilchard with a dollop of jam at the side of the plate. A plate of bread and marge was there for those who were first in, and all thoughts of table manners were forgotten. After her basic training she was sent to Devizes to specialise as a wireless operator, though even now this was mixed up with square bashing and blisters on heels were the order of the day. She soon acquired the nickname 'Spike', having nearly impaled herself on an antimine spike which was on the beach in the coastal areas; at the time she was on the Norfolk coast for a practice firing camp.

Her first operational site was at Southampton, while there she was sent home on compassionate leave as her mother was ill. When she returned, she sported an engagement ring on her left hand. Her stated reason for going on leave was naturally taken with a pinch of salt by her friends, all in good humour of course. When she applied for leave to get married she was asked for her fiancée's name and rank, she replied 'PO'. When her subaltern looked at her and said, 'Petty Officer, I presume,' she replied, 'No ma'am, Pilot Officer'. As a married woman she was entitled to have leave whenever her husband was on leave. Being an officer, he was entitled to more leave than she, so she did quite well.

The occasion Alice Lofty will always remember was the night of the 21st January 1944, at the time she was with 508 Battery which came under 160 HAA 29 Bde. On this day 95 German aircraft attacked London, and the Home Counties. It was the beginning of the `Little Blitz' and continued to April 1944. On the 21st a world record number of rounds was fired by the anti-aircraft batteries of which 508 was one, firing in total no fewer than 1,677 rounds. Again in June during the V1 attacks, which lasted over 16 hours, the same gun sites fired over 1,000 rounds. At the same time as this attack on the 21 January was taking place, Bomber Command was attacking Magdeburg. On the 22nd the Evening Standard published a picture of one of the Lancaster Bomber crews who had been to Magdeburg, and below it a party of ATS women including Alice collecting empty shell cases from the previous night's firings. The view of how well the women performed and did their job one feels comes best from a Mr. Kent, who was also there and operating on the guns with a battery at Romney Marsh. In 1944 he remembers on one occasion when `Doodle Bug' attacks were at their height. On this occasion there were two ATS predictors working, one a blonde Welsh woman named Meggy had a problem keeping up with the `Divers' as the rockets were known, so many were coming over the air was raining with shrapnel from the gunfire, a piece came down and through the tent she was working in, it stuck in the plotting board just like a knife, and only inches from her hand but her only comment was 'That could have ruined my nails.' "They were equal to the men, and at times better than the men, and I hope you can give these women a place in history where they bravely belong," Mr. Kent told the author forty odd years later. On one occasion east of Beirut in the Lebanon, Mr. Kent remembers they were operating a control post on the Beirut to Damascus road and in one of the worst snow storms for many a year, the snow was 20 feet deep and they were ordered to close the road. Suddenly a ATS Corporal turned up and said she was a staff car driver to a Colonel and the staff car was stuck in a snow drift about half a mile away, the Colonel had sat in the car and let the ATS woman struggle through to get help. Besides the weather conditions there were wild dogs and wolves in the area. They went back and rescued the Colonel, but if it had not been for the Corporal he would have frozen to death. For the next two days they were snowbound, and meals were cooked and prepared by ATS women.

Flora Freeman joined the ATS also in 1942, and when the bugler blew 'Lights Out' on her first night it sent shivers down her spine, it was a crisp moonlit night, and as she remembers now thinking 'You're in the Army now for sure.'

When she tried on the groundsheet, or gas cape, it went right down to the ground, but it did have its uses in keeping the condensation or rain from dripping on her bed on occasions.

Vera Rose, joined the ATS in 1938, at the age of 16 and when the war started in 1939 she was taken by lorry to the Chatham area. They slept each night in the area where the officers eat their meals each day, so they had to get up early pack their bedding away and set up the tables and chairs ready for the officers' breakfast. Their mattresses were called palliases and filled with straw, not the most comfortable mattress to sleep on but better than none. The meat each day was cut up by an officer who had been a butcher in civilian life, and in WWI been awarded the VC.

Violette Szabo joined in September 1941 and became a predictor with 481 Battery at Oswestry. She was married at the time and after she left the battery to have a baby, her battery moved to Liverpool Docks, and then later to Mary Churchill's Hyde Park battery. This however was not to be the end of her war; she later joined FANY and was trained as an agent to be sent to France. Sadly, she was never to return, as she was arrested by the Gestapo and her fate was to die in a concentration camp.

On a lighter vein, Dorothy Keegan served in the ATS Band, when the band was formed they were sent to Wellington Barracks to be trained in marching as a band by the guards. The Bandmaster was a man named Morris and he and the band were to give many concerts to the troops throughout the war, and to take part in the Victory Parade in London at the end of the war.

In 1941, came the first women despatch riders, four women from FANY and the ATS, all were drivers at the time in York. They were sent on a REME mechanics course at Camberley, here they were kitted out with khaki knee breaches, thigh length socks and motor cycle riding boots. The motor cycles, or mounts as they were known were 250cc Nortons. A sergeant on the course, Joan Barton could ride a motor cycle very well, but not a push bike.

In 1943, Dorothy Rawlings was a despatch rider at Harpenden, but this time instead of the general issue tin helmet they had been issued with a crash helmet, round and with a thick leather lining inside, goggles, and lipstick.

On one occasion when she delivered a message she was stopped by a guard on the gate. When she explained her errand, he let her in, but on the way out he again stopped her and said, "I can't make up my mind if you're a peculiar woman or a queer man."

She had started her ATS service driving ambulances and was married to a soldier in the Welsh Guards. Later when serving with 124 Mixed Transport Company at Morden in Surrey a V1 bomb dropped near her hut and 32 people were killed. Dorothy was wounded and spent a lot of time at the Queen Victoria Hospital, and then East Grinstead Hospital, her injuries ending her ATS service. On the 24th February 1945, the King granted his daughter Her Royal Highness Princess Elizabeth a commission in the ATS with the honorary rank of second subaltern. The Princess was the first woman member of the Royal Family to join as a full active member of the services. She began as 2308732/Subaltern Elizabeth Alexandra Mary Windsor, aged 18, eyes blue, hair brown and height five foot three inches. The instructions from the King regarding his daughter was that she was to be treated the same as the others. She began her training with No 1 Mechanical Transport Training (MTT) and soon became an expert in adjusting carburetors, grinding valves, and decarbonizing engines.

On the 27th July 1945, she was promoted to Junior Commander. In her training report it said she was extremely quick to learn, was not rash, drove with consideration and thought for others on the road and with every care for her car.

In 1945, Eileen Heron was sent on an NCO's course in preparation for taking over as Motor Transport (MT) Sergeant. While there, the King and Queen came to visit their daughter and they all fell for the King, who was tall, handsome and simply charming. Princess Elizabeth, she remembers, was small, neat and sweet, plus highly intelligent.

Corporal Patterson enlisted in 1944 at the age of 17, and wanted to be a driver, but when the RSM had stopped laughing he said that at five feet two inches she was too small to be a driver[2]. He went on to say, "I want you for the Regimental Police," and there she stayed until 1947. On one occasion she was sent on a patrol to Bicester. When the lorry arrived to take them back, the driver had been drinking and was not capable of driving so, although she had never driven before, she drove the lorry back to camp, via a field and haystack.

Sergeant Hella Logobrodski was born in Germany, her father a Polish Master Tailor. In 1932, Hitler began to persecute the Jews, in as part of his intention to clear the way for his Master Race. In 1938, after trying for five years to get visas, her uncle in England finally succeeded, enabling her father to make a fresh start in the UK. As they were about to leave all Jewish adults were being taken into "Protective Custody", and on a mass scale, houses and businesses were destroyed. Her mother was released but her brother was taken in her place. During the next two weeks her mother was able to book five passages on board a British ship from Hamburg to Hull, a few days before the departure date her father and brother were released and they all sailed to the UK together. On board they were overjoyed to see a portrait of the King, it was, and only then that they knew they were safe. When the war started her father and brother

---

[2] Princess Elizabeth was only an inch taller and one wonders if the RSM would have laughed at her

volunteered, and were accepted as Air Raid Wardens, she volunteered for the ATS, being a friendly alien was accepted, but, it was six months, and August 1941, before she was able to report for duty. She still did not have good command of the English language, so she went into the pay department, where she felt figures would be the same as in Germany, but as she admits today it was only pure determination that got her there. So much so, that she ended her Army service as Chief Clerk to the Assistant Director of the ATS (ADATS) at District HQ. She was also awarded a GOC in Chief's Certificate for good service. Modesty was very strict, one could wash up as far as possible, and down as far as possible, but one could not undress in front of other women. One bath with only five inches of water was allowed per week per girl, though cigarette coupons could be exchanged for an extra bath.

By the time the war ended her English had improved greatly, and she enlisted for a course in Design and Pattern Cutting at the Tailor and Cutter Academy only to find that having qualified for a position at the end of the course, vacancies were only open to men.

Doris Drell became a typist in the War Office, and messed in Central Hall, Westminster. She had to do one nights training while here, and was taken on the firing ranges, firing the standard .303 rifle, although this was illegal as the women were noncombatant, under the terms of the Geneva Convention. She later went to work at London at London District being based in Knightsbridge Barracks, and living in the Royal College of Organist's near the Albert Hall, each morning a spell of PT meant running around the Albert Hall itself. In May 1945, a VE Day party was arranged, and all her family were able to get home on leave, her brother and father being in the Army in the European Theatre. Her father lined them all up in the living room according to rank, he a CQMS, her brother a Staff Sergeant, another brother a Flight Sergeant in the RAF and she a Corporal in the ATS at the end.

Eileen Wailer joined the ATS before her 18th birthday and became a 'grease monkey' as was the name for driver/mechanics. She was posted to a motor cycle depot at Crystal Palace. While walking through Hyde Park early one morning she stumbled on the bodies of a black American soldier and a young girl. It was later discovered that they had committed suicide, and the woman was pregnant.

Eileen was later posted to Scotland and on one occasion when coming home on leave to Abergavenny, a long trip even today. She discovered the train was not going to stop at Abergavenny and as the train went through the station she jumped. Although it was not going all that fast she was still picking herself up by the time the train had gone out of sight. At the time an ATS officer was lodging at her house and one night she asked Eileen to go down to the fish and chip shop for her. She picked up what she thought was her raincoat and was amazed to find when she arrived at the chip shop she was being saluted, when she looked down at her shoulder she realised why, in the rush to get out she had put on the wrong raincoat and was in fact wearing the officer's coat with the pips on the shoulder.

Everly Lucas' father was furious when she volunteered for the ATS; he had served in WW1 and did not as he thought like the idea of her serving in the trenches with rats running over her legs. Her training was done at Peninsular Barracks where they were billeted in the old married quarters. The walls were so damp that you could write your name on them. The sinks were blocked with black water, which turned out to be from coal dust. A large tea chest was full of cornflake boxes which were full of used sanitary towels. The toilet cistern was frozen solid despite which the toilet had been used time and time again. They were told to light a fire but were not told what to light it with. It was so cold they went to bed with all their clothes including gloves. Breakfast was at 6.30am in a huge noisy and grubby canteen. The plates were washed after use in lukewarm water with food and grease floating on the top. She was issued with a greatcoat which nearly reached the ground. It was a case of cutting off the bottom and soaking the hem in water then putting the coat under the mattress to flatten it.

After her baptism of the Army she was posted to a signals section on a Ack-ack Battery Brigade HQ, she also became a part time, unpaid PT instructor. The shirt collars were bleached and starched at the local Chinese laundry, and the ties dyed to make them darker[3]. It was common to be pulled up by the MP's for wearing silk stockings instead of the lisle issue ones.

---

[3] The author notes that, in his time, it was the other way round.

53

Sgt. Joan Mortimer and LAC Bill Brooker at the Salt Box gun post, Biggin Hill, 1940 (Crown Copyright).

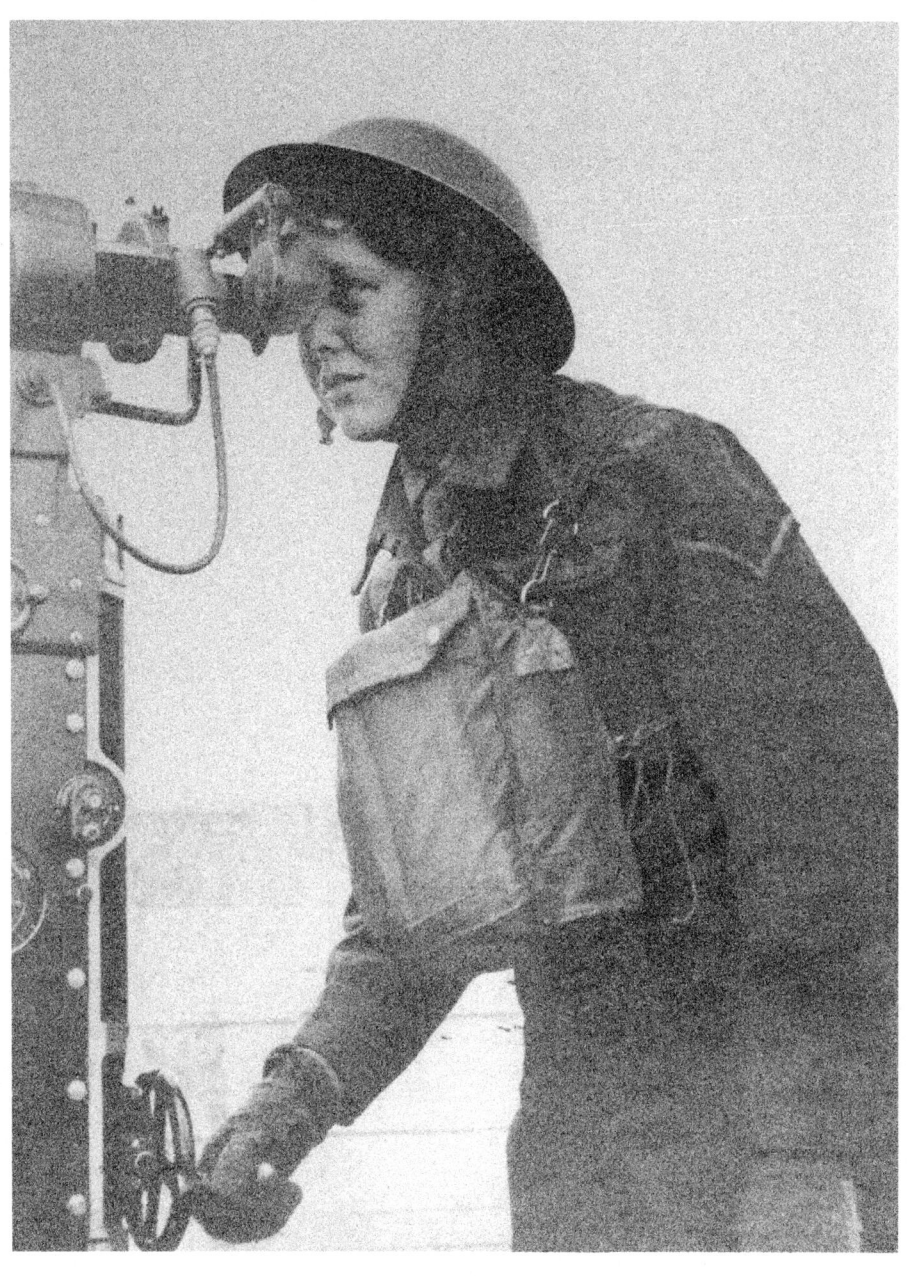

A look of intense concentration as an ATS woman uses the AA predictor (Author)

Above: Mary, the Princess Royal took her ATS duties seriously, meeting and then inspecting new recruits as they arrived from the station (Author). Below: A pre-war ATS camp at Witches Hill, possibly 1938/39 (Author)

Above: Pay Parade (Author). Below: Sick bay at Ripley (V. Falkner).

Left: Jean Petrie in 1943. Right: Pauline Leslie (front row, centre) and friends (Jean Petrie).
Below: 523 Hy. M AA Battery, A Section, Raynes Park, London, November 1944 (F. Pooley)

Left: Wartime searchlight (Author). Right: Alice Lofty. Below: ATS women at Westminster Abbey, November 1987. Alice Lofty is on the right (Alice Lofty).

Above and below: After a raid on London on the night of 21/22 January 1944 (A. Lofty).

Above: Waiting for Parade. Below: Antwerp: an unusual setting for a wedding in April 1945. (F. Pooley)

Above: ATS band, March 1945 (D. Keegan). Below: Sgt. Joan Barton (left) (J. Barton)

Above: Queen Elizabeth is clearly fascinated by the mechanical knowledge and prowess of her daughter, Princess Elizabeth in 1945 (now, of course, HM Queen Elizabeth II) (Crown Copyright). Middle left: The White House drill parade (M. Lewis), right: Pte. LD Baker (LD Baker). Bottom: 41 VRD, Scotland 1945. Pte. Waller aged 19 on right with the Princess Royal, centre (Author)

Above: Three photos of Sybille Knot-Nugent. From left, as 'acting unpaid' Lance Corporal; two stripes up, 2 Queens, Guildford TC; Subaltern (S. Phillips).

Above: PT time! (Author). Right: B Lambert posted to Llandrindod Wells in July 1940 after returning from France (B. Lambert). Below: Fall in! (Author).

Above: The two Elizabeths - Queen and Princess (Author). Below: The King and Queen's visit to the Ordnance Depot at Chilwell, Notts (M. Waggott).

Above: HQ staff at Dalbeith.

Below left: Predictor training (Author).

Below right: Vera Falkner (V. Falkner).

Above left: Each Training Centre had a Salvation Army canteen. "...They did a wonderful job helping the girls to settle, particularly after conscription came in!" Above right: Quartermaster's Stores staff (Author). Below: Sometimes the Mk.1 Eyeball was the only means at hand of detecting and identifying enemy aircraft (Author).

Above: Heavy anti-aircraft battery (Author).

Peggy Riley joined the ATS to become a switchboard operator. No other job interested her, but as we who have served in the forces know you never get what you want, it is what the Army wants. She had served a two-year apprenticeship at an electric motor works during which time she had become a very competent solderer. When she was being interviewed for a job as a switchboard operator she was asked why she was so desperate to become one, and why she felt she was good enough. Without thinking and to her own detriment she said, "Because if it broke down I could mend it" this simple but truthful statement was the very one that would not enable her to become a switchboard operator. After training one day she was told to report to London for an interview, it was she was told something to do with the War Office. She duly reported to an address in Baker Street, when she arrived she was told to get on the back of a motor bike which then drove around the streets and then dropped her off again, she is sure where she was dropped off was the back of where she had started. Her interview was not very satisfactory; all the officer wanted to talk about was her soldering ability, and she to talk about being a switchboard operator. When she returned to her unit in Leicester she was none the wiser as to what it was all about. But, later she was told she had been selected for a special posting and sent to Welwyn Garden City, on arrival she had to ring a given phone number. The instructions she got were to report to the Old Welwyn Police Station. Here she spent the night and the next day was taken up, through the village to a large country house which was surrounded by a large fence, suddenly while walking through the grounds her arms were pinned behind her back, and a hand went down into the front of her blouse, she shouted "It's only a doughnut!" On her way she had bought a doughnut to eat later, it was obvious someone thought it was perhaps a grenade. The doughnut was returned to her and she was told not to try it on again. A good start and a friendly greeting.

The unit based here was the Inter Services Research Bureau (ISRB) and she was to work in the Radio Communications Division (RCD), the assembly workshops were in a camouflaged but in the ground of the house. She was given a metal box, a tray full of components and a soldering iron. Her training involved making receivers for radios that operators were to use in the field in occupied territories[4]. Each joint had to be soldered in such a way as the operator's life depended on it, if it came adrift in the field an operator would be helpless. The only concession ISRB made to the ATS Command was to allow one officer under escort to a secluded hut to hold a weekly pay parade. "We got used to low flying small aircraft dropping packages, and then seeing figures running to pick them up, we learned they were the suitcase radios, they were being tested to see how they stood up to the drop."

On one occasion she had to visit one of the laboratories in the grounds of the house, here she met a Norwegian serving the RAF, and who was known as 'Little Willie'. Whilst a POW of the Germans he had worked at the idea for carrying a concentrated radio receiver, which was the smallest radio set she had ever seen. He was there working on the prototype. In the village near the house, which was called 'Frith', they were selling postcards showing the house on them, the women were sent into the village to quietly buy them all up, no doubt with the excuse they were sending them home. The only connection with the outside world were the regular despatch riders, and the Colonel's car.

After three months there, the unit was posted to Wembley, in North London, their new abode was the Boutex Knitting works. One day, a man noticing signs of life in the works assumed it was once again open for business and tried to place an order.

The safest way to drop sets was for the case to be lined with foam rubber which was glued in with Bostick, a filthy job but necessary. The ATS women seemed to think the WAAFs should do it, and probably the WAAFs thought the ATS should do it. On one occasion they were all taken to a cafe in the village for a lecture, the blackouts were drawn over the windows and a guard put on the door.

The lecture was about the work of the agents in the field, and the climax of the lecture was photographs of agents who had been caught by the Gestapo and had been tortured or killed. Many of the women made for the door when they saw the pictures, but they were turned back by the guards and made to look at every one. The powers that be seemed to think it would have a marked effect on the people making the radios, and that their work would continue to be

---

[4] in the TV Series 'Wish Me Luck' these radios were shown in suitcases.

of the highest order to help the agent avoid being caught. When radios fell into enemy hands the wavelength was modified on the next batch to be sent, this to avoid a leak in the organisation due to the Germans listening in. In some of the sets, hidden in the chassis were good luck messages. They were usually spotted on inspection and removed but nevertheless the thought was there. They were soon getting so much work that the factory next door was also taken over. While working in this special unit Peggy met and married a soldier in the REME and they went on to have three children and four grandchildren.

As a postscript, in 1988, while on holiday in Scotland Peggy pulled up their motor caravan and a little man came running up. He had locked himself out of his hire car, and in conversation it turned out that he had been an agent during the war and had dropped into France with one of the suitcase radios.

Lillian Reed joined in 1941 and her first posting was the Military College of Science in Rhyl, North Wales. There, she worked in the officers' mess catering for Canadians, Poles, Norwegians amongst others. The staff who worked there had to wear blue tabs with MCS in white letters across the top of the left-hand breast pocket.

Whenever she went on leave she was asked what she had won, she always said as a joke that it was a secret. She today remembers the morning drill parades along the promenade in Rhyl and being watched by holidaymakers. Later in her service Lillian volunteered to be a medical orderly in a military hospital, there one day she was to see the brutal end of being in a war, a man was brought into who had baled out of his aircraft and the chute had not opened. She cried all day, the incident brought home as the man had the same surname as her.

For Private Baker, February 1945, will always be a time for memories, as her fiancé was due home on leave from France and they were to be married on the 12th February. All the arrangements were made; a wedding dress and dresses for the bridesmaid had been borrowed, and two US soldiers were to be guests, one of whom was to be the best man. But, when the wedding day came no bridegroom, he was on his way from France still, five days before he had sent a message to say he would be one day late and could they delay the wedding until then, but the message did not arrive until the evening of the 12th. The wedding was rearranged for the 13th but the reception venue at the Wood Green Gaumont Cinema was not available on the 13th. In many ways this was a blessing as later that day a V2 rocket dropped very near it.

Joan Freeman joined at the age of 17 and served in the Regimental Police. On one occasion while escorting the top brass on an inspection the RSM spotted a couple who were known as the 'Odd Couple' and who had just got married. They were enthusiastically cementing their marriage in a ditch. The RSM said to Joan "Corporal get those two in the guardroom" how many one asks spent their honeymoon in the guardroom? At the end of the war she was one of the ATS women chosen to welcome home prisoners of war from Belsen, they were brought home by plane from Europe and welcomed with tea and biscuits, one man gave her a small toy he had made while a prisoner.

Private Hields went to the Albert Hall on a bitterly wintry night only to be greeted by a grumpy attendant saying, 'No seats left' but a second attendant then said, "So and so has not arrived so use their box, take them up there," she had taken a friend with her. And so, they were taken into a box at Albert Hall, when they stepped into the box everyone looked up to see who had arrived, they were met by two ATS privates. On another occasion she and the others were told to paint the floor with lino paint for a VIP inspection, to do the task they were given a one-inch paint brush. On the day a record player and records were brought in also rugs, armchairs, and even flowers. Even the coal was polished. She asked for an interview with the inspecting officer and told her that the conditions were not normally like this, but only for her benefit. The result was a posting to the dreaded Western Command at Chester, where the camp was run with a rod of iron by the RSM.

Joyce Maguire for the greater part of her time served in the pay section of the ATS on her last leave before demob she decided to go to the Isle of Man by boat, in winter time and the crossing was very rough. For her return trip she was flown back, which in those days was quite an adventure.

There were a number of ATS women who served abroad or came from abroad to serve in the ATS. One of the first to go abroad was Betty Lambert who joined up in December 1939, she wanted to be a driver as did many, but there were no vacancies, so she became a telephonist. Out of the 300 women who passed out in Brighton volunteers were asked to go abroad. It was not until 1941 that it became compulsory to serve anywhere in the world if required. In March 1940, she and the other volunteers were transported to Southampton, where, they boarded a troop ship, at the time their destination was a secret, later it turned out to be Le Havre. From their they entrained for Le Mans, now better known for its motor racing. Their arrival caused a great stir amongst the men of the BEF which they became part of. They were looked after by a ATS Sergeant who had served in WWI, who did not let her chicks stray in the direction of the men.

One morning about the 14th June 1940, they were told to get their kit together and were taken to a railway siding, where a train consisting mainly of horse wagons awaited them.

On the side was written '5 Chevaux, 40 Hommes', which meant five horses, and 40 persons. At the rear was a French third class carriage, this is where the 40 ATS women were accommodated, and the men were ushered into the horse boxes. When they arrived at St Maio they were packed on a Belgium ferry and arrived back in the UK on the 17th, some two weeks or so after the main evacuation had taken place, they must have been one or if not the last party of British troops to leave France.

Today, Betty is the only female member of the Dunkirk Veterans Association. Her husband served in the Army during the war, and after and so for some 24 years she related to the Army, serving in her own right, and as a wife.

Having joined in 1942, Margaret Scott Laws left in November 1943, on the troop ship Arundel Castle, bound for Kenya. Here, she was attached to the Command Pay Office and was still there when VE and VJ days came in 1945. She also took part in the Victory Parade in Nairobi and returned to the UK in June 1946. They were welcomed at Southampton with bands and cheering crowds, also by the WVS with tea and buns. It was then that she knew she was back in the UK, and home.

In September 1944, Nancy Hillier went to Italy as a Junior Commander, to work as Welfare Officer with the Allied Command and Military Government. She was sent to the Province of Frosinore which took in Cassino the area of much bitter fighting. Her work consisted of reorganising welfare and medical services and supervising refugee centres for the many evacuees from the damaged part of the province, and to the undamaged part. In May 1945, when the German lines had been broken, she was sent to Sienna which was flat and a rice growing area, whereas Frosinore was a complete contrast, being mountains up to 4,000 feet. She soon became known as "La Capitanesse", which she liked being called very much. To enable her to carry out her work she was given a Fiat coupe of 16 hp which was her pride and joy. Many POWs turned up while she was there, with enough stories to fill many books. A cup of tea and a cigarette, plus the sight of a pretty English face was a great morale booster.

Myra Miller is now 77, and a grandmother, but still with great affection remembers her wartime service, she left for North Africa in December 1942, by ship from Liverpool. When she arrived in Algiers it was teeming with American troops. Her job was Welfare Superintendent in the NAAFI Club. From there she moved to Italy where getting bands to play in the clubs was her biggest headache. Ruth Crewe trained as an Army Kinematograph projectionist, a job which had more to it than meets the eye. She was sent on a six-week course to the North Polytechnic where, apart from learning how to operate a projector, she also studied elementary sound and optics. She was kept on as an instructor when her training was over and stayed for two years. Later the unit moved to Wembley and it was here that all the training films were made, one of its recruits being Peter Ustinov. Eventually a complete all-ATS AKS unit was sent overseas, consisting of a three-ton truck, and seven fifteen-cwt trucks, which were equipped with transformers for power as many of the field locations that films were to be shown had no power. Their journey to Ostend took three days because of mines. The ship's stores had not allowed for this and they were issued with tins of corned beef and dry biscuits. The bright spot was trying to catch sight of the ENSA party. One of its members was said to be Stewart Grainger the actor, who had, up to the time of his medical discharge, served in the Black Watch.

Their role was to go out and about showing films to isolate units. The films being shown then were 'The Road' films with Bing

Crosby and Bob Hope. Other service information films were a little embarrassing to some of the women, covering VD and how men should behave in such matters. Getting to these isolated units had its hairy moments, drivers losing their way, and on dark nights driving into ditches which lined many of the roads on the continent. In each lorry there were two women. But, there were no serious accidents and the unit was disbanded one year after VE Day.

Sybille Knot Nugent had joined the ATS in 1942, at the time she was living in Northern America, and joined through the British Embassy in Washington. She had heard of the British Volunteer Movement HQ in New York, and so volunteered, being one of 25 who joined from all over the USA. She arrived in the UK on the SS *City of Hong Kong*, the flag ship of the convoy, on board besides the 25 volunteers were 100 naval personnel who had been shipwrecked. On the fifth day, out several ships were torpedoed, and they were diverted to pick up survivors, transferring them to a corvette of the Royal Navy. This period was The Battle of the Atlantic. In all, the voyage took 15 days, and they landed in Liverpool on the 9th November 1942. From here she went to Guildford for training, and stayed on there as an instructor on the permanent staff, and could wear the cap badge on her tunic of the Queen's Regiment, it was the custom during the war and afterwards in the WRAC to wear the unit one was attached to on one's tunic,

She was later sent on an officer's selection board, a very testing weekend she remembers, she however did not want a commission only to become a driver, it seems no women joining wanted to drive, she tried her hardest to fail the board but didn't and her commission came through. She was posted to No 1 London District, and billeted in Queen Alexander House opposite the Albert Hall in Kensington. Her job was as company pay officer at Knightsbridge Barracks. It was 1947 before she would return to the USA, but she subsequently returned to live in the UK.

Whereas Sybille came over from the USA, Margaret Lewis travelled in the opposite direction, sent to work for the Joint Chiefs of Staff in Washington DC. She sailed in June 1943 from Gourock in Scotland on the *RMS Queen Elizabeth*, which of course at that time was a troopship and capable of outrunning the submarine threat in the Atlantic. The food she remembers was wonderful. "After the rationing in the UK the food was a foretaste of paradise as the catering on the ship was American, our stomachs were not attuned to such luxury after four years of rationing." When she arrived in Washington she was posted to the British Commander Lieutenant General G N McCready's office. There were no barracks available and so accommodation was in a large hotel, where an early morning telephone call substituted for the usual bugle. The morning inspections were held in the lobby of the hotel. One drill parade was held in the front of the White House. Just before she returned to the UK at the end of 1945, Field Marshal Sir John Dill, Head of the British Contingent, died, and the ATS formed part of the guard of honour at the military funeral in Arlington National Cemetery[5].

Madeline Stokes came over to join the ATS from Argentina, where her husband was employed by an English company. The British contingent in Argentina post was the largest in any foreign country outside the physical boundaries of Europe. By 1944, 2,280 British and Anglo Argentinians had sailed for the UK to join up. Of these, 400 were women, five of whom were lost to enemy action on the way over. She also trained in Guildford and then went on to Officer Cadet Training in Windsor. Her husband was in the RE and serving in the Far East. While serving she and her husband could wear shoulder flashes on which were written Volunteer from Argentina, others had British Latin American Volunteers (BLAV). In 1946, along with 600 other volunteers she returned to Argentina, but today lives in the UK.

Lance Corporal Grace Golland, serving with the Heavy Anti-aircraft, was awarded the British Empire Medal in 1944 for staying at her post while surrounded by smoke and flames from bombs dropped near her site which killed cattle in the next field.

When a Wellington bomber crashed near their depot Private Jackie Birrell, known as '...a tough little girl...', Lieutenant Joan Myall, Privates Eva James and Joyce Middleton all went out to help put out the flames during which time bullets were flying about from the aircraft's machine guns. They were very sorry they could not do anything to save the crew.

---

[55] Interment in the cemetery was normally reserved for US servicemen who had been awarded the Medal of Honor, and other distinguished Americans such as President John F Kennedy, who was assassinated in 1963.

In 1939, the Women's Auxiliary Army Service was formed in South Africa and in May 1942 the Women's Military Police, the first twelve women were passed out to undertake police duties between Pretoria and Johannesburg. In Australia, the Women's Army Service was formed to release men tor the combat areas of the war. It was the same in New Zealand, where they were called the Women's War Service Auxiliary and later the Women's Army Auxiliary Corps. For many, the end of the war was a lonely one, as Ann Morley remembers, "At last the day came I had to report to receive my last orders, I was the only one of my billet to leave that day as all my friends were on duty. I said my goodbyes to the officers and peeped in the operations room to wave goodbye to my friends.

It was a terrible feeling of being alone after all these years of being with a crowd, being given orders and not having to think for oneself. Having surrendered my army kit, I turned my back on the life I had led for the past six years. It was all a terrible anticlimax, I felt empty inside."

Ann had joined the ATS in 1938 and became an interceptor operator. In 1941 she married an airman who at the end of the war was looking after a Lancaster bomber which was displayed in Oxford Street. By then she was stationed at Boreham Wood. Having been in from the beginning she had a low number for demob, hence her leaving before the others in her unit.

Chapter 4 WAAF

The Navy and the Army each now had a women's branch of their own, but what about the Air Force? From 1934 to 1936, proposals for the formation of a joint women's service, such as the Women's Legion, to supply personnel for all three of the armed services was considered but never developed, partly because of finance and because of the decisions made by the Women's Reserve Subcommittee of the Manpower Subcommittee of the Committee of Imperial Defence. This was that a women's force in peace time was not needed, or desired, and their recommendation to the Government was that no money be made available to voluntary organisations. Only the Air Ministry appears to have regretted the decision; their case was that if war broke out and the UK had to be defended they would be in a different situation to the other two services, and would face immediate attack, (which happened in the Battle of Britain). The Air Member for Personnel, Air Vice Marshal Frederick Bowhill, felt that having such an organisation as the Women's Legion would mean that personnel were there ready at two to three hours' notice, on the lines of 'Lady Territorials'. He however was in the minority. In 1937 Amy Johnson, the famous female aviator, wrote an article in the Daily Mail, and notes were also submitted to the Secretary at the Air Ministry by William Courtenay the Air Correspondent of the Evening Standard, suggesting that women should be trained in both flying and ground duties in preparation for an emergency in the future. But because of the pressure on the RAF's training resources in training male pilots, it became impracticable, although later in the future there did emerge the Air Transport Auxiliary (ATA), in which women were admitted. Some WAAFS were allowed to transfer to the ATA for flying duties.

In 1938, however the need for women was realised, and the Cabinet Policy was reversed, but only to fill a noncombatant role. On the 6th May 1938, a meeting was held at the War Office to discuss the proposal for a 'Women's Auxiliary Corps' the word Auxiliary apart from the WRNS title seem to employ one who aids, as opposed to taking the lead and playing a part. This meeting led to the ATS being formed, and then the RAF companies within it. On the 23rd

August 1938, an Air Council letter addressed to the War Office supported the scheme for a common service but desired that women enrolled for duty with the RAF should be segregated in separate companies and should wear a distinctive badge to denote their affiliation with the RAF. At this stage about twelve trades were available, such as drivers, equipment assistants, photographers, cooks, clerks, draughtsmen, tracers and filterers. On the 27th October 1938, the London Territorials and Air Force Association suggested that the RAF companies should be affiliated to No 601(Fighter) Squadrons and to the Balloon Barrage Squadrons at Kidbrooke, in South East London. This was to be No. 10 (County of London) Company under Miss (later Dame) Katherine Trefusis Forbes, the first Director of the WAAF, who, when the ATS was formed, was appointed Chief Instructor. On the 2nd December 1938, the Air Ministry realised this was not going to work, and so advice was given that RAF Companies in the ATS needed to work closer with the RAF and much more RAF training be acquired. These recommendations were implemented in a letter of 19th January 1939, and clarified in letters to RAF Commands and Groups, also to TA Associations and to ATS officers. On the 25th April 1939, the Air Member for Personnel, Air Vice Marshal Charles Portal, wrote to the Secretary of State that it was essential to break away entirely from the Army owing to the different requirements of the Army and the RAF. He went on to say that the Army procedure of control differed vastly from that of the RAF.

Three courses took place at the ATS School of Instruction in London, on the 20th March 8th May, and 5th June of 1939, lectures were given on the RAF and its organisation, however, as these were conducted by mainly amateurs it proved to be of little use.

On the 20th April 1939, a letter was sent to the Rt Hon Sir Alexander Hardinge at Buckingham Palace by the Secretary of State for Air. It went on to say that it was generally felt that it would be very desirable for the Royal Air Force to have a uniform in the same style as the Army as at present, the only modification being the colour, which should be blue, and the material used. The letter ended by saying that a general proof should be submitted to the King for his approval. On the 21st April a reply was sent to the Secretary of State for Air, the Rt. Hon Sir Kingsley Wood MP, by Sir Alexander saying that the King had agreed that the RAF companies of the ATS would be better dressed in blue, and approved the proposal, adding that he would be interested to see a sample of the new material. In April 1939, Portal suggested that the time had come for a woman be appointed to the Air Ministry staff to maintain a liaison between the companies, and the Air Ministry. This was agreed by the Secretary of State, and the Chief of the Air Staff, Air Chief Marshal Sir Cyril Newall.

On the 27th June 1939, approval was asked of the King for the wearing of the new service dress uniform of Royal Air Force blue-grey colour. On the 28th, a letter came from Buckingham Palace to say this submission was approved but that the King did not care much for the proposed cap. His Majesty preferred the WRNS cap, and wondered if it would be feasible to have a similar cap for the WAAFs.

On the 28th June 1939, the Women's Auxiliary Air Force were formed, to take the place of the RAF companies in the ATS which had been. created the year before.

With effect from 1st July 1939, Miss Katherine Trefusis Forbes appointed Director - WAAF, with the rank of Air Commodore, and the title of 'Senior Controller' later the rank of Air Commandant. She was awarded a salary not to exceed £800 a year, to compensate for the income she was surrendering to take up the appointment. She held this job until 4th October 1943.

On the 2nd July 1939, the new uniform was seen for the first time at the Royal Review of the Services and Civil Defence Organisations in Hyde Park. The cut of the jacket and the cap, and rank badges, were the same as in WWI. On the 2nd August 1939 a letter was sent by the Secretary of State for Air to His Majesty to say that the cap was very popular with the members of the WAAF, and well received by them at the Hyde Park Rally, and he hoped the King would have a more favourable opinion of them having seen them at the Rally. The reply came on the 4th, saying that the King was pleased to hear that the women liked their caps, and, in the circumstances, he certainly did not wish to attempt to change the style.

In August, also came an assistant for the Director, Mrs. van Baerle, who had been a Deputy Company Commander in the ATS. In her duties she would be more or less an adjutant to the Director.

The uniform consisted of a blue-grey barathea jacket for officers, the pattern being the same as for the ATS, less shoulder straps. The badges of rank would be the same as for the men, rings of braid worn on the sleeve. A brass letter 'A', to signify Auxiliary, would be worn on the collar of the jacket. The shirt would be blue poplin, and have a straight collar, the tie would be plain black barathea. The stockings would be lisle, nontransparent in a dark mole shade. The shoes would be black calf, with Norwegian front and low heels. The raincoat would be in blue gaberdine and would button on the right the same as the men. For the members of the WAAFs as the other ranks were called at this time, the jacket was of blue-grey serge, and along with the skirt and cap would be designed on the lines of the ATS but, as with the officers, without shoulder straps. They also would wear the letter 'A' on their collar, in the main the rest of the uniform was the same as for officers. At this stage the women had no greatcoat.

The ranks were similar to the ATS. For the officers, these were: Company Assistant, Deputy Company Commander, Company Commander, Senior Commandant, Controller, and lastly Director of the WAAFs, these encompassing all the ranks given to the men from Pilot Officer to Air Commodore. The other ranks were Assistant Section Leader, Section Leader, and Senior Leader, which corresponded with the men's ranks from Corporal to Flight Sergeant, there did not seem at this stage to be an equivalent rank for Warrant Officer, later in October 1941 it was announced that an underofficer was also to be called Warrant Officer.

When war broke out on the 3rd September 1939, 48 companies of the WAAF had been formed consisting of 230 officers and 7,640 airwomen. Between September 1939 and December 1940, this increased to 14,546.

The first WAAF Depot was opened at West Drayton on the 30th October 1939. Although a standard uniform had been agreed for the WAAF there were very few available when the war began. The standard issue consisted of a raincoat, black stockings, lace up shoes, a navy-blue beret and black bloomers known as 'Anti-Passion

Pants'. The WAAFS at this time soon became known as 'Orphan Annies'. The minimum height for recruits was five feet, two inches, but in some cases, this was reduced to five feet, and in the cases of cooks this was lowered to four feet eight inches. The main recruiting place was Victory House, London.

The recruits were required to complete Form W.1434.A, be interviewed by a WAAF officer and of course take a medical for fitness. When all this had been done and the enrolment was accepted she would become an Aircraftwoman 2nd Class. She was given four shillings; two shillings for one day's pay and two shillings for one day's rations. Terms of Service were 'Duration of the present emergency'; for those who enlisted in September 1939, this would mean six years' service or more. She could change her mind up to the time of her enrolment, but once given a service number she would be 'for it' if she did not report and would be marked as an absentee.

In December 1939, a promise was made that all WAAFs would have a tunic and skirt by the end of January 1940. Also, in December, the Director asked about a greatcoat being provided for the women. In the freezing weather, the women badly needed one. On the 17th February 1940, it was stated that every effort to get greatcoats would be made for the coming winter, this coming from Portal, who later in the year would become the Chief of the Air Staff.

In January 1940, the ranks in the WAAF changed and became more in line with the RAF. The Director of the WAAF became an Air Commandant, and the ranks up from the equivalent Pilot Officer in the RAF were Assistant Section Officer, Section Officer, Flight Officer, Squadron Officer, and Group Officer. For the other ranks or airwomen, the ranks became as for the men in the RAF; AC2 and AC1 and then Corporal, Sergeant, and Flight Sergeant.

In July 1940, there were 11,170 women serving in the WAAF of which 1,589 were cooks, 1,400 clerks, and 1,400 mess and kitchen staff. In July, an overseas posting came for three WAAF assistant section officers (code and cipher) who were posted with an RAF Flying Officer at the request of the Ministry of Aircraft to the Office of the Consul General in New York to handle the typex cipher traffic of the British Commission, New York. Later in 1941, they became part of the RAF Delegation, Washington, in which a large cipher section was formed consisting of 19 WAAF officers.

On the 17th September 1940, the WAAF Depot at West Drayton, closed, but another opened on the 18th at Harrogate, Yorkshire and another at Innsworth, Gloucestershire on the 30th December.

In October 1940, the number of recruits accepted had risen to 14,454 of which 1,956 were in Bomber Command, and 4,235 in Fighter Command. The overall total strength of the RAF at this time was 410,425. The average weekly working hours for the Director was 45 over a six-day period.

On the 22nd November 1940, there was great excitement over the arrival of greatcoats for the WAAFs, and lots of scrubbing with tooth brushes to get the protective lacquer off the buttons. The WAAFs seemed to think that the King had noticed they did not have greatcoats the previous year, and that he had a lot to do with them getting them for the winter of 1940. They could not have sung 'God Save The King' with greater feeling.

On the 25th April 1941, came the Defence (Women's Forces) Regulations, made under the Emergency Powers (Defence) Act 1939. It was now compulsory for women born, in the years 1920/21, were to be liable for some form of National Service. Also, under the Regulations, WAAF personnel were now members of the Armed Forces of the Crown, and subject to the Air Force Act.

Previously, officers had only been appointed to officer ranks; under the Act they were granted full commissions. Also, under the Act WAAF, personnel could be posted anywhere in the world. Under Rule 6 of the Defence (Women's Forces) Regulations 1941 they could be charged with being Absent Without Leave (AWL), Desertion, and Disobedience to an Officer or Senior Other Rank.

The trades increased from twelve in 1939 to 54 in 1942. They varied from plotters, radio, balloon operators, police, parachute and so on right across the board, and they were to increase even further as the war went on. Between January and December 1942, recruits had increased to 78,337. On the 30th May 1941, another WAAF Depot opened at Bridgenorth; this was in operation until the 15th August 1943 when the depot at Innsworth was opened. The last one to be opened during the war was Wilmslow which remained open to the end of the war in 1945. Kathleen Evans joined in 1939, and her first posting was to the Anti-Gas School at Rollerstone. On one occasion when returning to camp she and her friends were confronted by those famous words 'Who Goes There?' by a sentry, to which they replied, 'Meet some WAAFS'. They soon learned the rules and regulations of the services, particularly in wartime and in those early days before ti1941 came into being. One WAAF, who looked like Jane of the Daily Mirror, stayed out late and did not book in on her return. The next day she was in front of her commanding officer and given the order 'Remove Your Cap!' Her reply was, 'Oh but I haven't done my hair yet.' It was at that stage of the war where things were not yet as real as they would become in the future.

An early sad event was when one recruit was walking back to camp with a friend but was knocked down by a passing Army lorry and killed. All WAAFs at turned out for the service, and burial was at a little churchyard in Shrewton.

Kathleen Daulby was sent as a recruit to the Grand Hotel in Harrogate, then to the depot at Innsworth for drill and marching. After six weeks she moved to Aldergrove in Northern Ireland, and then to Stafford where she was trained as a carpenter packing aircraft parts into crates. These were the sent to airfields all over the world. On one occasion for a CO's kit inspection she found that, after sending her washing to the camp laundry, she was one pair of knickers short. Her plea of innocence did not wash, and she was put on a charge and found guilty, losing two years' good conduct pay, a severe sentence to have on one's record. She had four brothers serving in the Army, in India and Germany, one of whom had the awful job of dealing with the horrors of Belsen. Her father died during WWII, having been gassed in WWI. After the war she married and had seven children and several grandchildren.

For Mary Chance, her father a Lieutenant Colonel, had served in WWI. In WWII his age was against him for regular service, so he commanded the local Home Guard Unit. Her brothers were all too young to be in the service, so she subsequently joined the WAAF. Having completed a secretarial course before the war she was offered a job in the clerical side of the service. She told them she did not want admin work, but had heard of a new department being formed, Photographic Reconnaissance & Interpretation, whose job was to look at recce photographs and mark them on a map of the area where photographs had been taken. It was also to study photographs of bombing targets after the bombs left the aircraft. One target she will always remember is Hamm. It was at this time that she met her future husband, W/C Cheshire, who was in charge of intelligence at Bomber Command HQ, High Wycombe. Her first memory was his hands as they reached over her shoulder to pinch a piece of her chocolate. He had been previously a Hampden bomber pilot and flew on a number of operations. In September 1940, he asked her to marry him, but she was given an ultimatum, to be a WAAF or a wife in civilian life. She chose the latter and within a month was back in civilian life. At the age of 28, she was to be the wife of the AOC Gibraltar. He went on to become Air Chief Marshal Sir Walter Cheshire, the Air Member for Personnel at the Air Ministry and retired in 1965 after 40 years' service in the Royal Air Force.

At the beginning of the war there was much trepidation about women being in uniform. A Group Captain said in 1939, "As an officer with 26 years' service, I seriously believe this is not a job for women. In war women could tackle the quieter civilian jobs and leave it to the fathers and cousins to fill the fighting services. Then at the beginning of the war came the news that the men of the RAF were to have women in the ops room, driving our transport, operating our telephones, in our offices and manning our signals even invading our messes; petticoats in the RAF". In the coming months he was going to have to eat his words, and to be shown how wrong he was to prejudge the capabilities of the 'ladies in petticoats'. It did not take long to see the first signs of women being equal of, and as courageous as, the men.

On the 31st May 1940, Corporal Joan Daphne May Pearson, a medical orderly, was serving at RAF Detling. At 1.15 am an Anson aircraft R3389W of 500 Squadron, flown by Pilot Officer D E Bond and navigated by Flying Officer R D C Chambers, was coming into land when Corporal Pearson heard the engine cut. She knew the aircraft was in trouble, so she got up and pulled on her trousers and sea boots over her pyjamas. By this time the aircraft had crashed into a field and was on fire, having undershot the field through a loss of power when the engine cut[6]. The area of the crash had rising ground with trees all around it.

Corporal Pearson ran towards the crash site and came to a fence, which two of the Anson's crew who had not been hurt were waiting, so they helped her over, Pilot Officer Bond had serious back injuries and cuts, whilst Flying Officer Chambers had been killed in the crash. The flames were by now fierce and it was impossible to get into the aircraft, and then the petrol tank blew up. She administered first aid to Bond having first to get him free of his chute but as she did this a 120lb bomb on board the aircraft blew up, upon which she shielded his body with hers as best as possible. The medical officer arrived dressed as she was, in trousers and sea boots over pyjamas. The pilot was taken away on a stretcher to a waiting ambulance which had managed to get through the fence, which had been broken down with axes. Her action was later mentioned in the House of Commons by Winston Churchill. She was later commissioned and spent the rest of the war in Bomber Command. On the 19th July 1940, by now an Assistant Section Officer, she was awarded the Medal of the Military Division of the Most Excellent Order of the British Empire for Gallantry[7].

On the 12th August 1940, things began to hot up for the fighter stations in the South of England. On this day RAF Hawkinge, just outside Folkestone, was attacked, West Malling in Kent had been attacked two days previously. The C in C of Fighter Command, Air Chief Marshal Dowding, had been sent messages commending the conduct of the WAAFs at Dover, Rye, Pevensey, Ventnor and Dunkirk (Kent) to name but a few. ACW2 Harris, ACW2 Saunders and Sergeant Ovington all had miraculous escapes at Ventnor when the roof of the operations room fell in during an attack. On the 13th

---

[6] The subsequent enquiry later put it down to Bond not knowing the airfield at Detling, having made a night patrol of the North Foreland.

[7] When the George Cross was instituted on the 24th September 1940, at the instigation of King George the Sixth himself, all former holders of the EGM, which had been created by King George the Fifth, became holders of the GC, and the EGM warrant ceased. The GC of course is equivalent to the Victoria Cross, the difference being one is awarded for gallantry in the face of the enemy, and the other under other, though equally hazardous, circumstances, including to civilians. As with the VC, the GC could also be awarded posthumously.

August, a direct hit was made on the operations room at Detling, Corporal Josephine Robins was in a dug out when it received a direct hit; four men were killed and two seriously injured. She immediately went to help the injured and administer first aid, staying with them until they were evacuated. On the 29th August 1940, she was recommended for the EGM, which as later changed to the Military Medal. Her recommendation was endorsed by Air Chief Marshal Bowhill, the Commander in Chief of Coastal Command, only a matter of two days after the incident. The Commanding Officer of Detling, said "I would like to bring to your attention the courage and bravery displayed by the WAAF personnel on the Station under intense enemy bombing on the 13th August".

Also, on the 13th, the station at Andover was bombed and attacked by JU88s, and several hits were recorded. Corporal Jean Mary Youle was working in the Signal Section, on duty at the Telephone Exchange, part of which suffered a direct hit. Despite this, she carried on with her task; she and others were subjected to heavy falls of debris and splinters and the concussion from exploding bombs. For her calmness and efficiency, she was recommended for the EGM, which once again was changed to the MM.

Jean Youle MM (second from left) at a Battle of Britain commemoration in more recent times (Author).

Jean had in fact enlisted in No 49 Signal Company of the ATS on the 21st July 1939, aged 18. She was posted to Andover on the 28th September 1939.

On 18th August 1940, ACW1 Joan Hearn was at Poling when 87 bombs were dropped. In 'R' block, every door and window were blown in and one of the main walls cracked, several 500lb bombs had dropped alongside the block. She was alone inside this block, controlling the telephones, with it threatening to fall about her at any moment. Despite this she remained at her post and kept the telephones working. On the 12th November 1940, she was recommended for the MM, again by Air Chief Marshal Dowding.

Mary Briggs was posted to RAF Tangmere as a WAAF plotter in the operations room, on arriving she saw the controller sitting on his dais overlooking the plotting table. His first remark was, "Christ I asked the Air Ministry for a watch of plotters and they've sent me a bloody beauty chorus." On one occasion, when very tired from working a long weekend stint she suddenly met the glare of the controller's eyes "What's that convoy at Canterbury for God's sake" he demanded. She quickly got the convoy back to sea. On the 16th August 1940, Tangmere was attacked by no less than 160 German aircraft, the tannoy came to life "Take Cover, Take Cover," and then the bombs began to fall. The station was left a shambles, with deep rubble everywhere. Eleven servicemen and 23 civilians were killed, and 20 injured. They were moved out to Chichester by bus and brought to the devastated station each day. Joan Mortimer, who in fact was called Elizabeth, it appears that official records could never get her name right, had joined the ATS in March 1939, and then the newly formed WAAF in June 1939.

She worked in the armoury of 601 (County of London) Auxiliary Air Force at the weekends. On the 23rd August 1939, she was called up and sent as a clerk to the Air Ministry, possibly because she had been the Conservative Organiser for the Eastern Area prewar. This posting however only lasted two days, as she did not want to be a clerk, and told them so, so back to the armoury she went. By this time 601 had moved to Biggin Hill, and some weeks later she followed them and reported to the Station Armoury. Her words of welcome came from the armoury warrant officer, but they were not in any way welcoming, rather they were more of an ultimatum: "One month's trial, if you're no good, out!" He started her on filling belts of cartridges, so much so that in the end she was sick of the sight of them. This was followed by lectures and exams, also practical work on rifles, revolvers, and machine guns. After this she was allowed to fit them into the aircraft. In October 1939, she was promoted from Cpl Class 2 to Sergeant and put in charge of ground defences and the telephone switchboard. If a raid took place it was her job to stay in the armoury, not the healthiest place to be during a raid. On 18th August 1940, the station was attacked with bombs and machine gun fire. The warning procedure was RED for an unexpected attack and YELLOW for an expected one, followed by a GREEN for 'All Clear'.

During the attack, her role was to stay in the armoury and man the telephones which linked up all the defence posts, as well as to dispatch ammunition to the posts as required. Below her office a large amount of ammunition was stored. Here she stayed throughout, encouraging the posts with such expressions as "Get them boys, go to it". As soon as the bombing had stopped she went out sticking red flags in unexploded bomb craters. When on the 20th volunteers were called for to help dig up these bombs she was the first to step forward and begin digging.

Also, on the 20th Lord Trenchard, the Inspector General of the RAF said, "As usual the WAAFs here have been exceptionally good. The bombs dropped were 1,000 and from a low height. The operations room was rocking with the explosions, but the women stayed at their posts with admirable coolness setting an excellent example to everyone. The really admirable behaviour of the WAAFs under the stress of air bombardment at very exposed stations is beyond all praise."

On 22nd August, Sergeant Mortimer was recommended for the MM by Air Vice Marshal Park, the Air Officer Commanding of 11 Group. This was strongly endorsed by the Commander in Chief of Fighter Command Air Chief Marshal Dowding on the 24th.

Sergeant Mortimer later suffered from bronchitis, pleurisy and pneumonia, the aftereffects of having been exposed out in the open during raids, and then having to live in a cowshed because the armoury had been damaged.

On the 10th October 1941, she was invalided out of the RAF and went to live in Tunbridge Wells. For a while she was an ARP warden until her condition prevented her doing so. After the war she worked with the many homeless Poles, who were without a country to return to. Then for a number of years she worked on a newspaper, the East Anglia Daily Times.

The RAF station at Manston was attacked no less than eight times during August 1940. On the 24th, it was attacked by 20 bombers with fighter escort. In the attack, seven men were killed, and many craters left on the runways. It was the worst attack on the station so far recorded. On the same day RAF North Weald was attacked by 140 aircraft dropping 100 to 150 bombs. Nine men were killed and ten wounded, having been in a shelter which suffered a direct hit. Despite the damage sustained, the station was once again back in full operation on the 26th.

During the attack on Manston, ACW2 Muriel Dean left the shelter she was in and used her vehicle to take casualties to the sick bay. This was probably a petrol-powered lorry, and not the healthiest place to be when bombs are raining down. At the time she was the only WAAF on the station. For her courage she was recommended for the MM, by Air Chief Marshal Dowding. On the 28th, Winston Churchill visited the station to see for himself the damage.

On the 30th at 12 pm, RAF Biggin Hill was attacked by high level bombers and damage inflicted on the airfield, the neighbouring village and nearby Keston. All power, gas, and water were cut off, but the casualties were few, thanks to Group Captain Grice, the station commander, who had seen the bombers coming and ordered all personnel not engaged in essential services to the shelters

In the raid on the 30th a WAAF shelter was hit and several WAAFs hurt, Sergeant Garside from Canada broke her back, but none were killed. The only female casualty was ACWI Edna Button aged 39, from Tasmania in Australia she was serving as a nursing orderly, she was killed by blast as she ran towards the shelter, having stayed behind to close the sanatorium windows. She was a Deaconess of a Methodist Church and is now buried in a cemetery in Orpington, along with a number of airmen killed in the attack, and Battle of Britain pilots who were killed and lived in the area. The WAAF officer in charge at the time was Wing Officer Felicity Hanbury, who was later to become the Director of the WAAF from 1946/49 and then, from 1949 to 1950, the newly formed WRAF. She had started her service career in the ATS at Kidbrooke, South East London. At 6pm on the 1st September, the airfield was once again attacked, this being the fourth time during the Battle of Britain.

Corporal Elspeth Henderson was posted to Biggin Hill as a plotter and was one of the first twelve WAAFs to take over from the men at the station. Their quarters were the former married quarters on the station. Before joining up in January 1940, Elspeth had been studying languages and

The grave of Australian ACW1 Edna Button, in Orpington Cemetery, Kent (Author).

taken secretarial training. At the time of the attack she was in the operations room at Biggin Hill and was the senior WAAF on duty, all non-essential personnel were ordered out, and the others told to get under the operations room table, or on the floor. The bombs were falling all around the operations room suffered a direct hit, but she managed to maintain communications with Group Headquarters until the line was severed. She then saw all her own personnel to the shelter. On the 6th September, her recommendation for the MM was endorsed by Air Chief Marshal Dowding the C-in-C Fighter Command.

After one raid the WAAF quarters had been destroyed and the women were sleeping in the local civilian air raid shelters, and subsequently a large house in Keston, until this was also hit by bombs. She remembers that when the ops room was hit the bomb although causing a lot of damage did not in fact explode. The ops

Above: Two views of a parachuite packing room (Author). Left: Audrey Tennant (left) with WAAFs and a Dodge truck, May 1945. Below left: Audrey (centre) with friends in Morecambe, 1945 (A.Baser). Below right: Gas training at Morecambe, 1942 (G. Astin).

Above: Anti-Gas School, Rollestone, December 1939. These are the first WAAFs to be posted to Rollestone, initially being destined for Boscombe Down where the living quarters had not been completed. The entire permanent staff consisted of 60 officers and NCOs. The women went straight there from home without training; their uniforms were makeshift and the camp rough and ready (K.Evans)

Left: Mr. and Mrs. Lack unveil a roadsign in honour of Helen Turner in 1974 (Mrs. Lack). Below: Inside a radar station. The WAAFs developed skills that they would not previously have dreamed of (Miss Holloway).

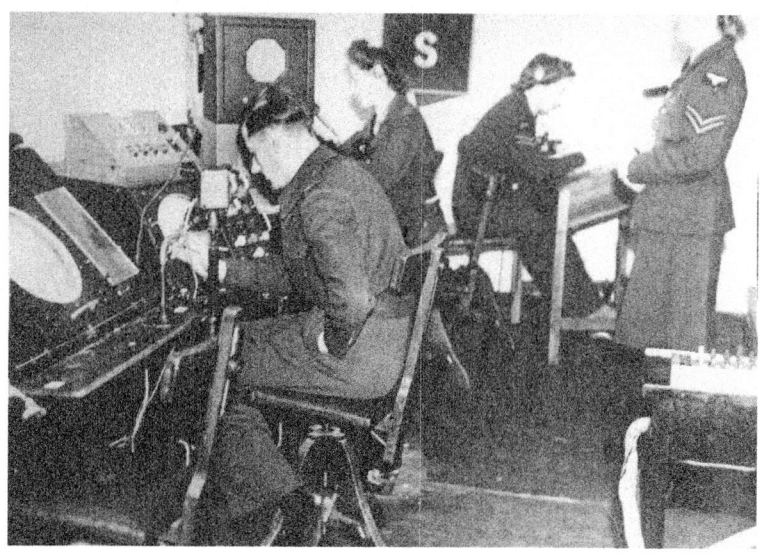

93

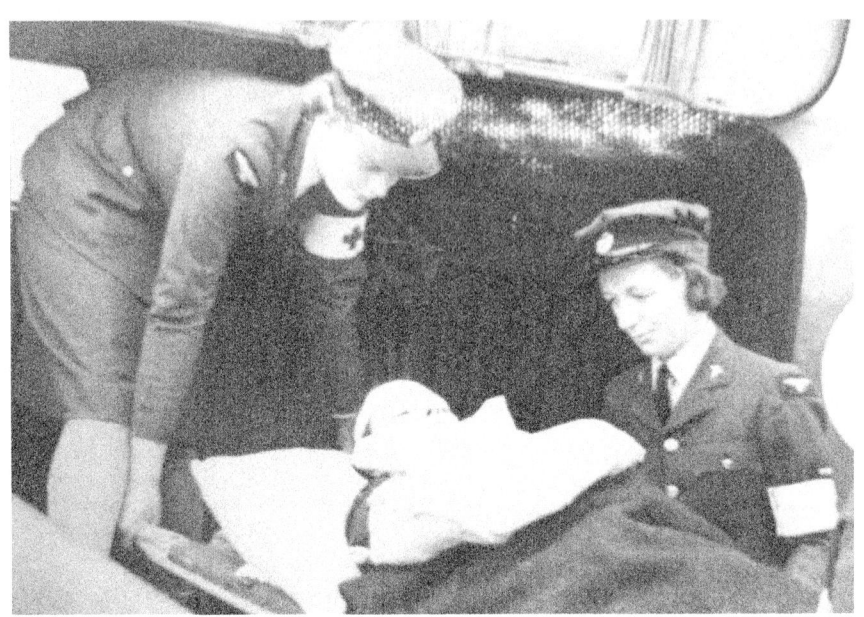

Above: A casualty being loaded onto an aircraft (Author). Below: WAAFs of a Barrage Balloon section (Crown Copyright).

Above left: Joan Hearn-Avis MM. Above right: Margaret McDermott, 1943. Below left: Jean Youle MM, 1942/43 (all via Author). Below right: Princess Maud, Duchess of Kent (G. Astin)

Top and middle: In April 1944, Halifax W7927 crashed into huts at Fairwood Common, Swansea (RAF Museum). The bottom photo shows the huts prior to the unexpected arrival of the bomber (Mrs. Baser).

Above left: Durridge Bay (Miss Holloway).   Above right: Inspection by Princess Alice: note the greatcoats (Author).

Left: Nellie Wylie , front right, marked with x (NR Wylie).

Below: Parachute   Section, Spittalgate   1945.   L-R: Liz Clark; Roni; Margaret; Joan; Marg; Betty; Dora (L Bond)

97

Above: WAAFs in a Plotting Room, a scene familiar from many a film about the Battle of Britain (Crown Copyright).

Above left: Field Kitchen Course at Halton, 1942. Above right: Asst. Section Leader E Henderson MM and Sgt H Turner MM. Below: WAAF Band (Author).

Above left: Edna Stafford, 1946 (Author). Above right: Irene Storer, aged 19, when stationed at Wattisham, Suffolk (I Storer). Below: WAAFs in Berlin, 1945, surveying the handiwork of their RAF aircrew colleagues (Author).

Above: Queen 'B', the Map Queen. Below left: ACW J Robins (later MM, centre left) and Section Officer Cope (centre right) who served in WW1(J Robins). Bottom left: Chorus line amateur dramatics, Pathfinders, 8 Group HQ, Huntingdon, 1944 (I Storer). Below right: Dorthy and Valerie Watson (Author).

Above left: Keep the aircraft serviced... Above right: Running up a Spitfire.

Below: Keep the guns armed! (Author)

Above: WAAFs on one of the Ruhr Dams, 1945 (Author)

room itself was moved to a shop near the airfield named 'Pantiles'. It later became the Biggin Hill Hire shop[8]. Today Elspeth says, "We certainly would not want to live through the Battle again, but we are proud to have been there, and to have helped keep the airfield operational. I, for one, certainly 'grew up' at Biggin Hill." When the operations room was moved to a house called Towerfield in Keston, where it remained for the remainder of the war, she moved on to a commissioning course as a code and cipher officer at Oxford.

One day she was called back to Biggin Hill for press photographs. At the time she did not know a lot about her award as, from Oxford, she had been posted to Dishforth and attached to Bomber Command. It was then that the announcement came of her MM. She was sent for by Group Captain Grice for a celebration party at Biggin Hill,

---

[8] A similar incident of the bombing of the ops room and its subsequent dispersal to innocuous premises off site is depicted in the 1969 film 'Battle of Britain'.

and on the train down she read of her award in the newspaper of a man sitting opposite her on the train. She was met at Kings Cross Station by transport sent from Biggin Hill. At the time an air raid was taking place in London, and she had only reached the Gray's Inn Road when her vehicle hit a traffic island. She suffered injuries to her hand and knee, resulting in her spending the next two weeks as a patient in Orpington Hospital, the nearest hospital to Biggin Hill.

She remembers her investiture some while later as terrifying. She was told she had to be hatless and not to curtsey to low as there was a bar at the back of the platform dais where the King stood, if she did not curtsey with her back straight the bar would be knocked off by her behind. All, however, went well. From Dishforth she moved to Topcliffe and then to Digby, and then back to Topcliffe. She was there when the first 1,000 bomber raid took place in May 1942, and remembers seeing the Cheshire brothers, Leonard, VC, and Christopher, who was later shot down and became a POW. After a further posting in the UK she was posted overseas to Cairo in Egypt, here she ended up in a tented camp at Heliopolis where she managed to see the Valley of the Kings, Palestine, and Beirut. When she left the air force in 1945, Elspeth went back to Edinburgh and became involved in the Festival, until she was married. She had two children and three grandchildren.

The third WAAF to be awarded the MM at Biggin Hill was Sgt. Helen Turner, known as Nell or Nellie by her family, and 'Jimmy' by her service colleagues. She had served in the RFC and the WRAF from 1917 to 1920. Prior to this she had worked for the GPO as a telephonist, which she continued in the air force. On one occasion in 1918, when a flu epidemic was raging in the camp she stayed at her switchboard for almost a week without being relieved, and only left when she collapsed and was taken to hospital. Her sister Doll also worked as a civilian telephonist with the RFC and RAF in Dover, when Nell left the WRAF in 1920 she worked at as a telephonist at the Savoy Hotel in the Strand, London. While there she met many famous people, one of whom was a ballerina who gave her some of her dresses, and Marconi once gave her a powder compact. She hailed from North London and lived in the Holloway Road for many years.

On the 1st September 1940, she was on duty in the telephone exchange of the ops room building, when the ops room was hit she continued to keep up communications until they were cut off and she was ordered to the shelters. Her memories of that day were, "We had to crawl out through the wreckage. I felt sorry for the youngsters in the building at the time it was their first experience of bombs and I did my best to cheer them up." On one occasion when the station was under attack she was carrying a tray of tea from the cookhouse to the switchboard office, but instead of running she just stood there holding the tray, feeling the tea was more important. This was the sort of spirit that was around in those days. On the 5th September 1940, she was recommended by Air Chief Marshal Dowding for the MM. Group Captain Grice the Station Commander said afterwards, "They showed amazing pluck. I am proud to have them on my station; their example during those two days of bombing inspired all around them."

Helen was the subject of a leading article in the London Evening News of November 2nd, 1940, and she later broadcast to the USA. Dame Laura Knight painted her portrait as one of a series of official war paintings which were exhibited in the National Gallery. This now hangs in the Royal United Services Institute, Whitehall. After the Queen visited Biggin Hill she later said to the senior WAAF Officer, "I hear your women are magnificent." The reply was, "Thank you, your Majesty, magnificent is the best word for them."

There were many incidents of how the women stood up and played a vital part during the sustained attacks on the airfields. When a Squadron Leader was hurt by bomb blast a WAAF ran to him and applied a tourniquet to his damaged, and bleeding legs, and then got him to safety whilst, all the time, the bombs were raining down. Her action, in the opinion of the doctors who attended to him, saved his legs being amputated. Sergeant Garside who broke her back when the WAAF shelter was hit was reported to have said, "Look after the others, don't worry about me, I am alright." After weeks in plaster her first words when she was able to walk again was, "Please may I come back to work?".

One WAAF driver, was driving an officer when a raid began, and bombs were dropping all around the car when she saw a bomb coming directly down upon them she swerved to the left and the bomb dropped exactly where they would have been. The officer said "I am certain we would have been killed if she had driven on and not swerved. As it was neither of us was hurt." In February 1941 and now a Flight Sergeant, Helen Turner was medically discharged from the RAF She was by now 52 and returned to her civilian job as a telephonist. In 1946, she married. On the 1st October 1953, sadly Helen died She was buried at St Pancras Cemetery, Finchley, North London. Her gravestone has an inscription naming her as 'Flight Sergeant Helen Turner'. She once said, "I'm all for London, 100%, I was born there, and my people live at Chaterway, Southgate. I think Londoners are doing braver things than I have done. They are, well, just like Londoners and I cannot say more than that. I have two loves; London and the RAF."

In 1973, plans were made to name three roads after the three WAAF MMs, Mortimer, Henderson and Turner, on the airfield at Biggin Hill. This was approved by the local council of the London Borough of Bromley, and the unveiling took place on the 25th July 1974. Present were: Mrs. A McWatt Green MM; former Section Officer Elspeth Candlish Henderson MM; former Sergeant Elizabeth Mortimer MM, and relatives of the late Flight Sergeant Helen Emily Turner MM. They were all treated to a fly past by a Hurricane and Spitfire flown by Squadron Leaders Peter Goslick and Mick Raw. Elspeth remembers being shown around the modern WAAF quarters at Biggin Hill, "Luxurious compared with what we had in 1940! We were deeply touched by the interest and friendship shown by today's RAF" Today, Helen Turner's MM can be seen proudly displayed in the upper gallery of the 'Battle of Britain' museum at Hendon.

The medal had been presented by the family in 1974, when the roads were unveiled. A signal came from 11 Group Fighter Command dated 3rd September 1940, exactly a year from the outset of war, 'On at least two stations alone the WAAF personnel displayed a courage and devotion to duty that was a fine example to many of the airmen.' From the Secretary of State for Air "I congratulate you on the fine courage and discipline shown by all ranks of the WAAF in recent actions. They are worthy of the great service to which they belong." The Commanding Officer of Debden said, "the RAF is proud to have them on the station" at Bircham Newton "I am very proud to be your Commanding Officer."

On the 5th September 1940, Air Marshal Sir Philip Joubert made a broadcast in which he fully mentioned how the WAAF had conducted themselves under fire. Finally, and the most important aspect of this period in the war was the report by the same Group Captain, who in 1939, had said he did not want "…petticoats on my station." now in September 1940 had a different opinion. "I have come to claim thank goodness that this country can possibly have such a race of women as the WAAF as I have on my station." The Battle of Britain set the seal on the role and contribution that the women could play. From then on, the number that enlisted and the vast amount of trades that became open to them, went well beyond all estimation, and it all stemmed from this period in the war when the country was suddenly under attack and fire.

On the 24th October 1943, Corporal Alice Holden was stationed at RAF Wittering as a radio telephone operator. A Wellington bomber DV 839 of 14 OTU crashed and burst into flames 150 yards from the flying control tower. At the time Corporal Holden was on standby duty. Without a thought for her own safety she ran to the burning aircraft, where by this time petrol tanks were exploding. On hearing cries for help coming from the rear of the aircraft, she found the rear gunner trapped in his turret and, with his clothes beginning to catch alight, she found the door and managed to open it, and drag the gunner Sergeant Dennis Buckley out, and to safety. Her action without a doubt saved his life, in fact he was the only survivor of the crash. The statement from Sergeant Buckley went as follows "On the night of Sunday 24th October 1943, I was the rear gunner of a Wellington which crashed at Wittering aerodrome. The plane burst into flames, I was trapped in the rear turret which was partially rotated owing to the crash. When I pulled the jettison handle to release the door it wouldn't fall away, it had jammed. I attempted to rotate the turret but without success. I smashed the window, pushed by head through and saw a woman running towards the aircraft. I shouted to her for help. There was an explosion and the flames started in the turret. The woman came to the turret, wrenched the door open and dragged me out of the turret and away from the aircraft. She then escorted me to the ambulance. Without her help I would have definitely have been trapped in the turret." On the 27th, three days later, she was recommended for the George Cross, a recommendation that was endorsed by Air Marshal Leigh Mallory the C in C of AEAF. Despite this she was not awarded the GC but the British Empire Medal instead.

A sad experience for Vera Pudge was typing a list of effects for a friend when stationed in Newcastle. The friend had married an Army officer and having seen him off on the train began to walk back to her billet across the moor, or common, near Fenham Barracks, days later she was found dead having been strangled. At the time she was in civilian clothes and for a while unidentified. However, her killer was later caught and hanged. While she was stationed at Catterick the classic film about the early bomber days, "The Way to the Stars", starring John Mills and Michael Redgrave, was made. Vera became an unpaid extra as she wandered about the film set. She also had her first boyfriend here, sadly as in so many other such cases, he was shot down on his fourth operation and is buried in France. In her own words, she completed her service career as a virgin. "We women in my group were threatened with the work house if we returned home in an 'Interesting Condition'. Honour was everything in those days." In 1946, she married a Canadian airman and left to live a new life in Canada but returned to the UK in 1949.

June Maxwell was sent after her initial training to the RAF College Cranwell, where she trained as a teleprinter operator, equivalent to today's computer operators. Each keyboard of the teleprinter was covered and one had to put one's hands under the cover to type. On one side was a chart of the keyboard, 'accuracy before speed' was the motto of the course. At the end of six intense weeks a test was set, the pass rate was 24 words a minute, with no mistakes allowed on plain language and figures. During her time here, June fractured her arm while doing PT which of course did not help with her work on the teleprinter. Each night after lights out she was swatting, and then up the next day early for square bashing. After passing her course she was posted to Cardington where she found eight to nine teleprinter operators. The teleprinter was the vital link with each station, group and command. The job meant knowing Morse code which had to be typed after it had come through a double tape speed. June ended up marrying the Corporal who repaired her set.

Gwyne Astin was also trained initially at Morecambe as was June, the NAAFI was the whole ground floor of what had been Woolworths. After training she was sent to London and the Met Office. Her training in weather forecasting was done in Oxford Street in a building which had belonged to a furniture making firm. After her weather forecasting training she was sent to RAF Mildenhall and Bomber Command. Her role was estimating the height of the clouds by standing on the top of a very high building. Within months she was posted to 3 Group Bomber Command HQ at Exning, Newmarket. When ops were on she had a lot to do as the weather forecast for the returning bombers was vital. It was here that she spent her 21st birthday, her friends buying her a set of silver spoons, which she still has today. She married in 1944, and as her father had died six months before she was given away by her mother. At the end of the war she went on one of the Baedeker, or 'Cooks', tours as they became known, to see the damage inflicted by Bomber Command in Europe, mainly Germany. She was driven to RAF Witchford and kitted out with a parachute. Each Lancaster took five WAAFs, and she sat under the mid upper gunner position about halfway down the fuselage.

Irene Peverett served as a WRAF in the Princess Mary's Nursing Service, 1942 to 1946. After being posted to Tangmere and then St Athan in South Wales she was sent on an ambulance course to Hendon, this was in preparation for the D-Day landings. The course asked for volunteers as air ambulance orderlies, and covered such things as working with the captain of the aircraft in the air in such matters as the height to fly when carrying wounded men with head injuries, and stomach wounds, how to use oxygen, and the most important thing, how to use a stretcher assembly unit, particularly in the Dakota. This aircraft could carry 18 stretchers and six sitting wounded. The nurses and orderlies carried parachutes, but they were only to be used by them on the journey outbound in which they carried freight, on the return journey with the wounded they would have to stay with the patients if the aircraft got into trouble, to the bitter end if necessary. They were issued with Red Cross ID cards for use in the event of being taken prisoner. After her course she was posted to Down Ampney in the Cotswolds, it was here that the paras took off in gliders on D-Day and after, the two Dakota Squadrons stationed there, 48 and 271. In all she made no less than 40 operations to Europe picking up wounded from Normandy to Nijmegen, in Holland. During these operations she flew with Jimmy Edwards[9], a pilot in 271 Sqn. The CO was a South African, Lieutenant Colonel P Joubert DSO DFC, known to all as 'Jouby'. The trip on the 1st January 1945, is the one that sticks in her mind; they were down to fly to Brussels taking freight and bring back wounded. As they neared Brussels a message came through on the radio that the airfield was under attack, in fact not only at Brussels but also Eindhoven, the airfields were being attacked by ME 109 and FW 190 German aircraft. "The sight that met our eyes at Brussels was frightening, the noise from machine gun fire was deafening. Jouby had come over to where I was sitting in the cockpit and said calmly "We must land or be shot out of the sky."" They did land and ran the gauntlet from the aircraft to the building, about 100 yards, but to Irene it seemed like miles. They ran a zigzag pattern with machinegun fire all around them; in the smoke around it was nearly impossible to see where one was running, Jouby[10] put his arm around her to protect her as best as possible.

Another WAAF who managed to get on operations was Flight Officer Rosemary Britten. She was an intelligence officer at Earls Colne in 1945, and her uncle, Major Ian Toler, was there commanding 'B' Squadron of the Glider Pilot Regiment. It was 24th March 1945, and the largest and probably the last airborne operation was to take place. Many of the intelligence officers, including Rosemary, wanted to be a part of this history and go on the operation in the glider towing aircraft. Somehow, and to her amazement, she was given permission by the station commander, and then by the CO of 296 Squadron, to be put in the ballot to go. She was detailed to fly with an Australian pilot Flight Officer Ron Lamshed, who was

---

[9] F/L Jimmy Edwards, DFC, became a famous TV and radio actor after the war. His trademark handlebar moustache was grown to disguise scars sustained when his Dakota was shot down at Arnhem in 1944.

[10] When VE Day came in May 1945, Lieutenant Colonel Joubert decided he would make some fireworks to help the celebrations. This he did by stuffing cartridges into a piece of drainpipe. Sadly, as he did, it blew up and he was blown to pieces.

number 17 in the takeoff order, Number five was the AOC of 38 Group, so she had to be kept right away from him, as well as Air Chief Marshal Tedder, who came to deliver a private message from General Eisenhower at the preflight briefing.

She was awoken at 3.45 am, for breakfast at 4.15 am, she had already, as was the rule, emptied all her pockets, and was left with a comb, her escape kit if needed, a powder and lipstick. She did not use makeup that much but if she was shot down in Germany she was to look as German as possible by using a lot of it. Her dress for the operation was slacks, her oldest tunic, a German scarf and a mascot called Ebenezer, which belonged to one of the other intelligence officers, he later insisted that it had saved their lives. The crew of aircraft 'D-Dog' carried her flying kit out to the crew bus. As she got in, she saw a Canadian War Correspondent sitting in the bus. Thinking he had stumbled on a scoop, he started to interrogate her about being the only women on the operation. In a sheer panic she gave him her name, but then appealed to his better nature to leave it out at least until the war was over, and he evidently complied, as nothing was written about her presence.

Once in the aircraft she stayed well-hidden as there were a lot of VIPs kicking about, but fortunately they all stayed outside, talking to the Glider pilots and troops waiting to board the Horsa gliders. Having taken off and arrived over Dover they found a stream of gliders being towed for a distance of 27 miles across the English Channel. Over Holland, they found great scenes of flooding, and there seemed to be no signs of life at all. However, as they approached the landing zones, Pilot Officer McGhan, the bomb aimer, started to take photographs of them. As they crossed into Germany, the green fields were speckled all over by hundreds of coloured parachutes. Rosemary spotted the wood near Hamminkeln, which she recognised from the briefing photographs. The actual landing zone was obscured by what she described as a very effective smoke screen; whether the enemies or the allies it was certainly effective. Their glider was detached and down it went with the others into the smoke below. As they turned away to port and just avoided another aircraft the flak started to come up puffs of black smoke she now knew she was in the combat zone. Suddenly there was an almighty crack and D-Dog leapt all over the place. They managed somehow to cross back over the Rhine, where at least they could if necessary to bale out into the battle. Quite what the Germans and in fact the allied troops would have made of Rosemary coming down in a chute at the height of the battle is beyond imagination. The pilot was by now holding the control column with his knees and dare not take his hands off for a second. It was now only held together by a quarter of an inch of metal. Sgt. Fred Humbly the Flight Engineer tied a hammer on to it as a splint. Although she could not see too much Rosemary realised that things were not working as they should on the aeroplane, the escape hatch was open, and she was instructed what to do if they had to bale out. Holland below did not look very inviting and she wondered how she would explain to a Dutchman what a British woman was doing there.

The tow rope had jammed, the idea had been to release it over the sea, but suddenly and most unfortunately for those below it came off over a Dutch village. The compass was u/s, as were the hydraulics, so Ron, the pilot, decided to look for a nearby airfield to make a landing. Rosemary, along with two other crew members, sat in the crash position in the rest bay with all the escape hatches open and the wind howling in. A fountain of evil smelling hydraulic oil sprayed over them, but they stuck it out and stayed where they were. Somehow, Fred had performed a miracle and got the landing wheels down, which Ron said had never previously done without hydraulics. He came in and made a perfect landing, the best his crew said he had done. The flak had burst inside the fuselage blowing the door away and peppering the aircraft all around and cutting a lot of the vital parts but somehow missing the crew, and the petrol tanks.

They had landed at B53 Merville, near Lille, in France, which was described as an American landing ground for lame ducks. They all climbed out, and with the usual American razzamatazz, out came the ambulance with a GI calling out, "Where is the wounded man?" One of the crew had a scratch on his hand and a great fuss of bandaging it up was performed; if he had been an American he would have got the Purple Heart. The fact that Rosemary was a woman meant questions were asked but it was smoothed over by saying the RAF always carried intelligence officers and that she was just a tame WAAF.

They were flown back to the UK in a Dakota, which was going to Honington, but Ron persuaded the pilot to fly to Earls Colne. The flight was very bumpy over the UK and Rosemary was nearly almost air sick. When they got back to Earls Colne, other crews were amazed to see them as they had reported D-Dog being shot down. It even got around that Rosemary was on board and her room had been sealed off as she had been reported as being killed. It appears that the Group Captain had rigged the ballot so that she could not possibly win. At first, he was furious, not so much with her but because his intentions had been misunderstood, but to her he was very pleasant and hoped she had enjoyed the experience! The story soon got to No 38 Group HQ and they rang up to confirm if it was true or not. The senior WAAF Officer known as Queen Bee said that there was no truth in the story and quickly rushed to see the Group Captain who in turn rang Group HQ to explain what had transpired. The result was Rosemary had to go to Group HQ where she was given an hour's lecture and threatened with having to appear before the AOC, and that if the story got out she would suffer the consequences. Rosemary thought that the WAAF officer giving out the lecture was in fact jealous of Rosemary having been on an operation when she herself had not.

When she arrived back at Earls Colne she, and Ron Lamshed were on the mat in front of the Group Captain and given a further warning that nothing must get out and to exert much caution over the incident.

In May 1939, the German airship Graf Zeppelin made a long flight along the east coast of England, tasked with intercepting transmissions from our radar chain, on behalf of an intelligence department the enemy had established, called 'Horchdienst'. In response, the British intelligence branch later known as the 'Y' Service was formed, tasked with picking up the German transmissions. It was first set up at RAF Hawkinge in Kent, and all the WAAFs spoke fluent German. This service was later moved to West Kingsdown in north west Kent, an ideal spot as it was the highest point in the county. The WAAF section officer in charge was Jean Conan Doyle, later to become Director of the WAAF. One memory she has is seeing five 'Y' operator Sergeants outside their billet in swimsuits and flying boots, which they were issued because of their exposed duties.

There were also several WAAFs dropped into occupied territory as agents, Flight Officer Sybil Anne Sturrock was parachuted into Yugoslavia on the 10th September 1944. She became attached to the Partisan 10 Corps in Moshlavina, and for the next ten months operated in an area surrounded by enemy held communications. Finally, she entered Zagreb on the 9th May 1945. For her efforts she was awarded the MBE in September 1945.

Flight Officer Cecile Pearl Cornioley, nee Witherington, was also awarded the MBE and the Croix de Guerre. Having escaped from France in 1940, she dropped into France on the 23rd September 1943, and worked with the Maquis in the Puy de Dome, taking part in the sabotage of the Michelin tyre factory at Clemons Ferrand. When her commanding officer and wireless operator was captured in May 1944, she took over the organisation and arranged 23 supply drops, undertaken by seven aircraft, and the planning of concentrated attacks on enemy communications on D-Day, the 6th of June 1944. On the 11th June, her group was attacked by 2,000 German troops supported by artillery, an attack which lasted twelve hours. The Germans lost 86 men, and the Maquis 24. The Germans did however manage to break up the organisation, being led to start from scratch. As well as organising resistance she helped escaping airmen to safety.

A number of agents dropped into occupied territory did not return; some were tortured after capture, some were summarily shot, and others died in the gas chambers at concentration camps. Section Officer Lillian Verna Rolfe landed in Orleans, France, by Lysander aircraft on the 5th May 1944. Her job was to ensure a radio contact with London and to arrange supply drops for the local Maquis. During her time there, her leader was arrested but still she kept up the daily radio contact despite the great danger in doing so. Then, on the 3rd July 1944, she herself was arrested and sent to the notorious Fresnes prison in Paris, and from there to Glincy. Nothing was ever heard of her again. Her name is inscribed on panel 277 of the Runnymede Memorial, commemorating airmen who have no known grave. Her twin sister Mrs. Helen Oliver lived in London at the time. Lillian had been living in Rio de Janeiro at the time of the outbreak of war and then came to the UK to join the WRAF. She had been born in Paris and when she arrived in France as an agent she found she had to restrain patriotic Frenchmen from shooting every German they saw. Members of the resistance were often known by more than one alias name, a street in Montages was name "Rue Claudie Rolf" after Lillian in 1956, and her sister was present at the ceremony. The name 'Claudie' was one of Lillian's code names. When she was awarded a posthumous award of the Croix de Guerre it was established that she, Violette Szabo, and Danielle Block had been put to death on the 5th February 1945.

Other WAAF personnel mentioned on this panel are Section Officer Cicely Margot Lefort who also came from Paris and was 46 at the presumed time of her death. She was also awarded the Croix de Guerre. Section officer Diana Rowden, whose code name was Paulette operated in France in 1943 and died on the 6th July 1944, at Camp Struthof Natzwerle. In 1946, a number of Germans were tried at a war crimes trial at Wuppertal for her death. On Panel 243 the name of Assistant Section Officer Nora Inayat Khan is shown. She had been born on New Year's Day 1914, in the Kremlin, Moscow. Her father, who was Indian, was well-known, and at the time a guest of Count Tolstoy. For a few years, she lived and was educated in Paris, including training at the Academy of Music. When she arrived in London after the fall of France she and her brother joined the air force, where she trained as a wireless operator. It was in 1942 when she joined SOE and left by Lysander for France on 16th June 1943, her code name Madeline. After some three months or so she was betrayed to the Gestapo and arrested. She tried on several times to escape but failed. Much of the nine months that she spent at Pforzheim jail was in chains. In September 1944, she was sent to Dachau concentration camp along with three other female agents. On 13th September 1944, they were made to kneel in the crematorium and shot in the back of the neck. On 5th April 1949, she was awarded the George Cross, and awarded a mention in despatches.

In July 1967, a plaque was unveiled at her old home in Paris, a message being sent by the President of the VC/GC Association, Brigadier Sir John Smyth BT VC, MC. It was read by Colonel Buckmaster, the wartime head of the French section of SOE. "I, and all the members of the Association, both holders of the VC and GC, will always revere Nora Inyat Khan GC and cherish her memory as one of the most splendid and gallant women in our history. In her life, and particularly in her incredibly valiant work for the resistance, she was always staunch and true to the cause of freedom and to the comrades who were working with her, and she faced death with the same courage she had always shown in her life." Her brother had also been an agent for SOE but was unaware that his sister was also involved in this work.

The TV series "Wish me Luck" portrayed two agents sent to France, one as a courier and the other as a wireless operator, whereas in fact only one woman was sent out to carry out both roles. The woman sent was Flight Officer Yvonne Cormeau, who in 1945 was awarded the MBE for her work in SOE. She joined the WAAF in 1940, after her husband had been killed in Belgium, and served in Bomber Command until 1943, working in the operations room at RAF Swinderby. In 1943 she was recruited for SOE and spent thirteen months organising arms, supply drops and training resistance workers. She would think nothing of cycling up to 100 kilometres in a snow storm. During this time, she posed as a child's nanny, carrying a radio, covered up in a basket on the front of the bike. Of the three agents dropped, she was the only one to survive. Her training took 16 weeks, during which she learned Morse, cipher and code work and how to repair her radio if need be. As well as this of course she had to learn to parachute, and unarmed combat and if need be, to slit a man's throat. This, she is glad to say, she never had to do. She left for France on 22nd August 1943 from RAF Tempsford, her code name 'Annette'. She worked in the area which stretched from Gironde to the Pyrenees. In thirteen months she sent back 400 messages, a record for one tour of duty.

Another woman who was given a WAAF commission was Countess Krystyna Skarbeck, who became known as Christian Granville and was given the code name 'Pauline Armand'. She was born in Warsaw in 1915 and at the age of 18 became a beauty queen. Her husband served in the Polish Cavalry and was killed attacking German tanks on horseback. Much of her work was in the South of France, and North Africa, developing an escape line for Poles, and on operations in Algiers. She was awarded the George Medal for saving the lives of two British officers, and the Croix de Guerre for saving the life of a French Officer, Major Sorenson. In 1944, in the South of France, she bribed and browbeat the local Gestapo to release Francis Cammaerts, Nora Inyat Khan and Diana Rowden. On 11th August 1945 she relinquished her WAAF commission and was given a gratuity of £100. She was then forgotten; even her own country, Poland, did not honour her in any way. However, in May 1947, she was awarded the OBE for her wartime efforts. She began her peacetime work as a steward on an oceangoing liner until 13th June 1952 when the ship docked at Southampton having sailed from South Africa. She booked into the Shelbourne Hotel in Lexham Gardens, London, and on the 15th, in the reception area of the hotel, she was confronted by a man whom she knew as he also worked on the same liner as herself. In a fit of jealousy, driven by infatuation, he stabbed her, and she died shortly after. When his case came up at the Old Bailey the trial took only five minutes. He pleaded guilty and asked for no defence; he was then pronounced guilty and sentenced to death by hanging. The sentence was carried out on 30th September 1952. As for Krystyna, who deserved a better post war life than she had, she was buried on 21st June 1952 at the St Mary's Cemetery, Kensall Green. Many people turned up to her funeral including the man she had helped escape, Francis Cammaerts. Twelve members of FANY were present. On her coffin lay her decorations, medals and her resistance badges, plus her small but well-earned parachute wings.

Margaret McDermott served as a nursing orderly on a bomber station at RAF Stradishall. At takeoff and landing times she would sit with a driver in the ambulance, or 'Blood Wagon' as it was known. On 29th March 1943, at RAF Chedburgh, two aircraft of 214 Squadron collided over the airfield while awaiting their turn to land, in a pattern known, then as now, as stacking.

One of the aircraft, Stirling BR663T, flown by Fg Off Dixon, collided with EF 362N flown by Fg Off Cooper. The rear turret was chopped off BR 663, taking the rear gunner Sgt. H Burt with it. Margaret and her ambulance were called out to look for the missing rear gunner in the surrounding countryside but returned having failed to locate him. Then came a call that the police had located him two mils west of the airfield. When they arrived it was, as expected, to find that Sgt. Burt was dead, his body lying ten yards from his turret. The other aircraft with Fg Off Cooper had crashed 17 miles away, the pilot being killed in the crash.

Audrey Tennant drove an ambulance for nine months working out of the sick quarters at Biggin Hill. On one occasion an aircraft crashed near the airfield, when she arrived bullets were exploding all over the field. All that was left of the airmen flying the aircraft was a decapitated and burned black torso. A ring found at the site of the crash had inscribed on it 'With Love on Your 21st Birthday'. The airman's birthday had only been a matter of weeks before; she just sat there in her ambulance and cried. At the sick quarters a loud bell would ring for a crash, and three short ones to denote a sweep. Her trade being a driver, she was expected to drive all manner of vehicles, such as a petrol bowser delivering fuel to the aircraft, and a snow plough clearing the runways in winter, to name just two.

In 1943, she was posted to Fairwood Common, near Swansea in South Wales. This was not too far from her home in Newport, now Gwent but then Monmouthshire. On 16th February 1943, a Ju88 dropped three or four bombs on the airfield killing two WAAFs in their sleeping quarters, ACW Irene Collett and ACW Pat Baxter, and injuring a further three. On 9th April 1944, Halifax W7927 of 1658 CU, flown by Sgt. Grubb, lost two engines in flight. As he attempted to land he found the runway blocked with another aircraft, he tried to restart one of the engines to gain power to climb and go around again. The engine restarted but was running badly and unable to make height he crashed into huts in a field adjacent to No 4 Site. The crew of eight were uninjured in the crash but the huts which were the WAAF sleeping quarters and accommodated at the time by WAAF drivers.

As many were on leave or out on late passes many missed the crash as it was 11pm when it happened. Audrey was sleeping in the reception hut nearby. On many occasions she had been asked to change huts, but decided she liked it better where she was. If she had changed she too would have been in the hut that was hit. One woman who was in the but was scalped by a flying window frame, and when she came back months later her hair had regrown but whereas it had been straight before, it was now curly, also before she had been a serious type of woman and she was now more outward and giggly.

Another woman had a fractured leg, and another was on the danger list. In all 15 were injured; one of whom, ACW Evans, died of her injuries the next day. Two WAAFs who had been out on a late pass found on their return a wheel of the crashed Halifax on their beds. Sister Vera Stone of the Princess Mary's RAF Nursing Service was one of the first to arrive at the scene. She had only just gone off duty when the crash happened having been on duty for twelve hours, but soon took control of the situation. A stove in the middle of the room had been knocked over causing many small fires which had to be put out. The aircraft was lying at the side of the hut, on board were smoke bombs although at the time this was not known. She managed by herself to get many of the wounded and injured out and administered them first aid. She then spent the rest of the night in the operating theatre until 5am when she had to stop due to exhaustion. This did not stop her being back at her post at 8am. For her splendid efforts on this night she was later awarded the MBE.

Beryl Sela-Morgan was a trained medical orderly and trained in aero-medevac (Evacuation by Air Ambulance). Her role was not only rescue and repair, as she put it, but also to administer preventative medicine such as vitamin and air sickness pills, and rum to keep out the cold. To help aircrew with night flying, ultra violet ray treatment was given to produce artificial sunlight. This of course affected in the main the bomber crews who operated at night. At night she would look after a ward of 30 beds and be ready to takeoff time for any accidents that occurred. The ambulance had to be despatched to the airfield to standby at the control tower at takeoff time. The crash theatre was always kept ready with gas cylinders. She would hear the heavily laden bombers takeoff for a target only known to those involved in the operation. Then it was time for an occasional sleep and then up ready for the crews' return. The aircraft would come back with gaping holes and shot up, crews wounded and needing urgent medical attention. All the medics were trained in how to get aircrew out of a crashed aircraft, which meant knowing where all the escape hatches were on all types of aircraft. The large camouflaged Albion ambulance would rush out to the aircraft, and the wounded were then brought to the sick quarters for treatment. If they were more seriously injured, they were taken to the base hospital. In the winter, with the flu scares, men were given gargles and aspirin to ward it off, as every man was considered vital to the task of winning the war. But the job of 'Nursing the men to fly' went on, even during the attack on the airfield themselves as often happened on bomber stations, as well as fighter.

Irene Storer began her balloon operating career in 1941. The outer fabric of a balloon was made of Egyptian cotton, two-ply, bias-cut, proofed and faced with aluminium. Inside the balloon was a diaphragm of thinner fabric. One panel in the balloon was not stitched but attached to a red rip cotton. The whole purpose of the balloon was to hold up the wire cable which was the lethal thing to the enemy rather than the balloon itself. It prevented dive bombing and kept enemy aircraft high enough for the anti-aircraft guns to get at them. On one occasion Irene burned her hands when the balloon shot up while she was hanging on to the rope. Another woman broke both her legs when operating the balloon. When Irene was promoted to LACW she moved to another site on high ground in Sheffield, from there to Derby. On one occasion a woman rang saying "Come and shift this balloon." It had caught on her chimney pot and was blocking the chimney and the smoke was coming back into the room instead of escaping up the chimney. It was explained to her that it could not possibly be a balloon on her chimney. What it was that she thought was a balloon was never discovered.

LACW Minnie Devlin tripped over a handling guy in the dark, whilst dashing to the tail-guy and broke her foot, which left her with a permanent limp. When Irene asked her why she was still working on balloons with her leg in this condition, she replied that she was waiting for a discharge, but before she was given this it had to be proven that her leg would not get better once again before her discharge was approved.

When balloons became obsolete Irene went on to serve in Bomber Command as an instrument repairer. In 1942, at the Coventry balloon site, a painting was unveiled. On the right of this painting, by Dame Laura Knight which can now be seen at the Imperial War Museum, is Irene giving instructions to the team launching the balloon. Irene died in 1986.

One WAAF nearly became airborne on a balloon. Queenie Masters remembers "I nearly went up with it as we were getting it in to a hangar for repair, I was still hanging on to the ropes when it started to get airborne. My sergeant gave a few choice words and I was badly shaken."

Georgina Webster began her service in IOC as an aircraft fabric worker at Colerne. She later transferred to balloons repairing them in a huge hangar near Glasgow. The balloon was inflated to assess the damage and on one occasion when she was inspecting one and inside the balloon, someone opened the hangar door and out went the balloon. Fortunately, it did not gain height but just moved along the ground. 'All I could hear was running feet and the FS shouting 'Get that bloody balloon down before it gets damaged' but no word about the terrified WAAF inside". Although Queenie comes from Lancashire, having met her husband who is a Scot in Glasgow, she has now settled and lives in Aberdeen.

The are many facets of war; some are in direct combat and others are in the wings keeping up the morale and spirits of the frontline troops. The latter was the role of 'Paddy' Black, who served in the RAF Gang Show run by Sqn Ldr Ralph Reader who, after the war, created and directed the Boy Scout Gang Show, and the British Legion Festival of Remembrance at the Albert Hall, later run by his son Bob. The Gang Show HQ was at Cadogan Gardens. It was here that she met Peter Sellers who then was much leaner than in later life and had a mass of brown wavy hair. He loved to mimic even then as of course he later did in the 'Goon Show'. At the time he lived with his parents in a flat in Finchley, his parents owned and ran an antique shop. Another member of the show was Tony Hancock, later of 'Hancock's Half Hour'. She remembers that there was little sign then of the immense talent he would later show.

With the show she travelled all around the UK and Europe entertaining the troops. One such place was Yugoslavia where the Gang Show entertained the Royal Ulster Rifles. She last saw Peter Sellers in 1946. Now when she watches Sellers or Hancock films it brings tears to her eyes.

In WWII radar was to play a vital part in the outcome of the war. In this area of the war the WAAFs played an important part. Dorothy Gray served on several radar stations from 1942 to 1945 around the coast of Britain, her training was undertaken at RAF Cranwell. The practical training consisted of working in a dark room, learning how to interpret the blips on the radar tube, which looked rather like a television set. Her first posting was to Holyhead where the radar station was near the South Stack Lighthouse. The watches were from 8am to 1pm, the second from 1pm to 6pm and the final watch 11 pm to 6am so it was covered 24 hours a day. When she was posted to Dale Castle in South Wales she found the local pub landlord did not admit WAAFs into his pub. The only thing left was a once a week trip to Haverfordwest, but if you were on duty, of course, you missed it.

Mary Holloway also worked on radar sets from 1942 onwards. When she was posted to Leighton Buzzard, she found her billet was a former workhouse. One WAAF there at the time became post war the Marquess de la Falaise, and another, Jean Dawney, a famous Dior model. During the nonflying time, the rest room floor became like the platform of a tube station, bodies were everywhere all catching up on urgently needed sleep. On one occasion when the transport broke down after the night shift finished, 30 dishevelled WAAFs walked down to the nearby Exminster railway station to catch the train back to Exeter. Going sick was quite a performance as it meant a ten-mile bus journey and a mile walk to the camp. You had to report sick with your tin hat, gas mask and small kit. If you failed to do so, the Medical Officer would refuse to see you.

Jane Lumsden trained at the Code and Cipher school in Oxford, probably the same one as Elspeth Henderson. Her training took three weeks, during which she was taught various codes and ciphers. The British version of the machine was called Type X and had a similar keyboard to an electric typewriter. Jane still today remembers pounding the keys, this spelt out plain language on one tape, and on the other a coded message. If you hit a wrong key, it spelt out nonsense on both tapes. Jane left the school a fully-fledged cipher officer. Eventually she was promoted to Chief Cipher Officer at No 5 Group, Bomber Command in Grantham, where three officers kept a 24hour watch. She also had to visit the cipher officers on 5 Group stations once a week; for this a staff car was provided but she preferred to use her own car for which she was given a petrol coupon and an allowance of a halfpenny a mile. She took her dog, a spaniel, along with her on these visits. On one occasion when a stick of bombs fell near the headquarters a white faced WAAF arrived with a message for her, "Try to be calm and not show worry." She replied,

"Don't worry, I think it's all over now." The WAAF retorted, "It's not the bombs, Ma'am, but a mouse which just ran across the passage in front of me." At the time Jean's surname was Train, and so she became known as 'Puff'.

On her officer door was the title, Flight Officer Train, and the names of three cipher officers. One day a 'wit' came past and said "Oh! Flt Off Train and her little miscarriages."

Cpl Beatrice Heaton Campbell, who now lives in Australia, was on duty in the ops room at No 13 Group in 1942 as a plotter. She suddenly noticed several raids appear on the plotting table, most of them were friendly, but one flying over the Northeast coast was thought to be hostile. It was Galashiels's Observer Corps who confirmed it as being hostile. By this time the 13 Gp controller had got aircraft airborne and they were on their way to intercept. The enemy aircraft was plotted onto the coast line and when it reached 13 Gp it was passed on to the next group as hostile. After about an hour and a half, word came that it had crashed in Scotland. A loud cheer went up in the 13 Gp ops room on hearing this news. The pilot turned out to be Rudolf Hess, one of Hitler's closest advisers. He was captured and remained a prisoner in the UK for the remainder of the war, after which he was incarcerated in Spandau prison, Berlin, for the rest of his life.

At the beginning of the war television was in the throes of deve10pment at MX Alexander Palace. When the war started it went off the air, the programme at the time being a Mickey Mouse Cartoon. A small group of servicemen and women spent many hours every day watching enemy television at secret points on the cliffs of Beachy Head in Eastbourne, Sussex, an area very exposed to gales and storms. From 1942, when the early tests were being made from the Eiffel Tower in Paris, to August 1944, when the first programmes were broadcast, a daily watch was kept. Valuable intelligence could be acquired, such as how the RAF bombing raids were affecting the production and morale in Germany. The weak signals were picked up by WAAF German speaking radio operators, and then passed to 60 Signal Corps.

Dorothy Warr was a plotter but could not bear the thought of working underground, so she carried on as a driver with 419 Squadron. She felt by driving the crews to their aircraft she was very close to what was going on in the war. To this day she still has an Ice Hockey Championship Medal which belonged to a FS George Mologzi who hailed from Canada. It was his lucky mascot and he always gave it to Dorothy before taking off for an operation and then on return she gave it back to him until his next op. To him it was something to aim at and a method of trying your hardest to return. He would say to her "Dotty, put this in your pocket, near your heart". When he finished his tour of operations he gave her the medal, which he had inscribed 'To Dot' and then kissed her. He was later killed after being posted from 419 Squadron to a training unit and is now buried in Stratford-upon-Avon. She had hoped one day to return the medal to one of George's relatives. Dorothy often went on air tests with the crews. On one aircraft, flown by a Plt Off Fawcett, her name 'Dorothy' had been painted.

Peggy Wells was also a driver with 622 Squadron where she became the 'B' Flight Commander's driver. On one occasion as she passed an aircraft of 'A' Flight one of the crew about to takeoff cut his finger badly. She drove off to the sick quarters to get dressings for the man's finger. The crew, it must be said, were not keen for her to enter the aircraft on superstitious grounds.

Despite this and wearing a skirt which she had to hitch up, she climbed into the aircraft and bandaged the man's fingers, so he was fit for their take-off. The crew later returned so there was no bad omen over her entering the aircraft. She also drove a tractor with 75 Sqn, delivering bombs to the aircraft for bombing up. Driving at night needed a sixth sense as well as perfect eyesight, and sometimes she would find a Lancaster breathing down her neck as it came out of dispersal.

When Nellie Wylie first joined the WAAF she had problems knowing her left from her right; although her salutes were straight from the manual, they were given with her left hand instead of her right as is the custom and requirement.

On one occasion, a pay parade in which one salutes with the right hand and takes the money with the left, she marched up to the pay table and when the officer called out "Wylie", she replied "Sir, 2102243" in the usual manner and as by the book, then promptly spoiled it all by saluting with her left hand. From there on she acquired the nickname of 'Crafty'. She began her course as a motor mechanic at the MTM Weeton, which took twelve weeks. She was then posted to the MT Section at RAF Wittering, the first female mechanic to be posted here. At first the men were none too friendly, but later all was well, and the women were accepted. When she was demobbed on 7th February 1946, after three years' service, the following was written in her discharge book: "Her skill, keenness and general ability at all times has been of the highest order. Employed in service, repair and inspection of motor transport of all types, and has proved herself equal and often superior to the average man on the same work."

Joan Packham joined the WAAF in 1942. The Wrens, she remembers were top dogs and all the women wanted this service as their first choice. The ATS were considered the common lot, so she went for the middle of the road option, the WAAFs. She was asked on joining if she spoke any languages or was good at science. To both she replied 'Yes'.

From there she became a radar operator, then later a 'Wrong' or Radar Operator Mechanic. This meant moving from operating them to repairing them, which was equally important. On one occasion she got a blip on her screen which was identified as being friendly, and the Navy at the Humber were informed accordingly. Shortly after, the phone rang, and it was the Navy calling back. The RAF officer who took the call burst out laughing; the Navy officer had said "Excuse me, Benton, are those friendly bombs being dropped here as well?"

The Wrong would have to clean the plugs and help with the day to day maintenance of the sets; as one was closed down to do this another took over so that continuity was kept. On one occasion as she was about to close a set down she noticed an SOS on the screen, which looked like a melting icicle. She promptly reported it and was told to stick with it as her set was the only one which had picked it up. It came right into land from the sea before she lost it. After about an hour and a half a signal came through to say the SOS was from an aircraft which had landed safely. The signal was from the squadron CO with his thanks. On another occasion, when a mechanic or Wrong was working on a set, he used a screwdriver in the wrong place and was blown across to the other side of the room. The wall stopped his progress and he just slid down to the floor. He was completely unhurt and began to giggle. At the time Joan's husband was in the Royal Engineers and in 1943 she left the WAAFs to have a baby. She had served for 22 months. In the late 1940s she had a stroke of luck, winning the football pools and a considerable amount of money.

For Liz Bond, her ambition was to become an equipment assistant, but this trade was full at the time, so she went into the parachute packing section for the aircrew and one of the most important sections. "We had no idea what a parachute looked like, and here we were to begin packing and servicing them, all rather nerve wracking. Particularly when you saw how large they were, and all this had to be put in a small bag and correctly, as it might save a man's life one day". As well as servicing the chutes, they also looked after the dinghies and Mae West life jackets, important pieces of aircrew kit, as if you came down in the North Sea and they did not work you were in trouble. The women also had to have a knowledge of knots and splicing. At the end of the course there was a written examination. When it was over there was a profound sense of relief. The corporal in charge of her billet went grey overnight.

Liz's first posting was to 13 OTU at Bicester. Her billet was a pretty little cottage in the village and later, a mansion. Her next posting was to 16 OTU at Upper Heyford. The parachute section was next to the hangars where the Wellington bombers were housed, the stove in the room was not for their behalf but for the parachutes which were hung from the ceiling. It was an eerie sight at night to see those long white sheets hanging down. The man on guard in the area would have to go in and make sure all was well during his patrol. In her autograph book, a cheeky little cockney, Peter Booth, wrote "Thanks for some of the best moments of my life spent with you and the gang of the pars section, I go, I come back." This was his last phrase. He became a casualty statistic of the war and did not return from operations. Another boy, as of course they mostly seemed to be then, asked her to look after his library book until he came back from a trip to Cologne on the 1,000-bomber raid of 1942; he also failed to return.

From missing crews, many flying log books were now piling up. Her own cousin Royce, serving with 44 Squadron was killed over Holland, and her boyfriend at the time, who was serving with 49

Squadron, went missing on the now famous Peenemunde raid of August 1943. He had only two operations to fly before completing his tour. He and his crew do not have a known grave but are recorded on the Runnymede Memorial. She also joined the station band as a side drummer. When she moved to Spittlegate she met her husband Mike, who had just returned from East Africa where he had finished his tour as a wireless operator. On one occasion Flt Lt Tate had to use his parachute, which Liz had in fact packed for him. He was said to be connected to the family behind the sugar-refining company, Tate & Lyle. He gave Liz a number of gifts to show his thanks. To sum up her service in the WAAF Liz said "What a wonderful feeling of comradeship which bounded us together. But never forget the boys and women who were so young and gave their lives for you and this country. I can still hear the WAAF's marching feet down the lane. We were very patriotic".

Noreen Dunbar, later King, served with 115 Sqn at Witchford and spent the whole of her career in the WAAFs in the flying control tower, the hub of any airfield. Her father having served in the Army in WWI was an intelligence officer at Mildenhall and her boyfriend, a Czech, was serving in 311 Sqn. In 1943, having completed two tours of operations, he became an instructor, but while on a training flight his aircraft crashed into the sea and he was killed. With shock, Noreen's mind went blank and she put the whole thing out of her mind, all her thoughts were on the job, getting crews off and then safely back to base. Although she married in 1946, she never forgot Frank, whom she had met when her father brought him home for the weekend to the family home in Newport, Monmouthshire. When he was killed they were already engaged to be married and looking forward very much to a future together.

In March 1943, Flt Lt Myers Wayman DFC was killed flying a Mosquito with 139 Sqn. His father was the Mayor of Sunderland. In memory of his gallant son he presented a cup, which was to be known as the Sunderland Cup, to the WAAF. It was decided to use it as a competition cup, to be competed for each year for the best all round WAAF unit in Bomber Command.

The WAAF expanded to 79 times its original strength. 95% of the WAAF were replacing airmen, of which 70% were in skilled trades. The number of WAAFs serving abroad increased; officers were sent to the USA, Canada, West Indies and Bermuda, and all ranks to the Middle East, Egypt, Palestine, East Africa, Seychelles, Iraq, Cyprus, Aden, Italy, India, Ceylon, Gibraltar and Malta. Serving in the ranks of the WAAF were Dutch and Belgian women, and some from Greece and Cyprus. In Palestine, 300 women were recruited, forming up in Jerusalem. Women from Poland were also recruited. They wore the same uniform as the British WAAFs but had their own cap badge and buttons. American women came over to join the WAAF before the USA eventually came into the war. One such woman was attending morning service at the Guards Chapel when it was bombed on a Sunday morning in June 1944, she and her husband were both killed.

During invasion time Edna Stafford worked at Norfolk House where the invasion plans were being drawn up. It was here that she met Gp Capt. Gleave who had been badly burned during the Battle of Britain. He said, "I had a row with a German", the title of his book. On 21st September 1944 she was taken to Heston airfield with all her kit, from where she was flown to Paris, then to Versailles where her office was in the 'Trianon Hotel'. General Eisenhower and Air Chief Marshal Tedder, had their offices on the first floor, as did the American General Spaatz. Towards the end of April 1945, by now in Rheims, she began to see the first senior German officers who had been taken prisoner, General Jodl and Admiral von Friedeburg to name but two. On VE Day in Paris, as in the UK, people celebrated the end of the war in Europe. Decorations and streamers were everywhere and bands playing. On 24th May 1945, she set off bound for Germany and landed in Frankfurt two hours later. She was once again back on the staff of Eisenhower and Tedder[11]. It was here that she met her future husband. He was the station hairdresser and had a shop in Bad Eilsen, which had been the HQ of the Luftwaffe. She soon became in charge of the typing pool, which consisted of seven typists for 50 officers.

Edna and her boyfriend decided to get married before returning to the UK, and the wedding was arranged for 2pm on 15th June 1946. Her wedding dress was loaned by a German woman and her

---

[11] The HQ was known as BAFO, or British Air Forces of Occupation. At this time Air Chief Marshal Sholto Douglas was in charge of all Air Forces in Germany.

headdress was made of orange blossom which had been picked fresh from the trees. Her wedding car was decorated with white carnations, and the car escorted by two white helmeted motor cyclists. The reception was held in the WAAF mess where a German band played the Wedding March as they entered. On a table was a three-tiered cake. Their honeymoon was spent in Brussels. When she later returned to the UK and her home in London, her mother opened the door and she entered for the last time as a WAAF. As the door closed, so did the last three years as a servicewoman.

Mary Briggs also went abroad as a code and cipher officer. She was posted to Washington in the USA and became part of the British Mission there. She sailed on the *Britannic* from Southampton, the ship being escorted by two warships and three destroyers. However, during the voyage two of the escort ships were sent to intercept the German battleship *Bismarck*. They embarked in uniform and disembarked in mufti or civilian clothes, as the USA was not in the war at that time. When, in December 1941, Pearl Harbour was bombed, bringing the USA into the war with Japan and Germany, the hotel guests suddenly saw the women arrive in uniform; up to this time they did not know they were even in the services.

After a few months, Mary was posted to Montreal to code the movements of aircraft on their way to the UK. She later served in Newfoundland, Labrador and Nassau until VE Day. The flight from Montreal to Newfoundland was eventful in that she accidentally pulled the rip cord of the chute under her seat and she was engulfed in a white canopy. While in Newfoundland she had an accident and shattered her knee. To help her recovery she was prescribed a pint of milk a day to build up the calcium in her bones to help them knit. As there was no fresh milk in Newfoundland it had to be flown in each day. She had her own flying milkman. Her billet in Nassau was a wooden bungalow on the beach.

Flight Officer Sturrock sailed on the Queen Mary bound for Melbourne in Australia to join the UK Army and RAF Liaison staff. During the voyage 400 German POWs were disembarked in New York. In San Francisco she boarded the SS *Lurhine*, in peacetime a luxury liner, and set sail for Australia via New Guinea with 5,000 service men and women aboard. They reached Brisbane to a much publicised welcome. They were the first WAAFs to be sent out to

Australia. In the next two years, as Personal Assistant to Air Cdre Grice OBE DFC, she travelled all over Australia and New Zealand. She also paid a flying visit to the UK and was made a member of the 'Rare and Elevated Order of the Longest Hop' after a flight across the Indian Ocean from the NW Coast of Australia to Colombo. She flew back in a Boeing flying boat across the South Atlantic, dressed in civilian clothes to accommodate the stop in Lisbon, Portugal, which was of course neutral. She slept in the honeymoon suite which had been used by Churchill when he crossed to the USA. In 74 days she travelled 34,299 miles.

Arlette Harris tried to join the Air Transport Auxiliary (ATA) in 1943 but with so many applying from the WAAF and so few vacancies, she was not surprised when she heard no more. In September 1943, by now an officer, she was posted to HQ SACSEA (Supreme Allied Command South East Asia,). The journey entailed flying from Poole to Karachi, via Marseilles, Sicily, Cairo, Habboniych, Bahrain and then by DC3 aircraft to Bombay and Ceylon. Her journey to Colombo was by road. In South East Asia she became part of Mountbatten's staff based in the Botanical Gardens and later in Singapore. She was demobbed in November 1947.

Joan Lumsden looked back on her service in the WAAF and said, "I remember best the friendships made, the humour when things got tough, the common endeavour, and the excitement and relief when it was all over". On being demobbed they were given £12 10s to obtain a civilian outfit, the Treasury felt that £8 15s was sufficient but the Director of the WAAF stuck to her guns and they got the £12 10s in full. At the time the price of a cup of tea was two pence and a dinner at a good restaurant was five shillings.

The fundamental object of the WAAF was to keep the aircraft of the Royal Air Force flying. At the outbreak of war, it numbered less than 2,000 in only six trades and only one officer branch. This increased in 1943 to 182,000 women serving in 75 trades and 22 officer branches. It was estimated that, without the women, the RAF would have needed another 150,000 extra men, which would have had to be taken from the other services or industry. When a bomber crew took off with its crew of seven it left 24 WAAFs with a job and trade to keep the one aircraft in the air. This would include the basic maintenance of the aircraft, then arming and fuelling to name but a few of the many tasks they carried out.

The Royal Canadian Air Force Women's Division was the first women's military service unit to be formed on the North American continent. They were originally known as the Canadian Women's Auxiliary Air Force when formed on 2nd July 1941. It got its later title on 1st November 1942. In 1938, the South African Women's Aviation Association became in being; in September 1939 and the outbreak of war it became the South African Women's Volunteer Auxiliary Air Force Unit, attached to the South African Air Force. Its motto was 'At Hand Ready'. The New Zealand Women's Auxiliary Air Force was formed on 1st January 1944.

In 1949, Sir Arthur Harris, the former C-in-C of Bomber Command, sent a message from his home at the time in South Africa. It was sent to the ground staff of Bomber Command, including of course the WAAFs. In his message he once again endorsed how much he appreciated their wartime efforts and ended it with a PS: "Wish you were here".

Many of the wartime WAAFs became grandmothers, though often those grandchildren know little of their grandmothers' wartime service decades previously. Many of them felt their memories would not be of interest, or that they would be thought to be "Shooting a Line" and so many kept it to themselves.

In June 1989, the WAAF celebrated their fiftieth anniversary with a service at St Paul's Cathedral and, despite a bus and tube strike, over 1,500 ex-WAAFs turned up from all over the world. It took one ex-WAAF four hours to get there by taxi. As they came out of the cathedral it started to rain but this mattered little, they barely noticed it. They were back in those days of 40 years ago. In Eastbourne, Sussex, the ex-WAAF members of the RAFA Club had their own celebration.

For the main party they had a cake in the colours of the RAF, red, white and blue. In the middle of the room was a wartime billet bed piled high with WAAF memorabilia including a WAAF uniform. They were entertained by Gerry Marsden, a well-known singer and entertainer.

The work undertaken by the WAAF was long and often far removed from the urgency of operations and the glamour of publicity. The success of the service can be measured by the fine tradition they built up, providing a solid foundation for a permanent service, an example and inspiration of its members and today's members of the WRAF who they are in turn equally proud of.

The last word must come from Elsie Campbell who when a corporal and with another WAAF was walking across Waterloo Bridge when confronted by two RAF officers. Elsie hated having to salute but her friend said, 'Go on Elsie give it your best' Up went her right arm towards her cap. As she did so, she knocked her friends cap off and into the Thames. The two officers were convulsed in laughter; being aircrew they saw the funny side of it. "We were well brought up women, never been away from home and were never teenagers, but oh, how we quickly became 'women'."

Chapter 5 Air Transport Auxiliary

The Air Transport Auxiliary or ATA, as it was known was the idea of Commander Gerard d' Erlanger, a director of British Overseas Airways Corporation. With the Munich crisis in 1938 and war obviously looming, the idea was to form a unit, in which in the early days would involve delivering mail, news, despatches, medical supplies, act as air ambulances, and fly VIPs around the country. It should utilise pilots with 'A' licences, and with a minimum of 250 flying hours, who, because of age or health were not eligible to be called up for the RAF. In the Summer of August 1939 more than 1,000 holders of the A' and 'B' licences were contacted, of which some 100 replied. All at this stage were male pilots.

The ATA got its title on the 17th August 1939. For the purposes of administration and finance it came under British Airways[12] which at the time was based in Bristol. It was January 1940, when the first women enrolled. They were put under the wing of Pauline Gower who was to become the first female Senior Commander. She was at first given permission to recruit eight women pilots, whose requirement was a minimum of 600 flying hours. She herself had 2,000 and had been taught to fly by Amy Johnson.

At first the idea was for the women to fly the light aircraft, and the men, the heavy jobs. The first eight were Margie Fairweather, the daughter of Lord Runciman and a former instructor in the Civil Air Guard; Winnie Crossley a former stunt pilot in an air circus; Joan Hughes, a mere five foot two inches in height, but later to become the only woman instructor on all types of aircraft; Mona Friedlander, a former ice hockey international; Margaret Gunnison, a prewar flying instructor, Rosemary Rees, a former ballet dancer, and now Lady du Cros. Joan Hughes had learned to fly in 1933 at the age of 17. When she joined the ATA, she was the youngest member, though, despite her age, she already had 600 flying hours logged. To

---

[12] This was the original British Airways, as opposed to the national carrier formed in 1972 from BEA and BOAC.

them they were doing a useful job and flying was no different from driving a car.

The uniform for the ATA was adapted from the British Overseas Airways Corporation (BOAC) uniform in dark blue. On the left breast in gold their flying wings badge with ATA in the middle. Badges of rank were worn on the shoulder; a first officer wore three gold bars, and a second officer two bars. For flying, of course, they wore the normal kit which was not very feminine, but somehow, they still managed to keep the difference between them and their male counterparts. When in dress uniform, they looked, in every way women. The motto of the ATA was 'Safety and Punctuality' and they were always told "You are paid to be safe, not brave". When they delivered an aircraft to a unit they would often bring back one that needed repair. Some showed significant signs of wear and tear, such as bullet holes or other signs of combat. When flying such aircraft, they were given a red card, which said 'This aircraft is not totally airworthy, take it easy.' The women pilots soon grew from eight to 100, and the ATA as a whole had a backup groundcrew of 1,000. In the Spring of 1944 the women delivered twenty fighter planes a day to units in the south, including Spitfires, Tempests and Typhoons. In October 1941 came the first full-scale female ferry pool at Hamble, led by Commander Margaret Gore.

There were five classes of aircraft that the ATA pilots could qualify for:

Class I: Single-engined aircraft such as Tiger Moths, Spitfires and Hurricanes. No passengers could be carried, even if the seating arrangement did allow.

Class II: More advanced single-engined aircraft such as Typhoon, Tempest and Tomahawk.

Class III: Light twin-engined aircraft such as Ansons and Oxfords but again, not carrying passengers.

Class IV: Blenheims, Wellingtons, Dakotas and Hampden bombers.

Class IV-plus: Mosquito, Hudsons and Baltimores.

Class V: Fortresses, Lancasters, Halifaxes and Liberators (only a few female pilots got to this stage).

Peggy Eveleigh, ATA pilot, above left, in June 1944. Above right: With a Mustang at Hamble, March 1945. Below: In a Tiger Moth, 1944 (P. Eveleigh).

Above: Peggy Eveleigh flying a Spitfire in 1945 (P. Eveleigh). Below: Diana Barnato-Walker in 1944 (D. Barnato-Walker)

Jackie Moggridge, from Pretoria in South Africa was one of the first fifteen female pilots to enrol; she had tried when she was 17 but was rejected because of her age, although at the time she had 200 flying hours logged and was studying at the Aeronautical College, near Witney. She then joined the WAAF and became a radar operator. When the call came for pilots for the ATA she was asked to apply, and succeeded, in her own words, by "Fright, luck, or by good judgement to take-off and land a Tiger Moth three times!" The WAAFs did not want her to leave, as in their opinion, radar operators were just as important, but, as it took a lot longer than six weeks to train a pilot than to train an operator, the ATA won the day. On the 15th July 1940, she became the fifteenth ATA female pilot. Her first task was to ferry a Tiger Moth to Lossiemouth from Cowley, Oxford. There were four going up at the same time but only the leading aircraft had a map and Jackie was detailed to fly at the tail. It seemed at the time there was a shortage of maps. Every two hours during the trip they had to land to refuel. When she had landed at Carlisle and unbuckled her safety straps she suddenly saw three Tiger Moths taking off in the distance, thinking they were her three she buckled up again and took off after them. When she later landed at Lossiemouth the other three Tiger Moth pilots came over and said, "Jackie what are you doing here?" It turned out they were not her group at all, but three that had been stuck at Carlisle waiting for better weather. She was on her way back to Hatfield before the other three, who had started out with her, had even reach Scotland.

In 1944, she was detailed to fly an Albemarle aircraft to Herne Airport, in Kent. The weather was not too good, with fog and cloud en-route. Before taking off an RAF pilot, a squadron leader and his navigator asked if she could give them a lift, she said yes and in they got. When they got near Hem, and as she knew the area well she soon visually picked up the road that led to the airfield. When she landed a loud cheer went up from the staff at Herne. The Commanding Officer said they had been unable to fly for days because of the weather and yet the ATA women were up doing their stuff. They must now get up and do some flying themselves. The squadron leader who had hitched a lift thanked her and said, "May I ask how you found time to read a book while flying in such foul weather?" When she replied, "I was not reading a book as such, but looking at the aircraft handbook as I had not flown this aircraft before," he went a shade of white and quite speechless. At the end of the war Jackie went on to join the WRAF, as a pilot, and flew with them for ten years which included flying the Meteor then jet aircraft of the day. For her efforts during the war she was awarded the King's Commendation, having ferried more aircraft than anyone else, male or female.

Diana Barnato had been an ambulance driver with the Red Cross, when she applied to join the ATA as a pilot. She had learned to fly at Brooklands, where her father had been a racing driver before the war. At the time she was only 18 and the cost of flying lessons was £3 an hour. After six hours flying she went solo and, with only ten hours flying in, she applied, and was accepted in the ATA. Later in the war she married Wing Commander Derek Walker, a pre-war airman who had flown no less than four tours of operations, in the Middle East and Greece, and been awarded the DFC. On one occasion he and Diana flew to France and back, on the return journey and in severe weather they became separated in the cloudy sky. She set a course for Dungeness but failed to find it and so turned left and due west. Suddenly she saw land, and then the gasometer at Bognor Regis. She followed the river up to Chichester and turned when she saw the lights at Tangmere airfield where she landed. As she taxied in she saw the white and worried face of her husband as he came out to meet her. At the time because of the weather Tangmere was the only station open in the whole of the UK.

Sadly, on the 14th November 1945 her husband was killed as he tried to land at Hendon. The crash inquiry said he was lost at the time, but with his background, she doubts this can be true. When her father Barney Barnato died he requested he be buried alongside Derek at the cemetery in Englefield Green. Diana herself went on to fly a Lighting in 1963 at a speed of 1,250 mph and flew with the Adventure Corps up to 1980. She became the Commodore of the ATA Association, which had some 230 men and women members, in the UK and Europe, plus 79 US members.

First Officer Diana Ramsay based at White Waltham took off from Langley en route for Henlow in a Tempest, but en route her throttle jammed open at a speed of 300 mph plus. She tried to land at White Waltham by reducing speed and by climbing, and then putting her wheels down, however this had little effect, so she spotted a field cut her engine and made a force landing crashing into some short trees, over a ditch and ending up in a small clearing. When Diana Barnato and the Medical Officer reached her the aircraft fuselage was upright against a tree, at the top was Diana Ramsey looking for her headband which she always wore and had come off. She then, having found it climbed down, still clutching her flight bag. To get to the car that had brought Diana Barnato and the Medical Officer meant crossing a field of cows. However, Ramsey was terrified of cows and would not cross the field. The debris was so great from the crash that it seemed a miracle that anyone could get out alive, but the Tempest was a sturdy beast and seemed to wrap itself around the pilot protecting her. The trees she had hit slowed her down, and the fact she did not hit anything head on at full speed seemed to have a lot to do with her getting away so lightly.

There were, of course, many ATA pilots from overseas. The daughter of the Polish Marshal Pilsudski was a pilot in the ATA. Anna Leska also came from Poland, she lived in Warsaw and was at the start of the war given the rank of Wartime Pilot Officer in the Polish Airforce. In the early part of the war, when Polish Forces were involved, she flew as a liaison officer, attached to the HQ of the Polish Air Force. As the war progressed in Poland she began to move towards the Rumanian Border and when the Russians attacked from the east, and the Polish Government had to leave the country she received orders to fly to Rumania, where, she and the others sent were interned, and their aircraft handed over to the Rumanians. After a few months, she and her squadron commander and another officer were able to leave and got to France by car. When the fall of France came in May 1940, she was sent to the UK by sea and ended up in London. She worked as a clerk at the Polish Inspectorate of the Airforce, and the British Air Ministry. Her job was compiling information about Polish airmen that were arriving in the UK.

When she found out about the ATA she went down to Hatfield then the home of No 5 Ferry Pool. Having passed all the tests, she was accepted as a pilot in the ATA in January 1941. From Hatfield she went to Hamble, near Southampton, the home of No 15 Ferry Pool and ended the war at No 6 Ferry Pool at Radcliffe, near

Leicester. Thinking back today about those days, she said "I loved the work, the way of life and the people I associated with".

Section Officer Joan Witherby had learned to fly in Malaysia and got her pilots licence in 1938. When the war started she returned to the UK and joined the ATA. On one occasion when landing a Spitfire at Brize Norton the starboard undercarriage leg collapsed, having failed to lock correctly. Two weeks later When caught in cross wind her Spitfire drifted off to the port side of the runway the undercarriage leg on that side hit a pile of rock which were stacked at the edge of the runway the impact knocked the wheel off so she circled the runway twice and then came in and made a one wheel landing balancing the sole wheel on the ground until the aircraft had nearly run to a halt. In 1988, she joined the First Fleet Re-enactment ships at Mauritius and sailed to Sydney, 7,000 miles, as one of the crew.

Whilst flying an Anson, First Officer Wynne Eyton spotted a German U-boat off Beachy Head. When she landed at Shoreham airfield she reported her sighting and later learned that the submarine had been located and destroyed.

Betty Keith-Jupp managed to get into the ATA at the end of the war, having transferred from the WAAFs. In 1944, the ATA accepted and trained two entries from the WAAF, she was in the second entry. At the time she had been at Cranwell on a course and was accepted for flying training from scratch. On the 29th May 1945, she was instructed to deliver a Barracuda aircraft from Prestwick to Lossiemouth. When she started out the weather was fine, and she followed the east coastline, when suddenly she ran into fog coming off the sea and was suddenly flying blind. At the time she was down to 1,000 feet and knowing there was high ground to the left she swung the aircraft to the right and out to sea to try and get back on her correct flight path. But, in turning she lost height and hit the sea. She quickly released the hatch on the cockpit and her parachute harness as the aircraft began to sink. At the time she was only wearing her overalls and shoes, so she soon came to the surface. As the swell lifted her up and down she could see the coastline in the distance, but too far to swim. She started to call 'Help' and was heard by fishermen in the area who had stopped with engine trouble. At first, they thought it was the seagulls barking but then realised it was a human voice, so they called back "Hold on, laddie" and soon had her out of the water and back to Crail.

In 1943, a letter was circulated by the Air Ministry to Commands and Groups "A limited number of women are required by the ATA for training as pilots. Applications are invited from officers and airwomen of the WAAF who wish to be considered. The minimum requirements were:

Age: Over 20,

Height: five feet five or over:

Education: Matriculation School Certificate or Equivalent.

Full Mobility Medically Fit.

Before final acceptance candidates will be required to pass the medical and psychological tests of the ATA for application, service medical gradings will be sufficient.

Over 2,000 WAAFs applied but only 30 were selected. Firstly, a short list was made of 150, from this the lucky 30 were selected. Peggy Eveleigh had begun her WAAF service in Admin but was later recommended for a commission and sent to Cranwell on an officers' course. It was while she was here that she heard about the ATA wanting potential pilots. She had applied before but heard nothing further. On this occasion she exaggerated the amount of flying she had done, saying she had flown mostly in the USA which could not be checked in the UK. She had applied along with another WAAF officer Mary King. A medical followed, she was only five feet four, so she put a thick chiropodist's heel pad inside her shoe to pass the height test. Having checked on this Pauline backed her up, even so Peggy still feels she was lucky. When the war ended in May 1945, she went to London and Buckingham Palace to see the Royal Family on the balcony, she then spent the night in an already overcrowded London on the couch of the writing room at the Overseas League Club.

When she handed her kit in at White Waltham, and left for the last time, she felt she was leaving great chunk of her life behind. Suddenly she heard that the RAF Flying Branch of the Reserve were going to accept experienced women pilots, and on equal terms with the men. She applied and was asked to report to the nearest RAF Reserve Centre. This turned out to be one of her old stamping grounds, Hamble. She went along and was enrolled as the lowest form of life in the RAF, aircraftwoman. She was issued with a battledress, flying helmet, and other bits and pieces. The limit was 30 flying hours per year, if one could produce a good case this could be extended to 60. During the two weeks training she had to wear uniform, but thereafter she could wear civilian clothes. When she landed at Exeter she was confronted by at RAF officer who challenged her right to be flying. He had not heard of women being allowed to fly in the RAF Reserve. Another officer arrived to make sure what he thought was a man, got a haircut. One of the lectures given was how to behave in the Officers Mess, forgetting that all ATA pilots had been honorary members of RAF and Naval messes throughout the war.

On one occasion, Rosemary Rees was ready to take off in a Halifax with a 'stooge,' or flight engineer, when without a second thought she reached for the controls. However, the controls she reached instinctively for were those of an Anson and not the Halifax, as her recent flights had been on the Anson and her brain was thinking on those lines. She soon recovered and reached for the correct controls. Her flight engineer on this occasion was Freddy Laker, later Sir Freddy of Laker Airways fame. On one occasion she was flying to Scotland; the cloud at the time was very low but below it the weather was fine. She flew along the sands of the west coast when suddenly something dark flashed by her righthand side. It turned out to be Blackpool Tower. Many years later, when in Blackpool for the Conservative Conference, she often looked up at the Tower, and reflected on what may have been.

In January 1941 Rosemary and the famous Amy Johnson flew up to Scotland in two separate aircraft, Rosemary was to get to Dumfries and Amy to Prestwick. Neither had an aircraft to bring back on the return trip so they arranged that whichever did get a return would pick the other up. As it happened an Anson landed at Dumfries and was going back so Rosemary hitched a lift. In the meantime, Amy had picked up an Oxford at Prestwick to bring back to Kidlington. En route back she spent the night at Blackpool and then in bad weather set off the next morning. As she flew south the weather got worse and, in some places, it was snowing. All flying at Hatfield had been cancelled and as she tried to find a landing place she drifted out over the Thames Estuary. After four hours, she ran out of petrol. She did manage to bale out but landing in freezing water made her chances very slim. She had been seen coming down by a naval craft, HMS *Hazelmere*, but she was so cold in the water she could not catch the line that was thrown to her. The captain of the ship, Lieutenant Commander Fletcher, jumped overboard to try and get a line attached to her, but she was sucked under the ship and lost. He was then pulled back aboard but suffered a heart attack and died.

The role of the ferry pilots after the war was a clearing-up job, collecting aircraft from stations, some still showing signs of battle and having to be flown carefully. On the 29th September 1945, an Air Display was held at White Waltham, it was in aid of the ATA Benevolent Fund which had been formed to help the wives and children of those pilots who had been killed in ferrying duties.

During war there were 1,152 male pilots 166 females, 151 engineers, 19 radio operators, and 27 ATC and Sea Cadets who often acted as 'stooges' or flight engineers on the four-engine aircraft, or any aircraft in which the pilot required help. Of this number, 174 were killed, including seventeen women. The number of aircraft delivered is impressive; all types delivered 308,567 this included 171,934 single engines, and 25,000 multiengine aircraft. Of this number 4,000 were Lancasters, 9,000 Halifaxes and 86,000 Spitfires. The total flying hours flown by pilots was 414,984, covering 18,250,000 miles and with only three passenger casualties. There were four MBEs awarded to the women, including Pauline Gower, Rosemary Rees and Joan Hughes, two King's Commendations, one Commendation and four BEMs to the ground staff of the ATA, two parachute packers, one Motor Transport driver and one Ground Engineer. There was talk in 1945 of a WAAF flying branch within the RAF. In the main pilots would be taken from the ATA but it came to nothing.

In 1989, the RAF started accepting a limited number of female pilots and navigators for noncombatant flying training. Flight Lieutenant Julie Gibson passed out as the first RAF trained female pilot. Many more have since followed. One female pilot has already completed two tours of operation on fast jet fighters, including a tour with 617 Squadron, The Dambusters, flying Tornados.

Chapter 6 Military / Civilian Nurses

In all wars through the ages there have been those who go and fight and defend their country, and others, such as nurses, whose role it was to care and look after the wounded and sick, from those wars.

Within a week of the outbreak of the Second World War nurses had landed in France. They belonged to the Queen's Alexander Nursing Military Service and served on ambulance trains and casualty clearing stations located in small villages in France. When they were not attending to the troops they would often help the local French people. Many French babies were brought into the world or assisted into the world by British nurses. The medical fraternity of all nations and organisations were there to assist the sick and hurt, colour, creed or country meant little, only that someone needed help. In all, between September 1939, and May 1940, 1300 sisters and many nurses embarked as part of the British Expeditionary Force that crossed the Channel to France. When the evacuation came in May 1940, most of these women returned safely.

Hilda Cant began her nursing training at Ayr, in Scotland, and her medical training at Farnborough Hospital, in Kent. At the time of the Munich crisis, in 1938, she was by now a sister at the Park Royal Hospital in South East London. One of her friends, also a sister, was in the QAMN Reserve. When she decided to leave Hilda took her place. When war was declared in September 1939, she was issued with a travel warrant, and sent to Southampton to join a ship which was being converted into a hospital ship. The ship, the *Dinard*, was owned by Southern Railways and had been a cross channel steamer. When she arrived, the ship was not ready, so she and the others were put out in billets and told to report to the military hospital at Netley each day. It took workmen five days to convert the ship; inside it looked like a hospital ward with beds on each side. When it was completed, they set sail and spent the next few months bringing back wounded and sick servicemen from France. When it was completed, they set sail and spent the next few months bringing back wounded and sick servicemen from France. When the fall of France came in May 1940, their services were in great demand to get the wounded troops back off the beaches at Dunkirk. On the 28th May 1940, they set sail for Dunkirk and arrived without too many problems, however, as there was no berthing party on the jetty it meant the crew having to jump from the ship taking with them the ships ropes. On the 29th May, they returned once again and took no fewer than 271 stretcher cases. On this day Captain Ailwyn Jones reported being attacked by two torpedoes. The water being calm and clear meant he was able to see them in time and take evasive action. He also reported a number of near collisions with other ships. On 30th May they once again went into the area but on this occasion with bombs and shells falling all around the ship, and with the depth of water dropping all the time they had to cut the ropes and back out. On board the *Dinard* was a stewardess, 59-year-old Mrs. Goodridge. When the ships converted she was told she need not stay as she was a civilian. Her reply was typical of the spirit of the time: "If the sisters are going I will go as well." She went on later to be awarded a Mention in Despatches, the only award given to a woman for the evacuation at Dunkirk. Hilda remembers bringing billycans of hot soup and bread for the wounded and crew. One soldier brought aboard with his eyes bandaged said after he had heard Hilda speak "Oh, a female voice". The matron on the *Dinard* said to Hilda after she had fed the wounded soup and bread "Get those men a plate for the bread." Of course, men who have not eaten for five days do not care how the food is served, a chunk of bread and a mug of hot tea is all they required.

After the evacuation Captain Jones said "As captain of the ship I would like to express my admiration, and deep regard for the nursing sisters aboard. We recently made two trips to Dunkirk and two to Cherbourg, in each case being the last hospital carrier to enter and leave the ports. Our second trip to Dunkirk was under extremely severe conditions, bombs and shells dropping all about us and men being wounded and killed alongside our ship on the pier. During this episode the sisters were splendid, just carrying on under the able leadership of the matron, calmly and efficiently". When the evacuation was over the *Dinard* went up the west coast and Hilda was put ashore in Scotland. In Glasgow, she took a train for Shaftesbury and the military hospital. Later she boarded a ship bound for the Middle East, and during the voyage around the Africa coast she learned to speak French. Finally, she arrived in Cairo, and then went by train to Alexandria where she joined a base hospital. However, her love for the sea soon made her volunteer for sea duties once again and she joined a hospital ship, a former liner, *Llandovery Castle*. All the time she was sailing around the Med she was never sea sick; on one occasion everybody but she and the purser were laid low with sickness. After three years she was posted to India and the British Military Hospital in Calcutta. Here she stayed until arriving back in the UK on the 8th June 1945. She was sent to the Royal Herbert Hospital, in south east London, now converted into flats. On the 10th September 1945, she was demobbed at Regents Park Barracks and returned to her old job at the Park Hospital. Having spent so much time as a military nurse she found the life of a civilian nurse very mundane and not for her, so she left for good. Two vivid memories she has today is while in India, they were told never to smile at the Indian orderlies as they did not think much of women and if a woman smiled at them they would think the woman was soft, so she never did smile them.

It is a common sight to see dogs, cats, and even foxes eating out of dustbins in the UK. For Hilda, it was something a little more exotic; she saw a panther eating out of a dustbin.

It was in the summer of 1938 and, after Neville Chamberlain had brought back his now famous piece of paper from Germany suggesting 'peace in our time...', Alice Moody decided to join a nursing division of the St John's Ambulance Brigade in South Manchester. Just after she had been awarded a first aid nursing certificate the Civil Nursing Reserve was formed. By this time war was imminent and so she enrolled in the new unit and began her training. This consisted of spending many hours in the local hospital training to become a nursing auxiliary. The minimum requirement to have served in training was 60 hours. In May 1940, just before Dunkirk, she and 30 others were called up. They listened to a speech delivered to them at Manchester Town Hall by a woman in the uniform of a Red Cross Commandant.

She told them they were going to prepare a hospital for casualties and that the road ahead was to be hard and difficult. They were taken to a former mental hospital, 20 miles from Manchester. The padded cells were turned into linen and blanket stores, and the empty wards were furnished with War Office beds.

The CNR had a specific uniform but members of the Red Cross and St John's were allowed to wear their own. Finally came the day and the first convoy of wounded arrived, all were veterans straight from the devastated beaches of Dunkirk, their wounds still bound in initial field dressings which were by now caked in mud. They had very little uniform or equipment left, they were tired and some in extreme pain and discomfort. The inexperience of the nurses showed through as they plied these men with eggs and bacon, forgetting many of them would be needing operations to remove shrapnel and to clean wounds. It was an anaesthetist's nightmare as it proved almost impossible to find patients who had fasted properly prior to being anaesthetised.

The air raid precaution personnel taught the nurses to cope with air raids and gas attacks, and the Auxiliary Fire Service taught them to deal with incendiary bombs. This was done by approaching burning canisters on their stomachs protected by an upended dustbin lid in front of them, and then to direct a gentle spray of water on to the burning canisters with a stirrup pump, and a bucket of water. On one occasion the A.F.S. officer assembled them all in the ward for fire drill, the ward happened to be the fracture ward and of course most of the patients were in splints, on frames or in some way immobilised. As the nurses disentangled the big hose from its reel and carried it into the war somebody turned on the water supply and out came the water in such a force that the nurse carrying the hose could not hold it on upon which it proceeded to snake its way around the ward soaking those who could not get out of its way, with the patients being static this would apply to many of them. Several the patients had to have their plaster of paris reapplied, beds had to be remade and the ward dried out. The A.F.S after this gave them up as a bad job and they were not seen again. One of the jobs for the night duty nurse was 'Prep' or shave, preparing patients for operations the next day. On one occasion as she was preparing and getting her trolley in position, and the beds screened off the Air Raid Siren went, and so did the lights. All the trolleys had lamps on but nevertheless the patients were more than apprehensive at being shaved in delicate areas by the light of a small lamp, and with a cut throat razor. She heard a heartbreaking cry from the head of the bed

"Oh Nursie Please", it was little use however trying to reassure him, so she waited for the 'All clear'.

When she was on theatre duty one night an RAMC orderly and guard came along from the 'Glass House' the name for an army prison and said a soldier was being brought in for emergency treatment. When she asked what was wrong with him the reply was "0 out of love" she thought this was becoming a joke, that is until the patient appeared with his right arm in a sling. When the sling and dressing were taken off all was revealed, his fingers had tattoos on them and "True Love" was written across his fingers, that is all but one on the right hand, there the 'o' and the finger it had been on were missing, the circumstances were not revealed it was not the nurses business, but she could not help notice that the missing finger was his trigger finger.

Peggy Francis was recruited as a nurse by the Government. They were being recruited from all areas, many were married and left nursing; before the war, when a woman married, she had to leave the service. Peggy was now also enrolled in the CNR. In 1940, she reported to Leavesden Hospital, about five miles from Watford, at the time the patients had mental health issues. They were all evacuated to prepare for the overflow from London, mainly patients from London University College Hospital. Casualties were being sent from the bombing in London, which left beds free in the capital in anticipation of forthcoming raids. She remembered a Dutch seaman being admitted. Although he did not know it, his illness was terminal, and he had very little time to live. He wanted a new suit to wear on his return trip to Holland, a trip he was not destined to make.

A nurse at the time was Anna Wing, later to appear as an actress in the TV series 'EastEnders'. She persuaded him to have a dressing gown instead of the suit. A few weeks later, when he died, Anna called Peggy into a side room where she was listing the man's effects to his next of kin via the hospital office. She showed Peggy tobacco tins full of paper money amounting to £700 in all. This was witnessed as it was counted and recorded in a book.

The victims of an air raid on Boulogne were brought in, all in a bad way. They had come by train from the coast to Watford Junction, and then by converted buses to the hospital, a distance of five miles. The buses, because of the nature of the injuries, could only move at a very slow pace; as it was five men died on the way from the station.

Diana Hansford joined the Red Cross in 1938 and worked at a local hospital part-time in Bedford where she lived. She volunteered to go as a 'Mobile' with the Army and so she could be sent anywhere. She was furious with Hitler and wanted to do her bit. Diana was given £10 towards her uniform, which hardly covered the cost of three ward dresses, six aprons, caps, cuffs and collars, a walking out navy uniform, a ward cape, black shoes, stockings and, as she described it, a ghastly mob cap. Diana served at a few hospitals before being posted to France and sailed from Tilbury to Lille. One night, when called out to the casualties of a gun site which had been hit, they dressed in the dark having taken down the blackout frame. The result was when they got down to the wards they were wearing each other's dresses. She was there when D-Day came in June 1944, with thousands of aircraft flying overhead. They eventually moved into Germany following the advancing troops. They came across rubble everywhere, with trains piled up. In Munster all that was left was shells of buildings. After the attention of the bombers on various occasions through the war, the Americans had obliterated it at the end of the war when the SS troops who were holed up there refused to surrender. The nurses were never allowed to go out unescorted as there were still German snipers coming down from the hills around Osnabruck. She stayed in Germany until 1946.

Dorothy May White was a Red Cross VAD in Sussex in 1941. Along with two other VADs, she was on duty at the village hail when a high explosive bomb dropped on the district nurse's cottage, destroying it. They found the nurse in the crater badly injured but managed to get her on to a stretcher and into the village hall. Then a bomb fell directly on the hall itself, killing the already injured nurse, fatally injuring one of the VADs and severely injuring the other. Dorothy scrambled over the rubble and gave first aid to the other two, including using a tourniquet made from her belt. She then visited all the cottages to see if anyone was missing or needed help. All the time bombs were falling around her. For her efforts, in April 1941, she was awarded the George Medal.

When Janet Stevenson was doing her nursing training at Lambeth Hospital it was hit no less than fifteen times in bombing raids. She remembers going to the Elephant and Castle after it had been had been hit, Lyons Corner House had gone, also Woolworth's and the Post Office. All that stood was the Midland Bank. She joined the QANMS in 1944, and was posted to was posted to Brussels, and where she worked in an isolation ward. While she was there an outbreak of diphtheria broke out amongst the German POWs, which who by then comprised old men or young boys.

Joyce 'Topper' Brown was a VAD Red Cross Mobile. She had been nicknamed 'Topper[13]' as soon as she was called up. On the 13th April 1941, she was serving in the Military Hospital in Shaftesbury as a theatre and surgical clerk to the head of the Surgical Division, Colonel Harold Edwards. On the afternoon of this day she was asked to take a telephone call by the Hospital Exchange from someone who seemed agitated and disturbed. He told her there had been an incident in which several military personnel had been hurt. At first, she was a little skeptical as to the sincerity of the call. As she was serving at a 1000bed hospital with all the facilities for emergencies she at first thought it could be someone testing their ability to cope in an emergency, when, at four pm, a convoy turned up at the hospital, and her reaction was one of horror at seeing so many casualties. The extent of their injuries was quickly determined and then graded into more urgent ones needing emergency theatre treatment. The doctors and staff worked through the night. Amongst the injured were several senior officers from the Army and Home Guard. The incident had occurred at Imber Down, Warminster.

The RAF had laid on a on a display of ground strafing from the air to impress the army of air support inwar.in war. The plan was to place khaki clad dummies in a field, and the army officers to be in another field adjacent as observers. A Spitfire, piloted by a Czech airman, came over the hill as planned but fired upon the army officers instead of the dummies, he. He was later exonerated of all blame. In all such types of exercises there is an element of risk. There were 54 casualties, 31 officers and 23 other ranks. Of the 54, 11 Eleven later died, 22% of the total casualties, four very shortly after being admitted, and seven some days later. All but six had machine gun bullet wounds.

---

[13] Traditional military nickname for anyone named Brown.

Later in the war Colonel Edwards was promoted to Brigadier and posted abroad. Today he is a posted abroad. He retired as a consultant from King's College Hospital. Joyce went on to serve at Chatham Barracks, and then at the Military Hospital, Shearness amongst other postings.

Winifred Phillips was in a reserve occupation as a senior clerk in a London hospital, the Central Middlesex Hospital at Park Royal. It was a hospital with about 700 beds, and in the middle of an industrial area. On two occasions the hospital was completely evacuated, and the patients sent all over the country, some as far as Scotland, because the electricity, water, and gas supplies had been put out of action.

During the Dunkirk evacuation many French soldiers were sent to British hospitals, some badly wounded, others just needing a place to put their weary heads to recover from the battlefield trauma. They were visited by General de Gaulle. Winifred remembers him walking down the long corridors; to her he seemed a fine tall man, and every bit a soldier.

As far as regular nurses, there were some thousands of VADs, nurses serving that had been trained by the Order of St John, and the British Red Cross Society. They served with the Navy, Army, and the RAF throughout the UK and abroad. Some 4000 were serving with the Royal Navy, of whom over 800 were serving abroad. The VAD nurses serving with the Army were classed as tradesmen, nursing orderlies, Class III that is, once they had produced a certificate for first aid and home nursing. 4,028 enrolled in this way. In the RAF the number was much lower, with 413 being mobilised. They were employed in various categories, including Clerks, Cooks, Dental Dispensers, Operating Room Assistants, Room Assistants, Lab Assistants, and Radiographic Transfusion orderlies. All categories volunteered for overseas duties. They wore on their left arm the mobile badge and the distinguishing badge of the service they were serving with; a blue anchor on the left arm for service with the Royal Navy, and red braided rank badges for the Army, the RAMC cap badge, for the RAF a pair of gold eagles worn on the collar. When serving in India a pair of Tudor roses in red enamel of the Order of the Indian Empire were worn on the collar.

Top: Anna Wing and Peggy Francis on right (Anna Wing).

Above left: The work must go on! (Author).

Above right: Anna Wing as an actress in the 1990s (Anna Wing).

Right: The grave of sister Ethel Carter, TA (CWGC).

Above: Sister Cant (standing, left) with fellow nurses.

Below: Sister Cant (top left) on a hospital ship (H Cant).

153

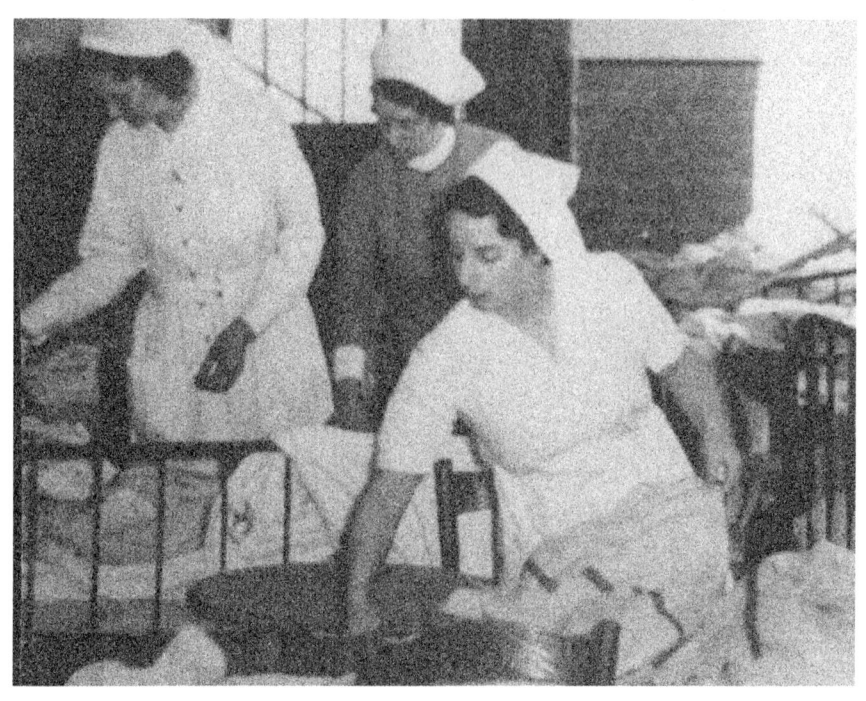

Above: Business as usual! (Author). Below: Nancy Stowell (N. Stowell).

Above: Children being checked by nurses in the Underground (Author). Below left: Entrance to the Military Hospital, Shaftsbury (VAD Somerset). Below right: Madge Aliey (M. Ailey). Botom: Members of St. John Ambulance (Author).

Above: Margaret McCarthy on left (M. McCarthy)

Moyra Platts was called up as a VAD hospital cook at the military hospital in Drymen, Dunbartonshire. While there, a remarkable incident in happened. A German airman who gave his name as Captain Horne landed on the Strathaven Moors, south of Glasgow. He was found to be suffering from an injured right ankle and having a duodenal ulcer. It soon became apparent he was not just an ordinary airman, as he was demanding to see the Duke of Hamilton. It appeared they knew each other as amateur aviators before the war. "I was acting cook at the time for the officer patients and had to push chicken through a sieve before serving it to him with his stomach trouble. It was called 'Hurst Diet'. The patient of course was Rudolf Hess. It was feared that once Hitler knew where his Deputy

Chancellor was, he would send an airborne expedition to kill him before he had time to negotiate with the British. Hess' mission in coming to the UK was to try and persuade the British to join forces against the Russians. The story of Hess being on a chicken diet got into the Glasgow Evening paper upon which the Scottish people were up in arms. The cry was why, 'Why should we feed a Nazi on fish and chicken, luxuries we have not seen for at least two years...?' Moyra and her colleagues kept quiet about being cooks at the hospital for fear of being torn limb from limb by the angry women nearby.

On another occasion a party of young German seamen from the sunken Bismarck were brought to the hospital to recover from exposure before being taken to a POW camp. They became interested in rehearsals for a hospital concert, until they heard a voice singing a German song, popularised by Elizabeth Slumman, upon which they raised their right arms in a Nazi salute and left. It turned out that Elizabeth was a German Jew, which was anathema to the Nazis.

Lorraine Williams also served as a VAD, having started in the Red Cross at the age of 6, and then in 1937 becoming a St John's Ambulance cadet. In 1939, she was she was evacuated to Eastbourne for a while but within a year she returned to Croydon and joined the services division of the 61st Norbury/Thornton Heath St. John's Ambulance. All uniforms and travelling expenses were borne by the members themselves. Her steel helmet, which she carried, wore a hole through her coat from constant rubbing. During the day she was a student at the Pitman Shorthand College. When the VAD was formed she became a leader for the fire watchers and first aid leader in her local district. She left college and began to work in the city just as the Blitz began. She volunteered for the gas decontamination squad at the Royal Exchange. Her dress for this was thin cotton pyjamas beneath oil skins, wellington boots, gloves, respirator, and steel helmet, looking at the end like something out of a horror film.

Each London St John's Division was asked to help staff the deep shelter, which very few people seemed to know about. The only outward signs of the shelter were the concrete ventilator domes. She was met and escorted to the two large tunnels that she and others were to help staff. The tunnels were such that one could easily get lost. Lady Mountbatten came to review them the staff before this took place; she was always very interested in the work of the Brigade. After a day in the office it was down to the deep shelter and back to the office the next morning. On one occasion she was so tired she fell asleep against the bus stop while waiting for a bus at Vauxhall Bridge. In those days it cost nine old pence (4p) for a return trip from Norbury to London Bridge. In recent times when her husband was travelling between London Bridge and Croydon his season ticket cost £1,000 a year or £20 a week.

At the weekend the Civil Defence would hold exercises; on one occasion where a make-believe casualty should have been being a note saying, 'Gone home to dinner'. Her husband was in the RAF and became one of the last Observers to be trained there after the before that flying role became Navigator. He took part in the 1,000 Bomber raid in 1942. Today her humble but proud Defence Medal, which one qualified for with a minimum service of three years in some form of home defence, means a lot to her, and she is glad she was able to serve her time in such, as she put it, an unassuming unit.

In 1939, just before the war, Malta was a lovely place to serve, renowned for its relaxing atmosphere and opportunities for picnics, parties, and dances. The Military Hospital was at Imtarfa. When the war started, a lot of the RAMC staff were sent home and their places were taken by VADs and men from the Malta Auxiliary Corps.

In February 1941, the Germans and Italians started bombing of the island and several patients at the hospital were killed and injured; the night sister was shaken but unhurt. On Easter Sunday, 13th April 1941, a full-scale attack was made on the whole of the hospital area but only a few minor casualties were reported.

Mrs. MacDonald served as a VAD in Malta, her mother was English and her father, who was Maltese, worked in the Civil Service. She did her nursing training on the wards at Imtarfa, the rest of the staff there having been trained at Guy's or St Thomas's in London. The matron was Miss Maud Buckingham. During the attacks on the island Mrs. MacDonald remembers the sky over Malta being black with flak from the anti-aircraft guns and the Germans and the enemy pilots flying so low that they could, and did, wave to the civilians. The Maltese children were evacuated to the small neighbouring island of Gozo, much as the children in London were evacuated to the country.

In March 1942, the hospital was bombed twice in one day, three soldiers being killed and one dying later, all members of the 1st Durham Light Infantry and were only there for a dental checkup. On 13th July 1942 the CO of the hospital Lieutenant Colonel Hamilton was wounded, as was his wife who later died of her wounds. On 23rd October 1942, a bomb was dropped and failed to explode, the part of the hospital near the unexploded bomb was evacuated. Four days later the bomb was defused. At the time there were 727 patients in the hospital. On 3rd November the main sisters' quarters were bombed, two sisters Miss Jameson and Miss Marshall of the QA's were wounded, and one sister walked out of her room into space and was injured in the fall. The air raid shelters were at first slit trenches and later built into the rocks by the Royal Engineers. The murmur of the Maltese nuns could be heard through the rocks. There was a lack of hot water and equipment and the constant sound of guns and sirens. Lunch was often a slice of bully beef. In one of the air raids a sister got a bomb splinter in her leg which was not discovered for some time; when she was seen applying a dressing to it, the splinter had gone right through her thigh.

Near where Molly Dixon was undertaking her nursing training, a German aircraft crashed killing all the crew; happily, no one in the hospital was hurt. The nurses were all issued with navy slacks and sweaters and then the warning siren went they gathered up their pillows and blankets and lay down in the corridors. As soon as the all clear came they went back to bed, only to get another siren for another raid and back to the corridor. Several the patients were soldiers with feet and leg injuries from stepping on land mines which had been laid on the beaches in Worthing. One and was always kept empty for emergencies.

Vera Penn was a ward sister at Horton Emergency Hospital, the surgical ward had 48 beds which were used for casualties brought back from the D-Day Landings at Normandy. The nurses also had to do fire watching one night a week, and emergency ambulance duties one night each fortnight. Night duty consisted of five twelve-hour shifts, on these shifts a ward sister would be responsible for 11 wards. The patients that were up and about wore a uniform of royal blue jacket, white shirt, and red tie. One young soldier of 18 and six feet four inches tall, had the whole of his left leg amputated after being hit by sniper fire on the beach at Normandy. His comments about it were "I guess I was too big a target". In 1948, she married an ex-soldier who had worked in her office on the ward; he had a 60% disability pension.

Lila Thornberry had two brothers in the RAF, another in the RNVR and one in the ARP. She herself was married with a child which prevented her enlisting in the regular forces. However, she did her bit by working the 1st Line Rescue Centre, looking after refugees left homeless after bombing raids. Then she became a VAD at the Royal Belfast Hospital for sick children. Later she received instructions to report to the Musgrove Park Hospital, which was then the American 5th General Hospital with 1100 beds available. When they moved out in came the 10th Station Hospital, followed by the 317th Station Hospital. While the 5th were there, General Eisenhower paid a visit, (at this time he had not become the Supreme Commander), and the entertainers Bebe Daniels, Kay Francis, Glen Miller and his orchestra and Mrs. Eleanor Roosevelt. But the one who stuck in her mind since was Irving Berlin the composer; he asked her and another VAD to sing and dance with him. They did to the tune `Alexander's Rag Time Band" and "I'm Dreaming of a White Xmas". After August 1944, the Americans pulled out and the British took over. She then went back to her former home duties. When she was with the Americans she wore a grey housecoat or overall with blue epaulettes with the American Red Cross insignia on the pockets. While with the Americans on one occasion, a coloured GI said to a volunteer shopper "Will you purchase me a tablet please?" the reply was "But we are not allowed to get you anything not prescribed by the doctor". She then spoke to a doctor who was on duty in the ward, and he came over to see the GI, asking him what he required. Once again, he said "A tablet, a pain", the doctor then said to the shopper "He wants a writing pad and pen!" In 1944, at Lewisham Hospital SE London, student nurse Mary McCrossan was awarded the British Empire Medal. On 26th July 1944, a flying bomb exploded on the hospital and a fire broke out, spreading rapidly. She, at the time was in D3 ward, and was knocked over by the explosion, hurting her wrist and leg. Despite this she freed herself from the rubble and helped carry patients from the damaged ward. She was later taken to St Alfred's Hospital and operated upon. Apart from her wrist and leg she was suffering from shock and loss of blood.

On 14th November 1940, Miss Marjorie Perkins was working as a work's nurse and in charge of the work's surgery at Pattison's Hoburn Ltd in Coventry. In the infamous raid on Coventry she rendered excellent service to the works casualties, and in the nearby street. On two occasions she was blown across the surgery by the blast of exploding bombs and suffered internal injuries and was for a while rendered unconscious. On recovery, and although in considerable pain she carried on dealing with casualties throughout the night. For her efforts on this night she was later awarded the George Medal.

At the Royal Northern Hospital in Holloway North London, a chest hospital, awards were made to Miss Catherine McGovan, the Assistant Matron, at the time being the Acting Matron. During bombing of the hospital and the area, she was badly cut but would only leave the hospital for attention when she knew everyone had been got out safely; to make sure she went around herself, supported by a policeman to make sure no one had been overlooked. She had served in WWI and had been awarded the Royal Red Cross decoration for her efforts. For her efforts on this occasion she was awarded the George Medal. At the same hospital was Patricia Marmion a staff nurse. At the time of the bombing she oversaw the men's ward when a land mine or heavy bomb exploded only 20 feet away. A patient who had been brought in the night before and had lost in the bombing five members of his family, tried to commit suicide by throwing himself into the street below, she prevented him doing so and led him back to the ward. She then carried on helping patients out of the ward and down the steps to safety as the lift at the time was out of action. Finally, she collected up all the dangerous drugs and took them to safety. Then and only then was she herself admitted as a patient. When the hospital was once again hit she jumped out of bed, and in her bare feet assisted other patients to safety. She was also awarded a very well-earned George Medal.

There were several nurses who served in the Far East, one Elizabeth Bonner served with the 53rd Indian General Hospital in

Kohima, Burma. on the 23rd March 1943, in a high wind a fire broke out in the kitchen of the Indian Wing and threatened the wards of the British Wing, however the fire was got under control and all was well. On one occasion a young private soldier suffering from TB and hoping to be shipped home, but unknown to him this was impossible as he was too unwell to be moved, wanted his favourite drink of soda water, which in the area was nearly impossible to get, he also liked fresh fish another rare item. Elizabeth however had a friend who was a tea planter in the area and made his own soda water. Suddenly one day he turned up with not only soda water but fresh fish. A few weeks later this gallant lad succumbed to his illness and died. The word came not long afterwards that the Japanese were only 40 miles away from the hospital and so they had to pack up and get out quickly. Their destination was Dinapore and that night was spent under canvas, when they awoke the next day they found to their horror they had camped in a Hindu Cemetery. During the Battle of Kohima, she was sent to Sylhet on temporary duty where the accommodation was marquee tents and it was the monsoon period, wind and rain were the order of the day. During this period Lord Mountbatten paid a visit and found all the nurses and orderlies trying to keep the tents on the ground. He soon sorted things out and better accommodation was found for them. In January 1978, as a member of the Burma Star Association she made a pilgrimage back to Kohimagmphal, on the site of her old hospital was the present Kohima Hospital, and on the site of her old sisters' mess had been were shops.

On the 19th February 1944, at 59 IG at Kegwima a very sad incident happened. Madge Hiley had been training for her SRN in a London Hospital when the war broke out. Having passed her exams, she decided to join the QAs; this she did and became a nursing sister in 1942. After a few months at a military hospital in Dorset, she was sent to India via South Africa. After three months in Calcutta she was posted to Kohima as part of the 14th Army. At a party here, she met her future husband, an officer in the Royal Indian Army Service Corps. They were soon engaged and within six weeks married, the marriage taking place in the local village the local Nagas forming a guard of honour for them. They also came to the reception at the hospital officers mess.

The organisation for the wedding had been undertaken by a Sister Ethel Carter who was in the Territorial Nursing Service or TANS as it was known. The sister in the hospital worked on a shift system, one on duty for the whole hospital one evening and alternate with another sister the next and soon. On the 19th, Sister Carter was on duty and was due at 8pm to finish her shift and hand her report into the matron. Madge and her husband were having a snack when there was a knock on the door, it was the matron enquiring if they had seen Ethel. Two search parties were made up, one led by the Colonel and one by Madge's husband. When the Colonel went to an unused ward he suddenly shouted out "Come quickly she is here" she was lying on the ground with her clothes in disarray; she was dead, having been raped and murdered. Gurkha soldier was put on guard outside the door of the nurses' quarters, it had been a Gurkha's Kukri that they had used to cut their wedding cake. They guarded the place so well that Madge's husband had a job getting back in. The civil and military police were called to investigate the murder, but within days the word came that the Japanese were coming, and the area was evacuated, the only thing that came out of the investigation was that she had been murdered by a left-handed person. The little church that Madge had been married in was destroyed by the Japanese on their arrival.

Margaret McCarthy also served in the Far East, spending a year in Calcutta*which seemed to be the launching pad for sisters sent out from the UK. She was also posted to Kohima, to No 53 1GS. While there she endured an earth tremor in which a medicine cabinet moved and nearly toppled over. In 1944, when the Japanese were approaching she and others also got the word to evacuate and put all her bits and pieces in a case and waited outside the sisters' mess for transport. They and the patients were taken to Dinapore where they set up a temporary hospital. While they were there, Lord Mountbatten came in by helicopter for a visit on his way to Imphal. When the fighting had subsided, they returned to their former hospital at Kohima.

As well as the Far East there were nurses serving in the Middle East. Mary Jones, who came from South Wales, was in North Africa in October 1942, at the time of the Battle of El Alamein and it was not long before casualties began to arrive. Three or four convoys a night, a bugle would sound when a convoy arrived, this could be at any time of day or night. "You did not think of the hours just got on with it". Today Mary is in her 80s and a member of the 8th Army Association. She had volunteered in 1940, after working as a nursing sister in London. "I wanted a bit of excitement" she certainly got this along with the dust, sandflies, and mosquitoes for the next 2_ years. In 1940, she was posted to the hospital ship Atlantis, it was here that she met her future husband who was in the RAMC. She first saw action in the Norwegian Fjords on the Atlantis a floating hospital with 600 patients on board. They were attacked by enemy aircraft and 30 bombs were dropped. Later, when a captured German airman was taken aboard the ship he was asked why they had attacked a ship with the red cross on it, he replied that they were not trying to hit their ship but merely to make it move out of the way. This they succeeded in doing.

From Norway the Atlantis sailed to Alexandra, where the early days of the North African campaign were taking place. Each ward on the ship had 24 patients, one sister and one orderly. In 1942, she transferred to a field hospital at Quassasin in the desert. They were now at the mercy of the sand and dust. After a sandstorm the sand would have to be shovelled out of the wards. It turned the traditional red blankets yellow. There were rats and sandflies, and the bread had weevils in it. A wound having been bandaged would then have to be encased in plaster of paris to keep the bugs out. If the wound began to itch it meant they had got in and the plaster and bandages would have to be taken off the bugs cleaned out and fresh dressing and plaster put back. Evidence later showed that these bugs would help a wound by eating away all the bad. When the Black Watch arrived someone said, "Rommel's had it now". In 1943, she returned to the UK and married, after which she served at Brecon and Hatfield military hospitals.

In June 1944, on D-Day plus 8, she landed at Arromanches with 73 General Hospital, a tented hospital of 1,000 beds. The casualties now coming in were from the Battle of Caen. In 1945, she was by now in Belgium and told they were going to a place called Belsen. The sights she saw here are still vividly with her today. There were 10,000 corpses and 500 people dying each day. She returned to the UK and once again took up civilian nursing, which she did until she reached the age of 60. She was also, for 24 years, a Divisional Officer in the St John's Ambulance. Along with her Africa Star she also had the Atlantic Star for service on a troopship at the start of the war and the France and Germany Star for her service in Europe at the end of the war. She was also awarded a Certificate of Merit signed by Field Marshal Montgomery for outstanding service in the field. She117is known by the 8th Army Veterans in South Wales as 'Our Mary'.

Nancy Stowell served as a sister in the Princess Mary's Royal Air Force Nursing service, or PMs as they are known. Before the war she had been in the QANS but after a disagreement she resigned. Her nursing had been at St Thomas', so she knew her stuff and when the war started as she did not like to ask the QANS if she could rejoin so she joined the PMs. The hat they wore was known as 'Dick Turpin' hats because they were black and four cornered. In the 1939/41 period she was ill and sent to Torquay to convalesce. From there she was posted to Newquay then Hastings, with its barb wire beaches.

In 1944, she sailed from Liverpool on the Queen Bermuda, 250 WAAFS, and 3,000 troops aboard. Most of the trip was spent sitting with one life jacket on. She spent Xmas and the New Year of 1944/45 on board. Her first posting was the hospital in Bombay, and then Delhi attached to an army hospital. From there she was posted to Calcutta, where she was when VE Day came in May 1945. She was then flown to Dum Dum and then Burma in a Dakota aircraft. In Burma she was based at Akas, an island from which supply drops were being made to the 14th Army. The buildings were built on stilts and the food very basic. It was here that she suffered gall bladder trouble, and was sent home by ship to the UK, and later an operation at the RAF Hospital at Halton. They said when they saw her that she looked like someone who had come out of Belsen she was so thin. Despite her illness she stayed in the PA's until 1960 serving for 22 years.

Dame Helen Wilson Cargill retired in May 1952, after 29 years' service in the PA's during this time she was matron at several hospitals. In 1944, she became matron of the 2nd Tactical Air Force Hospital in Normandy. It was a tented hospital of 200 beds and based at Bayeux. From there it moved to Brussels and a 400-bed hospital, a former German hospital. She returned to the UK in May 1945 and took over as matron at the military hospital at Ely. In July1948, she became matron in chief of the PA's and in 1949 Honorary Nursing Sister to the King and was made a DBE in 1951. She had also been awarded Royal Red Cross decoration 2nd Class in 1941 and 1st Class in June 1945. Dame Helen was born in 1896 and trained at St George's Hospital from 1919 to 1922.In 1924 she was awarded her SRN and became a sister in 1926. She was one of the first 60 to join the PA's, she had been promoted to Staff Nurse on the 7th June 1923. In 1969, she died at the age of 73, having had a remarkable career in military nursing.

On the 23rd March 1945, Sister Sheila Margaret Greaves was awarded the George Medal for bravery at Anzio, at the time she was serving with No 15 Casualty Clearing Station. An Arab thief was disturbed in the Middle East by a sister. A wire fence had been erected around the sister's quarters, but this had been cut at one point to allow them to get in and out with their friends without being seen, on this occasion it also allowed an unwanted intruder in. It was pointed out to them that the wire was for their protection and not to pen them in.

In 1945, Elsie Gordon was the editor of the Nursing Mirror. In this capacity she travelled a great deal with the nursing sisters. They were part of three evacuation flights, or CAEU as they were known. Each flight had its own medical and surgical officer, four nursing sisters and surgical and medical equipment including eight ambulances and nine three-ton lorries with trailers. The sisters worked on a rota system, three out of the four being on duty at one time along with seven male orderlies.

Just after Normandy a RAF General Hospital was set up with white painted tent walls inside to give more light and a concrete base for the operating theatre. Later this became a modern hospital in Brussels. It had previously been a German hospital and when they arrived the beds were unmade; caps and belts and other equipment were lying around. The wards were cleared, and the pictures of Hitler taken down off the walls. At the hospital there were 36 PA sisters. One ward had been for German officers only, with single and double-bedded wards within the main ward and had a lounge in the centre. The hospital was heated with gas fires, but the nursing staff quarters was spartan and cold. All electricity was cut between 8pm and 8am each day for economy on coal.

To become a sister in the QAs you had to be SRN and in 1940 they could wear rank badges equal to the men. In 1941, they became commissioned officers of the women's forces. The age limit was 35 and part of their uniform was a red cloak and so they became known as 'Red Capes'. In 1939, there were 640 and in 1945 there were 12,000. The PM's had in 171 in 1939 and 1,215 in 1945. In 1943, they also became the equal of their male counterparts in the RAF. A sister was equal to a Flying Officer (in the Army this would be a Lieutenant), a senior sister would be a Flight Lieutenant (or Captain in the Army). A matron was equal to a Squadron Leader (or Major in the Army), Principal Matron a Wing Commander or Lieutenant Colonel, Chief Principal Matron would be a Group Captain or Colonel and the Matron in Chief an Air Commodore or Brigadier.

In the RAMC there were 150 women doctors. In 1949, the QAIMNS became the QARANC or Queen Alexandra's Royal Army Nursing Corps. In New Zealand there was the New Zealand Army Nursing Service formed in 1911. South Africa had the South African Military Nursing Service formed in 1914. There was also the Australian Army Nursing Corps. Also, in the Middle East was a unit known as Hatfield named after Lady Hatfield Spears and May Spears who wrote under the name of Mary Borden Ambulance Unit.

When the war broke out the ambulances of this unit went out to France, the women who drove the ambulances were debutantes who came out in 1937. In France they worked with French units. When France fell they managed to get out on the last civilian ship after a 15-day hike across France. The famous French General de Gaulle was got out of France with the help of General Louie Spears, the husband of May Spears, who in fact came from the USA. Along with French doctors, 15 women drivers were sent to North Africa to cover 1,000 miles. The men already serving there thought it was a miracle seeing women in the desert. The golden rule, they were told, was if you broke down stay with your vehicle. On one occasion one woman fixed a faulty water pipe, with her stockings and when the word got around she was never short of stockings from then on.

Driving in the desert could be hairy with minefields etc. The living conditions were primitive, often a dug out with a tarpaulin top. One woman made a dressing table out of a tea chest and a mirror. There were desert storms of course which brought everything to a standstill, getting to one's tent or dug out meant crawling on your hands and knees and wearing goggles to protect your eyes. For medical operations a tented lorry was used.

The Germans would usually make their bombing attacks coming out of the sun in the morning and afternoon. When they arrived outside Tobruk they were the only women in the combat zone. From North Africa they went to Italy and to Naples. The nurses were called 'Nanny's' by the drivers, but of course if they wanted to go anywhere they had to ask the drivers to take them so it paid for them to be on good terms with them.

Getting to Naples was not easy as the liberty ships were not allowed to take women dressed as men and so they were sent by the RAF All arrived in time to unload their cars but were promptly given 15 days confined to barracks or CB as it was known. During the Battle of Cassino they were put up front of attacking guns in order that they could keep up as they were with the mobile hospital and surgical units. On one occasion a shell came through the operating theatre tent, a man being operated on was lying on the ground with his intestines hanging out; they were put back and he lived. Two of the women landed with the Canadians in the South of France, one a nurse and one a driver. The remainder came on a landing craft. In the victory parade in Paris, in which General de Gaulle took the salute members of the unit were invited to take part. They did in their polished staff cars; when the wounded saw them, they shouted 'Vive Spears', but as de Gaulle had fallen out with Spears he did not like this as he thought they were shouting for General Spears and they were asked to leave the parade.

Chapter 7 The Home Defences

On 9th April 1938, details were announced of how Air Raid Wardens would carry out a nationwide census, to ensure that every man, woman, and child in the country would have a gas mask if needed in case of emergency. All houses were visited to ascertain the type and size of gas mask required. It was to be carried on the shoulder in a square cardboard box, a few inches square weighing very little and resembling a picnic lunch box. The Services had a gas mask, but it was called a respirator instead, and carried in a canvas type shoulder pack. On 17th February 1939, Sir John Anderson, the Minister for Civil Defence, announced rates of pay for full time workers in Air Raid Precautions as it was known then, and the Auxiliary Fire Services in the event of a war. The men would get £3 a week and the women £2, over a million men and women would be employed in this work. The annual bill would be about £85 million. Women who worked in the ARP or Civil Defence as it was later known, full or part time, would be employed as wardens, ambulance drivers, clerks, telephonists and in the nursing services.

Charity Bick in 1940, lived in West Bromwich in the Midlands. She was fourteen at the time and wanted to become a messenger in the ARP. However, although the minimum age was 16 her father took her along to enrol. When he told them that she was only 14, she was promptly told she was too young. Her father then marched her round the building, took her back inside and suddenly she became16 and was enrolled as a despatch rider taking messages. This she did until she was 17½.

Her name, Charity, came from her being in a Quaker environment in the Midlands. Later in life she did not like the name and changed it to Anne. On 19th November 1940 she was attached to the warden service at Post B13 where her father was the post warden. On this night she was on duty as a despatch rider when the siren went. Shortly after, incendiaries began to fall on the roofs of the surrounding houses. Using a stirrup pump she helped her rather attack the fire that had developed. One had started on the roof of a pawnshop, so they went inside the shop and up into the livings rooms and then into the bedroom. The bomb had lodged in the false ceiling. The stirrup pump of the shop did not work but somehow by splashing water on to the fire with their hands they put out the fire. As Mr. Bick turned to make for the entrance his foot went through the false ceiling and Charity fell on to the bed below which broke her fall and she sustained only minor injuries. By this time the town was being attacked with high explosives and all communications between the control room, warden's post and depots had been severed.

The only means of communication was by despatch rider so Charity came into her own and delivered many messages to the control room. A high explosive bomb fell immediately opposite the warden's post and she was instructed to take a message to the control room asking for assistance. She borrowed a bicycle and started off but, on several occasions, she had to get off and lie in the gutter to shelter from the bombs falling nearby. In all she made three trips to the control room which was about a mile and a quarter away, all during the height of the raid. When the all clear came she returned to her post and stayed there for the rest of the night. On her last trip she was seen to be limping badly and was obviously in some pain.

For her gallant efforts on the 19th she was recommended for the George Medal. This was approved and in 1941 she was instructed to attend an investiture at Buckingham Palace, where the King would present her with one of the highest awards that can be awarded to a civilian. When she was notified of the award her father and mother were out working, her mother was a full-time nurse. The Civil Defence authorities promised her a uniform for the investiture, but this never arrived and so her mother collected all the clothing coupons she could. The instructions said uniform or dark clothing was to be worn.

And so, suitably clothed, she arrived at the Palace where a clip was pinned on her chest for the King to hang her medal. The recipients were lined up alphabetically, she was at the front and given instructions as to how to get to the investiture area. She could never tell her right from her left and soon got lost, not surprising as the Palace is a maze of corridors. Eventually she arrived in the right place and as the King presented her with her medal he asked her age, she said 15 which she was by now, although she had been only fourteen at the time of the incident.

When Charity became 17 she joined the WAAF and became an electrician. Later she transferred to the Administration side and served in the RAF for 20½ years. She retired in 1965 with the rank of warrant officer. Her RAF career over she then took up a new life in the Civil Service and stayed there until 1987. The medal that she received, now over 58 years ago, had been kept all that time in a cigar box. She was the youngest person ever to be awarded the GM and became known as 'Jimmy' because of the initials GM after her name.

Women's work in the ARP could be grouped under two headings, first ARP Services or Civil Defence General Services as it was later called, and secondly Social Welfare. They worked as wardens, helped as fire guard, manned first aid posts, mobile units, stretcher parties, auxiliary ambulance services and of course the Auxiliary Fire Service, later the National Fire Service. The women wardens performed the same duties as the men, including patrols and reporting air raid damage. The fire guards were formed to fight fires in their own homes and surrounding area. The mobile first aid units could be conveyed to the scene of serious casualties and were manned mainly by women. The welfare side included canteens, rest centres, clothing depots, and the rehousing of people who had been bombed out. There was also the Housewives Service which formed a valuable auxiliary to the official ARP service, and gave women at home the change to contribute to the work of the CD. There were shelter wardens whose job it was to keep order when the shelter was occupied during a raid and to encourage communal activities. The homeless people were taken to the rest centre until they could be rehoused or billeted.

Joan Aston was 17 when war was declared in 1939. She and her friend decided to volunteer for the WAAF but as her job in a factory making condensers for aircraft was essential war work she was not released. She was then designated to the ARP service as an ARP warden and went along to the local town hall for an interview and uniform. The ARP post was an oblong windowless brick building. The hours of duty were 7pm to 10pm and then 10pm to 7am during the night on a shift system. One of the two on duty would sit in the office and take turns to patrol the streets. She and her partner had a problem in that they found it difficult to wake up when the telephone rang during the night when a raid began. To get over this an ARP officer was placed on duty with them. One night a land mine fell a short distance away hitting and destroying three houses; many of her friends were killed, there was only one survivor and she had been found on the upper floor of what was left of the house, still sitting in the bath, her only injury a broken nose.

Linda Wray served in the CD in Hull and used to cycle three miles in the blackout when on duty. The reporting centre was an old police station and she was the head telephonist controlling all the messages sent in by the various air raid wardens and then alerting the appropriate services, rather like today's 999 calls.

Miss Ellen Wilkinson occupied the most important Government post that, so far, had been given to a woman in the war, that of Under Secretary of State to the Ministry of Home Security, the Civil Defence, was directly under her control. In the Evening News of 30th April 1940, it stated that hundreds of women in the Borough of Wandsworth were eager to play a part in the National Defence Programme, and they became the Wandsworth Housewives Service. They took an elementary course in first aid and anti-gas precautions. The whole idea was that there should be at least one trained woman who could be relied upon in every street. They were to cooperate with the local air raid wardens; no examinations were involved, if the woman completed her course she would be presented with a special badge by the Women's Volunteer Service which we shall hear more about later in the book.

When the Munich crisis came in 1938, Mabel Winter was working in a fancy goods factory. One day the forelady asked if there was a war would anyone know what to do in an air raid. No one did so she asked for volunteers to join the ARP. On their way home from work one day Mabel and her friend called in at the local police station. All the ARP training was done under the supervision of the police. The training took two weeks during which time they learned to use a stirrup pump in the event of a fire, and first aid. At the time and only being make believe they enjoyed their training, but not so much when the balloon went up and it was for real. Mabel and her friend passed the course and were issued with identity cards by the Chief Constable of Manchester. Their first allotted task was to go around the sector issuing leaflets, and then delivering babies' gas masks, which could only be issued by a female warden. It was an awful contraption; the baby was placed inside, and the mother would have to pump air in by hand. If for some reason she had to stop pumping the baby would die from lack of air. She and her friend were the only two female wardens to cover six sectors, which owing to their daily job, they had to do on Sunday afternoon. Some people they called upon were not at all happy or cooperative, but if they refused point blank they were reported to the police.

When the war started on 3rd September 1939, the training stepped up and met far more often. Mabel had two brothers who had served in WWI and her own son was serving in the RAF and had been taken prisoner at Singapore. It was two years before she knew if he was alive or dead. Despite the lovely summer of 1939, there was an air of black depression. The winter that followed was bitterly cold. On one occasion in early 1940, while training for future air raids, one man acting as a casualty had been put on the top of an old fashioned outside lavatory, and it was their job as wardens to locate and get him down. They didn't so he eventually climbed down and wrote on an adjoining wall "died and gone home".

All the traffic including trams and buses stopped when the siren was sounded. Not even a torch or lit cigarette was allowed on the streets. The first job of a warden after the siren had sounded was to sign in for duty. He or she then made a tour of their sector to see that all the blackouts were in place and no lights were showing. We have all heard many times the expression "Put that light out". On one occasion a woman left her front door open at night and during a raid so that the light from her house was streaming across the road. Mabel asked her to either put out the light or shut the door. She was met with a stream of abuse and a refusal to do so. In the end Mabel pushed passed her and closed the door, leaving the woman locked out in the chilly night air. The result was that the woman reported her to the Chief Warden, who promptly asked her to resign which she refused to do, all the other wardens supporting her actions. This included the Chief Inspector for the District who said she had done the correct thing in closing the door. The woman had apparently got in by climbing through a window. She obviously learned her lesson because she did not leave her door open again during a raid. The Chief Warden was later dismissed but not over this incident. On another occasion, when on duty outside an air raid shelter, a little girl ran out crying. When asked what the matter was she said there were two men in there. Mabel went in to find two drunk Irishmen causing a disturbance. She ordered them out, but they refused and said she had no righto order them out. She then said, "If you do not leave this shelter I will call the police with my whistle." She was terrified, and her knees were knocking but she tried not to show it. She was 4'11" and they were very tall, burly men. For a few minutes they stared her out, but then they walked out. Everybody thought she was marvellous, although no one offered to help at the time. Times don't change in many respects.

The first uniforms were a navy-blue drill overall, but later a heavy Melton overcoat ideal for night patrols. People would ask you to go in for a brew up or go and get a clean nappy for the baby, or even refill a hot water bottle. Some nights it was quiet but others the air was full of German aircraft noises and the anti-aircraft guns trying to shoot them down. She was once hit by a piece of red hot shrapnel, luckily it hit the corner of her steel helmet, which weighed 4½ lb., and which after wearing it for some time gave you headache, but on this occasion, it did save her from significant injury.

During the day Mabel worked in a factory making uniforms. They worked an eight-hour shift with one day a week off. In 1941, she was offered a full-time job with the ARP as a telephonist in a rescue centre. They were given prior notice of a raid and out on a "Yellow Alert". When the "Red Alert" came the siren would be sounded. One raid among many on Manchester on one Christmas Eve stuck in her mind to this day. It began at 10pm and ended at 6am. Her own home suffered some damage in the raid. One woman was dug out the rubble with her eyes burnt, it was like 'Dante's' Inferno' and 'Hell on Earth' as she described it. The Germans were after the railway station but failed to hit it.

When the ARP became the CD she and all the staff were transferred to an ambulance depot. Here she stayed until June 1945. By this time, she was all alone, her brother and mother both having died during the war. If you left the CD during the war you were eligible for service in the armed services. Her rations when she found herself alone were 2oz butter, 2oz sugar, 2oz tea, 2oz bacon, 2oz margarine, one egg per week and one pot of jam per month.

Plus, one got one shilling's worth of meat per week. Bread, strangely, was not on ration until after the war.

Ruth Wilson's mother ran a CD canteen and she helped her mother along with others to keep it open night and day. During the day, Ruth worked in the Town Hall, where her father was the Town Clerk. Petrol was on ration, but they were in the car pool taking stores to various service canteens and acting as chauffeur to members of the St John's Ambulance who visited the hop fields in Kent to give first aid to the hoppers and their children who lived in huts near the hop fields.

Katie Haig is proud of the fact that she was born within the sound of Bow Bells, making her a true Cockney. During WWI her school was bombed, a 500-lb. bomb dropping on her unoccupied desk. The school was about a mile from Petticoat Lane. When WWII came in September 1939 she was living in Stratford and became a volunteer warden. Today she remembers helping people out of the wreckage, dead and alive. Two small shops she owned were bombed in the early days of the bombing and her son was evacuated to Somerset. She was not in good health having had TB and a thyroid operation. She had left school at the age of twelve and began work in a draper's shop making cloth covered buttons.

Susie Body was a postwoman driver at Tadworth and an air raid warden. She had a rare blood group and on the eve of D-Day, in June 1944, she was sent for late at night and taken to the nearest town a few miles away to give blood. Several days later she was told that her blood contribution had gone out with the troops on D-Day. On one occasion a bomb fell close to where she lived and although not on duty she decided to go out in the street and investigate, that is until she fell into a bomb crater outside her front door.

When war broke out Violet Hall was living in Newport, Monmouthshire. Besides her husband who was serving in the RAF she had two children, an uncle serving in the Home Guard, and an Aunt who had two sons. She, along with others, would fire watch once or twice a week and when the sirens went would go to the local air raid shelters. On 1st July 1941, a German plane that was being chased by an RAF fighter jettisoned a sea mine which landed directly on Violet's house. Her husband Claude, daughter Barbara, and her uncle, aunt and their two sons were all killed. She herself was buried with her son for7 hours. When she came out of hospital she was taken back to see where her house had been, you could have put two buses in the crater left by the explosion. The chickens in the area were running around without any feathers. When the rescuers found her and her son, the water from a fractured water main had reached her chin. As they carried her son out the siren went again, and a voice said, "Leave everything, the siren's gone". But a man named Bert Goring and the police stayed on and got her out. All she knew of one of the policemen was that by the light of a torch she saw number 7 on his tunic top. She later met Bert when she recognised his voice while in a shop. When she filled a form in for insurance purposes she was given £5 10 shillings for the funeral of her husband and daughter. The Company said it was an act of God, though others might have described it as an act of Hitler. The RAF however paid for a headstone and agreed the two children's names should be on it as well as her husband they had lost a child before the bombing incident. Her husband is now buried in the Christchurch Cemetery, Newport.

Mrs. Gwendoline Park enrolled as a warden on 17th May 1938 and was employed for whole time service on 31st August 1939. On 26th August 1940, she was on duty at Harlington Warden Post when lights from flares were noticed over the post, so she left the post with the idea of warning residents in the area to take cover. She had succeeded in warning the occupants of about four to five houses when the bombs began to fall, and she was forced to take cover in the doorway of her own nearby house. When the bombing stopped she immediately returned to the Warden Post to make her report but found the telephone wires had been cut and Mr. Channing, another Warden, had been wounded in the foot. She managed to bandage it for him and they then returned to the scene of the bombing. A small fire had started on the roof of a house, which was adjacent to the house that had been bombed. She and another warden using a stirrup pump were able to put the fire out. As they were doing these another five bombs fell nearby. She then, along with Mr. Channing, entered what was left of a bungalow and rescued and gave first aid to a woman and her child. She was later recommended for the George Medal but given instead the British Empire Medal, as was Mr.

Channing who despite having an artificial arm had played a major part in the rescue. Both medals were gazette on 17th January 1941.

In the same gazette, Mabel Hedgethorn and Eunice Richards were awarded commendations. On 5th November 1940, a Navy drifter was cruising between Brightlingsea and Clacton when it was attacked by an enemy aircraft with bombs and machine gun fire, several the crew being hit. A Naval first aid party set out in a speed board but for some unknown reason it never reached the drifter. A call was then sent to the report and rescue centre for a first aid party to be sent out. Dr. Alister MacQuarrie, the medical officer, Mabel, Eunice and two others set out in a speedboat. At the time there was a high wind raging at gale force and a very heavy sea it was also extremely dark. Because of the high seas and the boat being overloaded Mabel and Eunice were transferred to a yacht nearby, the others went on to the drifter and then the speedboat came back for Eunice and Mabel. When they arrived, they found three of the crew suffering from severe body injuries and bleeding badly, one of whom died on his way to hospital. The wounded were taken on board an ambulance ship and thereby the doctor and his party including the two women given first aid. They were all completely drenched and had worked by the light of a torch and in boats that were being tossed to and fro.

There were women in the Fire Service during the war. When the war began it was called the Auxiliary Fire Service or AFS, later the National Fire Service or NFS. Betty Murphy joined the Fire Service and worked 48 hours on duty and 24 hours off. The AFS and later the NSF was run on the lines of the Navy, with expressions such as scrub the decks, and eating in the galley. Her job was on the switchboard and, when a call came in, to press the bells and get the fire crews out; also, to collect information about aircraft that had crashed on returning from bombing missions, or on take-off.

On one occasion a call came in to attend a house fire. When the fire crew arrived the family in the house were sitting down quite calmly eating their tea. When asked where the fire was they replied 'Upstairs' and carried on eating. The fire turned out to be a smouldering mattress which when the firemen opened the door the draught caused the smouldering to become a fire and all that was left to do was to get it out of the house via the bedroom window. In the circumstances the firemen were not at all happy when they arrived back at the station. Now this same situation would probably mean a fine for the householder or being sent a bill for the fire service. The pole which they used to exit from the crew rooms to ground level where the engines were, ran through the men's locker room and the firewomen on the station were dared to try out the pole. Betty, being curious, agreed to take up the dare but only if the men's locker room was empty at the time. Unknown to her, the men had told the Divisional Officer and he was standing waiting for her when she came down the pole.

One or two of the women retrained as despatch riders. Riding a motorbike for a woman was quite an experience and had previously been frowned upon in some quarters. Firewoman despatch rider Gladys Marsh was commended by the fire force commander for outstanding devotion to duty while attending a flying bomb incident. She donned her top boots, crash helmet and goggles to go to the scene of an incident as courier/assistant to the fire force commander. When her duties with him were finished she rushed away to administer first aid to the injured. On one occasion she entered a room which contained people who had been bombed out of their homes and said "Doesn't anyone here need bandaging? This is my last bandage and I'm not going to take it back".

Vickey Kilford joined the Fire Service in 1941 and served at Woolwich and Sydenham. She had, in WWI served in the Women's Army Corps and when posted to New Cross Fire Station she was one if not the oldest serving firewoman. In all she served 02 years in the fire service. Joyce Mannheim was among the first intake of women in the new formed National Fire Service and served from 1941 to 45. She spent most of that time in Manchester Central Fire Station manning a hundred-line switchboard. Discipline was very strict, woe betide anyone who attempted to bend the rules. The weekly dances within the station were great fun, but not quite so funny when the bell went, and your partner suddenly did a disappearing act down the pole.

Marie Lee served in the National Fire Service from 1940-45 joining as a telephonist/mobile and later becoming an instructress at the Manchester Training Centre. From there she went to B Division as assistant group officer. After attending the NFS College at Saltdean,

Brighton she was promoted to group officer and took over the whole of the Carlisle area, 2,700 miles. As well as ARP training there was training in the London Volunteer Ambulance Service, a section created to help in any emergency if war broke out. Lectures were given at County Hall, London on anti-gas precautions, first aid and some driving practice.

Miss Robinson became a driver with the LAVS on 3rd September 1939 and was based at 126 Ambulance Station, which was at Invicta Road Infants School, London SE3. When she arrived at the school she was met by the station officer, Mrs. Rogers. Of the people who reported some 127 were to be drivers and other attendants. They were issued with gas masks, haversacks and steel helmets and assigned a vehicle. Some had specially prepared ambulances, others were a mixture of vans and cars which had been lent or commandeered. Many of the attendants had been nurses and at this stage there were more women than men. At first, they were obliged to wear their own clothes but were later issued with an arm band and badge, navy blue cotton coat and cap for which one had to sign and promise to replace if it was lost. Today she still has the printed receipt for one steel helmet, cost 5/6d, lining 2/-, chinstrap 1/-, civilian respirator, and face piece 5/9d, container 1/- and haversack 9d. One woman's coat and LAS badges cost 10/-, with a belt 10/3d, women's cap and badges 3/4d and one ARP (home office) silver badge 1/3d.

During the first year of the war, Station 126 like others was waiting and preparing, studying first aid, and creating imaginary incidents which may arise when the balloon went up. The location of hospitals and the upkeep and driving of various vehicles, and the study of motor mechanics at the SE Technical Institute. For Miss Robinson the chance to handle and fire the Lee Enfield rifle at the gun club in Blackheath. In off-peak hours they became table tennis experts, played darts, cribbage, chess, and solo whist, and other did needlework or knitting. The balloon went up in September 1940 when the south east was severely bombed. She herself was directly involved in that her uncle's house had received a direct hit, and her cousin and her sheep dog Jimmy were both killed, her aunt and uncle somehow survived. Several places in the Greenwich area were hit, including the baths. 1W° of 126 Station personnel were awarded George Medals for this incident.

In November 1940, the ambulance station in Invicta Road was demolished by a parachute mine, she at the time was not on duty. None of the personnel there were injured as they had all taken cover in the coal cellars under the school hall. They then moved to Station 123 at Vanburgh Park Drill Hall, which no longer exists. Only two weeks later, after they had left Invicta Road Infants School, the very same coal cellars were penetrated by bombs and destroyed. After a few months they moved to permanent quarters at Christchurch College and remained there until the end of the war. In April 1942, she transferred to the Regular London Ambulance Service and was posted to the Brook Ambulance Station where women drivers were replacing the men called up for the services. She had to take her driving test three times before she passed on 4th June 1942. When she became a full time regular driver she was allotted a special ambulance, a 73 Talbot which had agate gear change.

At this time the Brook Station dealt with fever cases, which included scarlet fever, measles, mumps and even smallpox. They wore whitecoats and took the patients to fever hospitals such as Hither Green in south east London. They also carried private patients, many maternity cases, for which a fee of 12/6d was collected. On one occasion on 6th September 1943, they were sent to a house in Eltham to take a patient to the Sidcup Maternity Hospital, on this occasion Miss Robinson was acting as attendant. She told the woman they had collected to call if she needed help. They had only just started when she did just that and called for help. She had started to have the baby. Quickly she had to remember her midwifery lectures and eventually a beautiful baby boy of 9lbs was born in the back of the ambulance. On another occasion while taking a patient from Woolwich to Shepperton she had a puncture. When she set about mending it, she found that someone had removed the jack from the toolkit. She managed to summon help from an Army lorry on the other side of the road, they were able to fit her up with a reconditioned tyre, but when she arrived back at the Brook she found the tyre had started to crack.

On 27th July 1944, she set off to collect a patient from Lewisham Hospital and then to the patients' home at Forest Hill. As they waited in the hospital a VI bomb passed overhead and then suddenly cut out. As it did it turned back in the opposite direction towards the centre in Lewisham and crashed on the clock tower in the centre. The casualties killed, and wounded was high. When they returned from Forest Hill the scene of devastation was horrific. On 11th November 1944, a V2bomb hit the Brook Ambulance Station. She had just left that morning and said goodbye to the receptionist, Stella. As there was no bus in sight she decided to walk. As she did a No 89 bus came up in the opposite direction to what she was walking. Just after it had passed her the sky lit up and it sounded like there had been an earthquake. When she looked back the bonnet of the bus was on fire and the conductress was lying lifeless on the pavement. Where the reception had been there was now a heap of rubble. The receptionist Stella had been killed, she was only 20 at the time. Another woman died later, and a number were hut. Their next base was to be their last, it was the Trafalgar Tavern, Greenwich where the second floor became the ambulance station. The ambulances were kept in a shed across the road. This is now the site of the Trident Theatre.

Edna Perry wanted to be more than just an ARP messenger, so she lied about her age and volunteered for ambulance duty, at the time she was only 17. She found the first aid and midwifery training tough, but she did get through and began some gruesome spells of duty. It was at this time that she began smoking to calm her nerves, although when driving it got in her eyes and made them water. Not the best conditions to have to drive through a churchyard to avoid missing the bomb craters in the road, and with an expectant mother giving birth in the back and bombs still dropping around her. On one occasion a mother gave birth to triplets, two women and a boy, in the back of the ambulance. When she was trying to catch up on some much-needed sleep she was awakened by her mother saying, "They've bombed the canal." Edna replied, "I hope they haven't hurt it". Her mother said, "We'll all be drowned".

Edna had a dislike of water and so got up and put on her uniform greatcoat over her blue and white spotted pyjamas, and her wellies and tin hat and reported to the ambulance station. The canal was at the bottom of a steep hill in Birmingham and the water was pushing down the side streets bringing the biggest rats she had ever seen. A lot of people were trapped by the crater from the bomb blast. She helped get them out by using a large van and anything that would float. On another occasion when many bombs were dropped and her schoolfriend lost her feet which were severed by the fin from a dropped bomb. It was Edna's ambulance which took her to hospital. She was later fitted with artificial limbs and taught herself to ride a bike and to swim.

After the war Edna married a man who had come home from the war wounded. When a German fighter came over one day and began to machine gun everything in sight she dived under the table, remembering to take her dinner with her. When she got up the wall behind where she had been sitting was a row of bullet holes. One night the BSA factory in Smallheath was bombed and the night workers buried in the rubble. After an extensive search the area was sealed off. Edna had known many of the people who were killed and buried that night.

Coventry was bombed on 14th November 1940; Edna would always remember the devastation, fire, and loss of human and animal life. Some 250 people were killed and 800 injured. When Edna and her colleagues arrived, the bombs were still dropping, and fires raged everywhere. The next four days were spent digging, looking for possible survivors. Their bare hands were their only tools on many occasions. When they arrived back in Birmingham they had to report to the general hospital to be deloused as the filth and dust had drawn everything out of the woodwork and they were alive with all manner of insects. Edna was so tired she could have slept for a week but because the Germans kept up the onslaught it was back to work as usual.

Edna had her own share of tragedy during the war, losing her boyfriend, a sergeant air gunner, and her brother Edwin, a Wellington bomber pilot with 70 Sqn RAF. He went missing on an operation from Italy to Hungary. It was his fifth operation; he was only 20 years old. Both men were killed within four months of each other.

In 1943, Nora Gaskin was a Civil Defence Ambulance driver based at the Town Hall in Shanklin on the Isle of Wight. Her working hours were 5am to 8pm five days on and two days off, then a night shift of 8pm to 8am for five days. During the war the

Gloucester Hotel was the home of Shanklin Fire Brigade. During a raid, known as tip and run by the Germans, it received a direct hit killing most of the occupants. Nora worked many hours bringing the dead back to Shanklin Town Hall, where a temporary mortuary was set up in the basement. The work was made more harrowing for her as she knew most of the victims. The stretchers used for the victims were painted green and made of half inch wavy wire mesh. The next day when she set about cleaning her ambulance there were still particles of bloody flesh caught in the mesh. But she and many of the other women just took it as a part of everyday life at that time.

When war was declared, Rae Wagstaff volunteered to join the Wrens but owing to an asthma condition she was considered medically unfit, so she joined the ambulance service. Her first duty was spent alone in what was called the Spike or workhouse. Her job was to paint large cardboard notices stating Men Gassed, Women Gassed, decontamination area, etc. She started her ambulance duties without an ambulance, so to fill in the time she learnt to drive a corporation dust cart in which changing gear was a major operation, one had to hold the steering wheel with the knees and change gear with both hands. After a month she was given a Daimler ambulance. The first few months were spent taking expectant mothers to hospital or picking up dunks and taking them to the local police station along with a police escort.

In 1941, Mrs. Weston was told that the council needed ambulance attendants, but when she was asked if she had any first aid certificates she replied "No", but she did have some nursing experience having worked for a doctor. But she was turned down and instead offered a job as a cook in the canteen. She in turn refused this job and with the help of the local Red Cross hospital she acquired her certificates and became an attendant with ARP ambulance service. There were two wooden huts in Erith Council yards, one for the women and one for the men, but often the women slept under the council offices and when the telephone went for a call out the men would come and wake the women. In 1942, the raids came nearly every night. The one that she remembers was in Bexleyheath. When they arrived, the local ARP had already done what was necessary. All along the pavements were black bags with blood running out from them, and the ambulances were lined up the length of the road to take the bodies away. The system of awards to ARP personnel worked on the basis that a person's name was put forward to an independent committee and they took a vote as to whether the person got an award or not.

Mrs. Mabel Armitage was an ambulance attendant, and with two drivers, Betty Coverton and Ruby Sandford, she was recommended for the George Medal, but by two votes to one the award was lowered to the British Empire Medal. On 7th September 1940, they had been called to assist in a severe aid raid at West Ham. They were sent t o a local factory shelter, where women and children who had been bombed out were sheltering. They managed to move about five families from the shelter, the roads were covered in debris, there were burning buildings, bombs and incendiaries falling all around.

Joan Westerly was serving in the Coventry Emergency Medical Service and was on duty from 14th November to 7.45am on 15th November and made 11separate journeys from the depot to different areas that had been bombed. Despite this she was on duty again at 10.15am. In 1941, she was also awarded the Ekaterina MacAulay volunteered for ambulance service at Shoreditch. There were seven ambulances and two cars. Her wage was £1 1s 9d of which twelve shillings was taken up paying for lodgings, and eight shillings for food. In 1940, the ambulances spent most of their time waiting for bodies to be dug out of the rubble. She stayed in the ambulance service until 1945, her husband was in the Merchant Navy.

The idea of the American Ambulance Great Britain was formulated by Mr. Gilbert H Carr at an executive committee meeting of the American Society London in 1940. It was decided by the committee to raise a fund for the purchase of ambulances for Britain. All American organisations in London were invited to cooperate and in six weeks no less than $140,000 had been raised by Americans in London. The fleet of ambulances consisted of 300 ambulances, surgical units and first aid mobile posts. Many of these vehicles were to go through the blitz in London, many bore the scars of that battle. But out of 400 British women involved only three were killed, two in the London blitz of 1940/41 and one in the bombing of Exeter later. The cost of maintaining the fleet was borne by American subscription and handled by the British War Relief of America. The cost worked out at £2,000 per week. The ambulances were painted grey with a red stripe and had a badge of British and American flags emblazoned on the sides.

In the early days training was carried out at a training school in Leeds where the AAGB drivers had to pass a very severe test before qualifying. In the course of its great humanitarian work the fleet travelled over twelve million miles averaging 100,000 miles and carrying 4,000 patients per week. The women were between 21 and 45 years of age and were required to purchase their own uniform, a uniform which resembled the one worn by the ATS, or FANY. They, however, wore on each sleeve the crossed flags badge as on the side of the ambulance. On each sleeve they had a rank badge, ranging from lance corporal with one stripe to a captain with three pips.

Joan Willis, later Lady McDonald, whose father was an Admiral of Fleet, became an ambulance driver, with AAGB in August 1940 and reported to an ambulance garage in Hammersmith. She remembers the ambulances were Packards with Ford V8 engines. At first, she worked with a mobile first aid unit and one of her first patients was an old lady aged 70 who had been buried in her bombed house for 17 hours but was still cheerful when dugout. Joan had joined the ambulance service after her fiancée, a pilot in the Fleet Air Arm serving on the aircraft carrier HMS *Glorious*, was killed when the ship was sunk off the coast of Norway by the German ships Scharnhorst and Gneisenau. In all she served for a year and throughout the blitz period which must have seemed like ten years leave alone one. She later went to South Africa with her father who was C in C of the South Atlantic Fleet and worked as a civilian cipher in the Naval office at Freetown. When her father was promoted she returned to the UK and began work in the Admiralty as a civil servant, her full title being Temp Assistant Civilian Officer, or TACO for short.

The plotters lived underground in the Citadel part of the Admiralty as plotters for the intelligence room. Here they worked on a 24hour watch with breaks for meals and an occasional chance to lie down on a bunk and get some sleep. Many of her father's friends would come in to ask her where the ships were before planning an attack.

The Women's Auxiliary Police Corps was formed in 1941 and women were recruited for driving, clerical and communications duties. They were issued with blue cotton overalls and an arm badge which had the letters WAPC. They had to be British subjects, physically fit, aged between 21 and 50, and not less than 5'3", although some got in who were much shorter. They worked a 48-hour week with a weekly rest day and twelve days annual leave. Some while later they were issued with the same uniforms as the regulars and a weekly allowance of 1/6d if boots had not been issued.

Mrs. Collings started the war with the Civil Defence and then transferred to the WAPC. Her husband was also a reserve policeman. One morning when she was on the early turn she suddenly burst out laughing. When her sergeant asked her, what was the matter she replied, "Do you know Sarge, I've come to work every morning leaving my husband in bed with the woman next door". This was her next door neighbour whose husband was away in the RAF and she and her three little girls would come to sleep in the brick shelter along with the Collings'.

The shirts that the WAPC wore were air force blue in colour and had loose collars and trying to put them on with a collar stud and drink tea in the mornings at the same time was not easy. She was only 4'10" so somehow, she had got in despite the minimum height being 5'3". On one occasion when the Germans first used flying bombs and the Red Alert went on all night she saw an alarming object in the sky and tried to keep pace with it on her bike. As she made her way to work, an officer who saw her was horrified and ordered her to get inside as it was Hitler's new weapon.

Norah Lee joined the Metropolitan Women's Police Force in 1940. The period of instruction was one week and was given by a female Police Sergeant. She was then sworn in and posted to the West End and Central Police Station, London. Coming from Lancashire she had no idea of getting about in London. Shortly afterwards the air raids began in London. The night shift was 7pm to 7am and she lived in a section house at Notting Hill. Most of her patrols were conducted on the underground system at Oxford Circus, Piccadilly, and Green Park. She was later transferred to Tottenham Court Road, being the only WPC to work in this area.

On one occasion after a holiday she was asked to report to her station as there had been an incident. It concerned a colleague who had been covering for a Bertha Cleghorn who had been injured and taken to hospital. When Nora arrived at the hospital she found that Bertha had been seriously injured and died that afternoon. It was her job, as duty WPC, to take Bertha's parents to identify their daughter's body, a duty that any police officer must dread although the fact that Nora knew Bertha must have been comforting to her parents. Bertha had in fact been hurt when a bomb exploded near the station and as she stepped outside she was hit by the blast and falling debris. She was late cremated at Golder's Green.

The number of policewomen in the Metropolitan Police varied from 111 to 152, covering an area of 700 square miles.

Betty Kelly started in the GPO as a teleprinter operator and stayed until 1941 when she joined the Salford Police. GPO volunteers were asked to man the exchange while a bomb was defused nearby. She volunteered, and, when she and another woman looked at each other, they burst into laughter, each had a telephone type mouthpiece-cum-headphone and gas mask, and on top of all that they wore a steel helmet. She had to leave the police in 1943, as her husband was very ill. At the time he was on a commando course in Scotland. When he had recovered she took jobs at various officer clubs and the US GI Club and American Red Cross Club. From there she went to a new US Officers Club opened by Lord Derby and attended by General Patton to whom she was introduced.

On 14th December 1942, the Daily Express reported that women were to be admitted to the Home Guard and would carry out all duties except combat ones. According to the Daily Mail on 29th October 1941, 50 women had volunteered at a factory to be what was the first Women's Home Guard although at that stage it was not official. Their uniforms had been privately bought. Although not official they were on parade four nights a week. The War Office said they were not to be recognised and the carrying of arms by women was not to be encouraged.

Isabel McGrahaw was living in Newport during the war and most women who were not in the Services were in the fire service, home guard or police. A woman in London is said to have started the idea of women being in the Home Guard. When Isabel wrote to her, she replied, telling Isabel to form her own group in Newport, which she did. Isabel had about 2030 replies to her plea and started a training programme. This included using the target practice ranges. She was interviewed by a Colonel Phillips who had served in the South Wales Borderers in WWI and was now a local Home Guard Commander. He arranged for them to have ammunition and the use of the ranges.

Ruth Colyer remembers joining the 'Women's Home Defence Corps' and learning to shoot, although her aim at the time went on became erratic as she was pregnant.

Another important organisation for the women was the Royal Observer Corps. Patricia Jackson joined the corps when she was 18, her father having been it prior to the war, and up to 1940 when he went into the Forces. Today, she counts the years served in the Corps as some of the happiest of her life. They worked in shifts of eight hours around the clock. One week 5am to 4pm; 12pm to 8pm, 8pm to 4am, and 4pm to midnight. There were three crews in all. These were joined by part time members who did four-hour shifts. They would think nothing in those days of walking to the corps centre, about 112 miles and in the blackout. Sometimes on arrival a raid might be in progress and the whole ops room would be a hive of industry and excitement. They would slip quietly into position at the ops table and plug into the outdoor posts reporting the information to them.

Patricia happened to be on duty the first night the V1 'doodlebugs' came over. At first everyone was mystified as to what was happening. Reports and sightings were coming in all over. They had been warned of an unspecified new weapon but were unaware of the form it would take. The code name given to reporting Doodlebugs was 'Diver'. When this was given everyone concentrated plotting them until they had been shot down or crashed.

Phyllis Parr decided to join the ROC in 1943 in the Colchester area. Women were first enrolled in 1941, at this time they were all volunteers. But when the men were getting called up in substantial numbers, women and boys were drafted into the Corps. Her training lasted two weeks and was spent at a secondary ops room. On her course were twelve other recruits all attending for the first time.

The operation room plotting table had a mass of circle dot figures, letters, and squares. The dots were the positions of the ROC posts and each was given a letter, e.g. A1, A2, A3. Then a circle representing a five-mile radius was drawn around each post and was issued for bearings when plotted by sound and marked to show bearings in degrees. The circles overlapped so that areas were duplicated. The whole table was marked in the National Grid lines of longitude and latitude designated by letters and numbers. Each took a place around the table having a tray of magnetic counters, numbers, letters and plotting equipment such as coloured arrows, sound shields and leaving counters. After training you were transferred to the main operation room centre. All telling, and reporting was done in set sequences in the most concise form and in the order required by the recipient which saved time and unnecessary chatter. The plotter's duty was to make sure that there was continuity in tracking aircraft, watching the movement of the aircraft and warning your posts of the approach of aircraft in their area. There was always great satisfaction in plotting an SOS and then finding it had landed safely. There was always great tension in the plotting of hostile aircraft.

In charge of the ops room plotting table was a supervisor and two orderlies. There female Billeting Officers looked after evacuees and were usually local school teachers. On 3rd September 1939, Hilda Cripps was rushed over to Rochford to the District Council Chambers and was sworn in as a billeting officer. The first evacuees arrived at 5pm mainly from the East End of London. They were not used to eating at the table and took their food out and ate it on the door step, old habits die hard.

Another role she had was Salvage Steward and arranging Salvage Depots collecting cleaning rags to clean the guns, four by two as they were known in the Army. Her garden was a dump for old saucepans and similar scrap. The aluminium was supposedly for making Spitfires. Her badge of office was red and made of plastic. In 1940, the area she covered was a possible one for by the Germans. In view of this an Invasion Committee was formed at Shoeburyness, a garrison town. The Commander came to see them and explain the situation and what was required. He said from his position and in the case of an invasion he would have to fight over and around them if necessary. They would have to become self-sufficient must keep the roads clear at all times.

A census was made of the residents and what equipment needed to be collected. Buckets, bowls, and a large detached house was required to act as a hospital, and another smaller one for isolation purposes. In a barn in the village a large supply of papier-mâché coffins was stored. A census was made of all livestock, sheep, and pigs, that would be needed for slaughter and all nonmilk producing cattle and non-egg laying hens, would be reserved for slaughtering if necessary. Fresh water was a problem if the mains was destroyed, but with the help of a builder she was able to ascertain the location of a great many wells, and with the help of Southend Water Company a number were checked and tested for capacity and purity. To get the water to the people horse drawn carts would be needed. For this purpose, farmers' carts were sterilized and would be used and were listed. A small yellow triangle was affixed to the local school, its significance being to show the military personnel that this was the headquarters of the Invasion Committee.

Marie Weavers was in the 'Girls Training Corps' a preservice organisation perhaps on the lines of the ATC or Army Cadets for the boys. It was set up to ease women into the services when their time came. They met two days a week, during air raids the meetings were held in the air raid shelter. At the weekends visits to hospitals and map reading exercises and on Sunday Church Parade.

During the war, in about 1942, a guard dog training school was formed by a retired Lt Col Baldwin who was a well-known and respected breeder and trainer of Alsatian dogs which he had introduced to this country after the 1914/18war. He worked under the auspices of Lord Brabazon, then the Minister of Aircraft production. He recruited staff from men and women who were breeders and trainers of Alsatians, he also recruited dogs on loan from the public, not only Alsatians but other suitable breeds as well. For example, all dogs that were provided for RAF stations were on loan from the public and were in due course returned to their owners. A roll of the dogs supplied was submitted to the officer in charge of records at RAF Gloucester. Teams of servicemen from the Army, RAF, US Servicemen and MOD Police attended the school for training with a dog and then passed out at the end of the course. They then returned to their unit for dog guarding duties on airfields, army installations and other areas as and where security was required, not only in the UK but abroad.

Violet Day was a breeder and trainer of Alsatians and when she heard of Col Baldwin's requirements she volunteered her services and spent the first few months at the kennels near Cheltenham, and then to Beoley kennels, near Redditch. The kennels here had been used for greyhounds before the war. The staff consisted of nine women and two men trainers, plus a male van driver. All breeds of dogs were accepted provided they were of a suitable size and were train worthy. When they arrived, they were housed in a bar and the trainers drew lots for them. Each dog would be given a tag on its collar with its name and home address. One owner in error put her own name on the tag instead of the dog's and until she could be contacted the dog was known as 'Mrs. Smith'.

The training was long and took place in all weathers. When dog fights occurred, they were often started by the male bull terriers and without any provocation. When this happened, it would take three women to hold each dog and another would put her hands around the bull terrier's throat and by pressing hard on its windpipe make it momentarily gasp for breath, at which point the other women would pull the dogs apart. It proved to be the only way to make the terrier release its grip on the other dog. The staff of course suffered many dog bites as part of the day's work.

One dog called Thorn, an Alsatian, had remarkable intelligence and could do many tricks. On one occasion a man trainer had his spectacles accidentally knocked off and called for everyone to stand still in case they stepped on them in the dark. He then sent Thorn to find them and in no time at all he returned with the glasses unbroken. When shut in a room and called from the other side of the door he would turn the door handle with his mouth, let himself out then close the door behind him by pushing it shut with his paws. To demonstrate the strength of his grip he once gave a public demonstration by having a tug of war with his trainer holding the dog's lead, he gripped a rope on the other end with four men pulling it against him. His work after training was rescuing people from the blitz, working with another dog he was attached to the Civil Defence. On one occasion he found no fewer than 24 buried people in South London. On another occasion he entered a burning house, stepping carefully over the fires seeking out trapped people, all this despite the smoke, flames, fires, and hose pipes belching water. When he was presented with the animal VC known as the Dicken Medal, the Queen wore a very long fur stole which Thorn sniffed at. When the King saw this, he said "It's alright my dear, he thinks it is a rabbit." After giving so much gallant service, his life was to end in tragic circumstances. His owner let him out of the car to relieve himself. As he went into a field in foggy conditions a shot was heard. The dog had been shot by a farmer who thought he was after the sheep. It was a sad and awful end for a very brave and wonderful dog who had served his country so well, he at least deserved to live his life out and die of old age.

One dog whom Violet looked after was a white Alsatian which was being trained for criminal work much as today's police dogs. One day she took him into a field and no sooner was he on the grass in the field and, no doubt thinking it was for more criminal training, he leaped up and attacked her. To protect herself she raised her left arm which he grabbed and hung on to the sleeve of the thin coat she was wearing at the time. She lowered her arm and slowly walked back to the path and the gate. As soon as they reached the path he let go of her arm and walked to heel back to the kennels. She later learned that some months later he had been returned to his owner, who in turn had returned him to the kennels as being unmanageable. The end of the story for this dog was that he had to be put down.

Later in the war the school was taken over by the Air Ministry and in January 1946, became the RAF Police Dog Training School. The dogs that had been borrowed were now being returned to their owners and a breeding programme of Alsatians was started. Over 400 puppies were bred and at the age of three months puppies were brought to her for rearing. Over the next nine months WAAF volunteers were recruited to assist rearing the puppies and giving initial training.

The puppy rearing section was set up in disused Nissen huts at Staverton and RAF Innsworth. They were used for whelping mothers and their puppies being fed on meat considered not fit for human consumption and identified by green dye splashed on it. Much of the meat was got from the local slaughter houses. After the animal had been killed and boned the meat was put into a bucket and it was not unusual for the meat to jump out of the bucket; being freshly killed the nerves were still responsive. To assist in the rearing of the puppies they used goat's milk obtained from a neighbouring farmer.

At the end of the war the dogs that had survived were brought back to the kennels before being returned to their original owners. This was not easy as many of the dogs had been posted all over the world and from place to place in the UK and the world. Many of the Americans were smuggled back to the USA. The dogs that had been abroad were put into quarantine for six months. Each dog owner received a certificate of merit for war service as a thank you for the excellent work they had done. Violet had married just before the war and had moved into a brand-new bungalow in Essex. Later in the war with her husband in the Army overseas, her own home and her parents' home were destroyed in the bombing. At this time, she found the love of dogs a great comfort. They lived in a government industrial hostel or whatever accommodation was available. As well as the emergency services there were many other organisations and jobs which were manned by women and their own way equally as important.

Hannah Lamb worked for the gas board. Her job was to read the meters and empty the box which in those days would have been full of pennies. After she had counted it she then had to work out the amount of gas used and take enough to cover this, any leftover, called 'Divvy', was refunded to the consumer. She wore a navy-blue uniform and carried the money in a leather Gladstone bag. Although they were called 'Meter Maidens', their official title which was on their cap badge was Gas Inspector.

In those days were few lifts and it was nothing to climb three or four flights of stairs to read the meter. At that time a lot of the elderly people lived downstairs because of the air raids, their beds had been moved into the parlour as it was then called and placed in front of the meter cupboard. This meant that to read and empty the meter the bed had to be moved each time. When a house had been hit in an air raid the meter still had to be emptied.

Another vital industry during the war was the railways on which ammunition, troops and vehicles had to be moved. Nancy Head served as a signalwoman and manned along, with another woman, a live line in Cumberland. She used to cycle three miles to the station each day, the early shift started at 6.30am and the late shift ended at 10pm.

Another form of important transport was the buses. Edna Williams who we had earlier heard about in the Ambulance Service became, at the tender age of 17, a bus conductress, or 'clippie' as they were known on the Birmingham Trams. She remembers a direct hit on her tram depot and many of the night staff being killed, severely burned, or injured. One night during a heavy raid they had to take cover in an Anderson shelter, it was here she sampled her first fag, the start of a lifetime of smoking. When the 'All Clear' came they left the shelter in the early hours of the morning to retrieve their tram only to discover a huge crater in which at the bottom was the tram, or what remained of it. So, between them the driver and her shouldered the tram pole and walked back to the depot.

Joyce Paton also worked on the buses in Cornwall. Her early shift started at 4.30am. It was the first bus out and took the workers to the dockyards. They also carried mail bags and boxes of flowers from Covent Garden, plus live chickens. On one occasion one got out and had to be chased around the bus. On another occasion she saw the wheel come off the bus and roll down the road. The driver managed to jam the bus against a hedge to stop. Later she was sent to Plymouth to work and not knowing the fares in her new area she charged a bunch of sailors 2d each which was a lot less than it should have been, a cheap trip but in her opinion justified for servicemen who may well go out and be killed later. When she overslept one morning the driver brought the bus around to her house and knocked on her door to wake her. The buses were 20 or 32-seaters. On occasion the 20-seater would carry 60 passengers and the 32-seater would carry 80.

When Plymouth was bombed, which was often, she had to put the passengers off the bus and take cover in the nearest shelter, then when it was all over collect them all up again and carry on. Her time on the buses ended in romance as she married her driver.

Elsie Ewing was a driver on the buses. Today professional female drivers are commonplace, but then it was a rare sight. She drove a bus for Worthington Motor Tours Ltd in Stoke and took workers to the ordnance factories at Echashall which was between Stafford and

Stoke, and in the evenings the US troops to Stoke for a night out. The bus was a 32-seater Bedford and driving it in the blackout and through rural areas was not easy, in the fog or smog as it was called then the passengers would get out and guide the bus with the aid of a torch.

Jessie Butler was born in south east London and when war broke out for a brief time she was working in a laundry in Lordship Lane, Dulwich. In 1940, she went for a job as a conductress at the London Transport Garage in Chiswick for training. Then to the garage at West Norwood and spent the next five years there. When she first arrived, the women shared the toilets with the men until separate toilets were built. When the bombing started in 1940 the buses were full of people carrying anything and everything, even cats, dogs and budgies in cases. They were making for the underground stations where they would spend the night. When she could not get through the crowded bus to collect the fares, the passengers would collect them for her and pass the money back to her. On one occasion while taking passengers to the Arsenal at Woolwich, the munitions factory, an air raid started, and bombs began to drop all around the bus.

During the war a Government scheme was started for expectant mothers. Thanks to the help of many women who gave up their country houses for them to be used as maternity hospitals, the scheme was able to work. Dorothy Nash's husband was one of the first to be called up at the outbreak of war and she and 200 expectant mothers were taken in a red double decker London bus to what was at the time an unknown destination. The upper deck was fitted out as a labour ward with a sister and nurse in attendance. Eventually they stopped at Colchester en-route for a break and then eventually arrived at the village of Ramsay and a large house, Michaelstowe Hall. Here they were welcomed by the matron and her staff. She only stayed here for a short while as the baby was not due until 20th September. In the meantime, she was billeted out and went to stay at Parkston Quay where she stayed with an elderly couple. Near the time that the baby was due she was taken back to the Hall for the birth and had a baby son on 19th September. From there she was taken to South Wales by her husband who was in the Navy. Sadly, on 16th April 1941, he was lost when his ship HMS *Voltaire* was sunk in the South Atlantic by a German surface raider.

Evelyn Jones was in 1941 also expectant and taken to one of the specially arranged maternity houses, this time Hemel Hempstead. The local villagers called the maternity bus the 'Blunder Bus', which was normally the name of a type of gun. The house she stayed in was at Great Gaddesden. After four weeks her son was born. One mother who was there said 'All those trees and cows and nothing else, we'd rather be at home with the bombs'. Only one thing marred their stay; the villagers always referring to them as 'Dirty Londoners'.

Daphne Julian was a Noland nurse (a trained Children's Nanny) looking after children at a war nursery in Slough Social Centre. Sleepy children between two and five years were brought in at 7am each day while their mothers went to work in the munitions factory at the Slough Trading Estate. The day was a long one, 7am to 7pm, and involved looking after 30 to 40 children who had to be fed, washed, and nursed each day. A lot of the day was spent in the air raid shelters. There were of course cuts and bruises and, on occasion, overwrought, overworked, and tired mothers. The fathers were away on active service. When the cook went on leave Daphne became the cook as well as a nurse, her special was steam puddings. Once a month a medical officer would come and look at the children and search for lice and nits in the children's hair. If any were found the treatment was a sassafras cap which was put on the child's head, then bound with a bandage for a few hours while the oil did its work. After that the hair was washed with a medicated soap and finally combed with a fine-toothed comb. The pungent smell of Sassafras stayed with Daphne for many a year. For this work she was paid 27/6d a week, from which she had to pay 17/6d a week for lodgings.

Mrs. Fugill was a head housemaid at St Andrews Hospital on Bow, East London. Some of the women workers at the hospital had lost everything in the bombing and slept at night on mattresses in the basement of the hospital. On one occasion she went looking for one of her housemaids, Patricia, who lived in but had not been seen all night. It turned out she had been killed in the bombing and the only way she had been identified was a yellow ribbon she always wore in her hair. She was buried in Bow Cemetery, the funeral being attended by her mother, brother, Mrs. Fugill, and the home sister. The hospital chaplain conducted the service.

Louise Palmer ran a coal yard, keeping warm of course even during war time perhaps even more so was important. Her husband Richard had been in the Royal Navy prewar but left to help Louise run the yard. However, being on the reserve he had to report each year for one week's training. In 1939, he left on 31 August and did not return until December. At the time the coal yard was well stocked, so she was able to manage and run the yard on her own with the help of two men too old for military service and a boy to do odd jobs. But, as the war went on stocks became low and supplies scarce. Some of her customers got in touch with the BBC. As a result, she was asked to go on the programme '*In Town Tonight*'.

In those days the coal was delivered by horse and cart. One horse she had would bolt on hearing the siren and come straight home to the stables. In the end things got too much for her and she wrote to the Minister of Fuel and Power and he was able to arrange for her husband to leave the Navy and come home nine months before the war ended. This she remembered helped a great deal. They kept the coal yard going until 1960. Where it stood is now a block of flats.

In 1939, Mavis Young was a pupil at Newport High School and in the Sixth Form waiting to take her school certificate which was much like today's GCEs. She wanted to be a school teacher and had already done some training at St Woolos Elementary School. In front of the High School was a barrage balloon which the children had an affection for, they looked rather like elephants floating in the sky. On one occasion a boy and girl from the school were killed when a German plane crashed on to their house. The streets outside the school were lined with 6th Formers as a mark of respect as the funeral cortege dove past. In 1941, Mavis went to St Hilda's College, Oxford, to read for a degree in history. While there she had to do her share of fire watching and firefighting drill. One thing she always remembers from those days was a notice which said, 'Never leave a body alone, it is bad for public morale'. No mention was made of what it did for yours.

Above left: KM Collings of the Women's Auxiliary Police Corps. Above right: WPC Bertha Cleghorn who, sadly, did not survive the war. Below left: Nora Bee (Author). Below right: Hot cocoa for a police officer in Salford, 1942 (B. Kelly).

Above: Women bus drivers and conductors (Author). Below: Leading the team from Bealey Kennels, Redditch, on a road walk. Bottom: Station 126, Septmeber 1939 (Author).

Top: Women's Home Guard.

Below: Mabel Winter, Civil Defence, 1941 (Author)

Right: Mary the Coal Horse (L. Palmer)

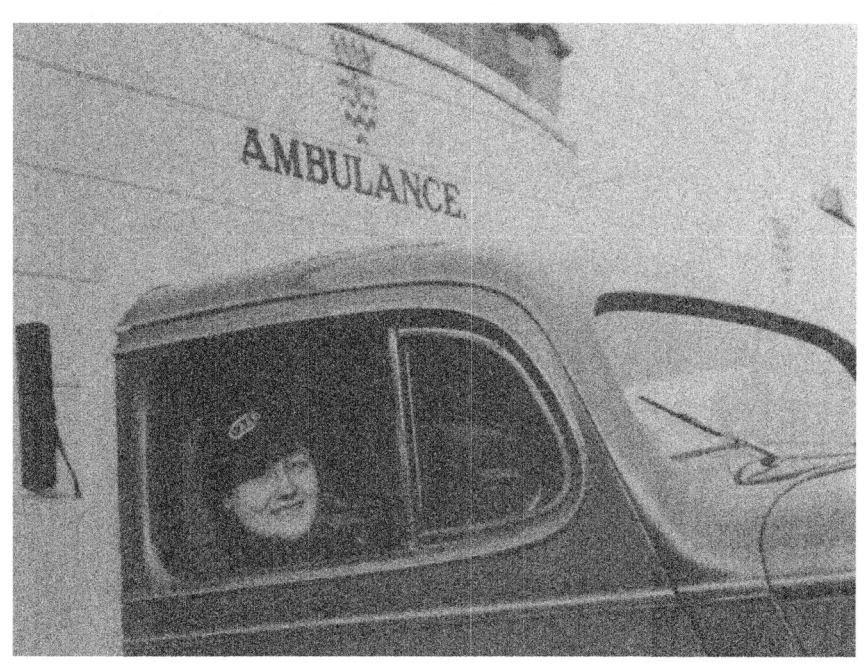

Above: Woman ambulance driver (Mrs. Housen).

Below: American ambulances in Great Britain (Author).

Chapter 8 Industrial Work

In 1940, Aneurin Bevin made a speech concerning the industrial workers; "Ever since we took off we have been extorting you to work hard. I have never done so much extorting to work hard in my life. We've got to do it to win the victory and I know you will do it, I have you to keep it up because the more you keep it up the quicker we will get this wretched job over. We are going to get it over on our own terms with you in the factory, and the soldiers, sailors and airmen on the job and the mercantile marine, trawler men, and all the rest of it. We'll do it and will do it cheerfully and we don't need to alter much. We all go along together with a mighty effort and show the Hitlers and Mussolinis that we cannot only work and fight, but we can be cheerful in doing it as well".

The women in the factories became known as Bevin Girls, much as the boys in the mines were known as Bevin Boys. It was the responsibility of the Ministry of Supply to recruit women for the factories, from them came a plea 'Women of Britain Come into Factories'. The Ministry of Labour set up labour bureaus and women could come in off the street and try out the machines they would work on. In 1938, and prewar, women in the factories were getting 25/a week, this later went up to £2 and in 1944 to £3/0/10d. The holidays had to be split. Monday, Tuesday and Wednesday would be taken, then six months later the rest of the week, Thursday, Friday, and Saturday.

The women working with TNT or other explosives found it made their hair and skin go a funny colour. Those working in the engineering factories found the oil got right through to their skin and the smell in their lungs. By 1943, over 7½ million women were employed in some form or another, of which 500,000 were in the factories. In April 1942, there were more than 40 ordnance factories employing 300,000 workers. In May 1942, the current rate of production of machine tools was six times the normal output, and the production of weapons of war had doubled. There was good reason to believe that the UK factories were turning out more munitions in proportion to the population than any other nation in the world. Aircraft production was three times as great as on the eve of war.

The aircraft had become much larger and more complicated, it took 15,000 items to make up one bomber, the production of tanks had doubled. In June 1942 alone the production of tanks, jeeps and other mechanical vehicles was at the rate of 257,000 a year and shipping were four times greater in 1941 than in 1939. In 1942, more than twice as many guns were being produced as was in the peak of production in WWI. Ammunition for the big guns was being produced at 25 million rounds a year and for small arms at the rate of two million rounds a year.

Margaret Coulson worked in the ammunition works at Chorley where the workers were taken to the factory by special train each day. She was fitted out with jacket and trousers, hat, and waist belt. No jewellery or hair clips could be worn, and one could not eat on the 'Lean Side' (inside the factory). She was put on No 1 Section P Line, the live ammunition section in the factory. Her job was to fill and clean detonators. A woman called Blue Band told her what to do and placed her on a machine. In the room where they worked was Red Band, whose job it was to make sure everything was being done correctly. During the day a Head Red Band would walk around each shop to make sure everything was ship shape. The detonators were picked up with tweezers and the women wore gloves. At the time of her accident, Margaret was working on a varnishing machine when there was a loud bang and her thumb began to hurt. The shock of the bang has stayed with her to this day and she cannot stand anything to do with switches. When her hand was better she was sent to the docks in South Shields, to a warehouse taken over by the Admiralty where she packed shells into boxes.

Linda Hayward was sent to the Royal Naval Cordite factory at Holton Heath. After a medical and interview which she passed, she was given a book on regulations in which the need for security was stressed. A talk was given on safety in the factory and she was kitted out with thick serge trousers, long sleeve tunic and mob hat which one used to cover one's hair. Each worker was given a disc with a number on it which was securely tied to the waist of the trousers. No buttons or metal objects were allowed. With explosives the greatest danger was fire. The shifts were 6am to 2pm, 2pm to 10pm and the night shift, 10pm to 6am, but this could often be stretched to a ten-hour day. The night shift people got £3/10s and the day shift less. They were told the income tax they paid would be paid back at the end of the war, but when Linda applied after the war she was told that being married her rebate had been given to her husband in one lump sum, including hers.

The women in the factory were aged between 18 and 40 and the men there were much older. They were taken each day by bus to the factory and on arrival checked to see if they had any matches before being allowed through. Then they had a three-quarter mile walk to the changing room and canteen. After 15 minutes a hooter would sound, and all the workers would move to a danger area, and yet another spot check. A telling off was forthcoming if any hair showed below the regulation area. From there to a changing area to change into soft shoes. If they needed to leave the floor for any reason they had to once again change their shoes. The smell of cordite was awful, until one got used to it; new workers were often sick, it got right through to their underclothes. The powder was fed into a press and it came out like dough; this was once again pressed into what looked like spaghetti and then cut into lengths and laid on trays to be taken back to be baked in large ovens. The job was out of doors and in all weathers. The small truck on a small gauge railway was pushed by hand, three women to each truck. She did this for two years of her total time in the factory. The one perk was the use of hot baths at the end of each shift, as she did not have a bath at her cottage so made full use of this facility.

Lily Webster worked in a munitions factory in Worcester. It was her first time away from home in London. Her mother was very upset when she left and said, "Don't take my baby away, she is all I have left". Her brothers had all been called up. Her first experience with landladies was not good, the first one she had gave little value for the money she was paid. When Lily moved to Stratford-upon-Avon things improved, but her landlady took some convincing that the bombing in London was as bad as the radio described.

Katherine Greig did not fancy the prospects of being in uniform, so she chose to work in an ammunitions factory in Aberdeen where she trained as a fitter. She later transferred to the BSA in Redditch where she was put on a machine pressing gun barrels for aircraft. She remembers a band coming and playing for dancing in the canteen at dinner times; the menu was a cheap meal, a glass of milk or a mild English beer. The dress in the factory for the women was green overalls or dungarees as they were known and the traditional turban to keep the hair away from the machines. The one part of working in a munitions factory during the war was the ever-present danger from fire and explosives.

Mrs. Phillips worked in a factory from 1940 to 1946, filling explosive detonators which were easily set off and a number exploded injuring many of the women. When a big bang came everyone rushed to see who was hurt; on one occasion they arrived to find a young woman being laid out on a stretcher, she had lost one hand and part of the other and had been blinded. All she said was "What will Mother do now?". Later she was sent to St Dunstans, the wonderful organisation for the blind, where she learned to type and sent a letter to the women in the factory to thank them for the collection they had made for her; she had typed it with her thumb which was the only thing she had left on the one hand.

Another woman who was hurt and pregnant at the time hurt her hands and stomach in the explosion. Her husband at the time was serving in the Middle East. She was doing the same job as Mrs. Phillips but on the next shift. Many more were hurt and at least two killed in her time. In a factory in Surbiton, Surrey the Women's Factory Group was formed; they were trained in first aid, cooking, clerical and transport. They also spent some time on the miniature rifle range in the factory.

Miss Pace was 19 when the war broke out and she was serving her apprenticeship in a print and book binders in Euston. Her boss was the husband of Barbara Cartland, who used to come to the factory with her daughter Raine, now Princess Diana's stepmother. Part of the work was contracted out and so the Official Secrets Act had to be signed. Overtime was spent in producing ration books. When she was 21 she was called up, much to the disgust of her father, and sent to a factory in Rugby. The sheer size of the factory terrified her after the Dicken's type building she had been used to in Euston. She could not see from one end of the workshops to the other, and everyone seemed to be talking in a foreign language. She took one look and cried her eyes out; all she wanted at that moment was her Mum and Dad. Her father said she was not to do any night shifts, little did he know she had been doing this every two weeks since she had started at the factory. Her Mother, being very practical, told her to make friends in Rugby as this was now her home. She remembers when 'Music While You Work' came on the radio the women would all sing at the tops of their voices above the noise of the machines. The bands who played on this programme were told not to play anything slow so as not to slow down production.

All the machine setters were from Wales; they had come to Rugby when the depression hit the Welsh Valleys. In off time periods she and the other women would go to Leicester and dance at the De Montfort Hall to bands such as Glen Miller. The local women were not too happy with the influx of outside women, which meant the factory women becoming very clannish. She found the night workers a great bunch, full of comradeship, records were played throughout the night and while waiting for the machines to be set up one or two were doing a bit of jitterbugging to the music. After 2Y2 years she was not keen to go back to London but go back she did just before the war ended and got married. In the market in Leicester they could chat up a stall holder for stockings and shoes without coupons.

Ruth Barber was, up to the Spring of 1941, working in a bakehouse. When her husband was called up she went to work on aircraft production at Ringway. One day she was working in a warm bakehouse and the next in overalls in a large aircraft hangar complete with toolbox. On the day she started 100 other women started as well, all were servicemen's wives. They started off learning to thread cables from the cockpit to the tail-plane on Beaufighters, the cables controlled the rudders and elevators. From there she and the others went on to assembling complete tail-planes all done by women. Eventually she ended up working on Lancaster bombers. The woman supervisor was very strict, and even removed the mirror in the toilet to deter them spending too much time doing their hair or makeup. They were all injected against flu to make sure production did not slip. After four years away, her husband came home and today they have celebrated their Golden Wedding Anniversary.

Mrs. Brown worked on an aerodrome which was very cold in the winter as it only had a coke stove in the hangar for heat. When she first went there all the overalls were men's and of course too big. Mrs. Brown's mother could never understand why she always wanted cheese sandwiches. The reason was, she was able to slide them on a piece of aluminium into the small tunnels on the side of the stove and so make cheese on toast! They occasionally used the forces canteen, until one of her friends found a big black spider in her rice pudding!

Their job at the aerodrome was servicing the RAF Training aircraft of the time, the Tiger Moth. The aircraft would come in for a full service after about 300 hours flying. Two men would work on the engines and two women on the fuselage and wings, which had to be completely stripped and overhauled. On occasions, the rudder and other parts would need a complete new cover. A woman would seam and stitch them together and hand-stitch around the outside. They were then dope, and inspection windows put in. This included working Saturday and Sundays. They were paid 8d an hour and the weekly pay was about £2. After the aerodrome was closed and she was drafted to the Rover Company who made tank engines. Mrs. Brown's job was piston rings and checking the cylinders. After 15 months she was drafted to another firm and put on a drilling machine and when that closed she went back to her original firm J Cash.

Colleen Edmunds began work in the Autumn of 1941. She began work as a navvy on an airfield. They were fitted out with men's wellington boots, bib and brace overalls, an oil skin mac and sou'wester. For certain dangerous jobs they had rubber gloves which came up to the elbow. The tools of the trade were a garden fork, shovel, and pick axe which were all full size as Colleen was careful today to point out. She also had a stiff broom with a head on it 2½ feet wide. The main job was keeping the runways clean and chipping off any split or chipped concrete. Later, she was given the job of pipe laying for drainage on the runway for which she received an extra one penny an hour. When she was promoted to Bay Joiner she received an extra 2d an hour. The Bay Joiner's job was to fill the space between the new bays with boiling lead. For this job they wore facemasks and the long rubber gloves. On one occasion she got into hot water for riding a dumper scoop truck. At the time it was pouring with rain and it was a mile walk to the canteen, so she jumped into the dumper for quickness to get there.

The ladies' toilet was a small wooden hut with two handles at the back and front just like a Sedan chair, as they moved further and further down the runway, so the portable toilet was carried along behind by two men. On one occasion this was done with someone still sitting on the seat.

Joan Stevenson volunteered for office work at the Metropolitan Works in Trafford Park, Manchester. Here she started work on Gaisle which was in the main works. The depot was involved in the construction of a component, known as a G Modulator 64 which related to radar and which helped the RAF bombers to accurately home and bomb targets deep in Germany. This was known in the RAF as H2S. On one occasion after the Dams Raid, Barnes Wallis and the 'Boffin Boys' as Joan described them, visited the depot. The area where the components were assembled was known as the cage. Joan's job title was Progress Clerk. When each of the units was tested the serial number was rushed to her to be recorded. In her desk was a small black note book which contained details of all the Top-Secret maintenance units all over the UK. It was her job to make sure that every unit had delivery of the modulators.

On Saturday 18th July 1943, at a Vickers aircraft factory, workers arranged with the management and the joint production committee to build a Wellington bomber in the record time of 30 hours. The Crown Film Unit filmed the bomber being built. The record-breaking attempt began at 9 am. Two sections of the fuselage were brought in where a dark-haired girl, Eileen Daphney, who used to work in the Rayon factory, was waiting to rivet them together. The fuselage parts were assembled in big frames called jigs. These volunteer workers were going to give the bonus they would make for this weekend work to the Red Cross Aid to Russia fund. The record they were trying to break had been previously set by them. It was a big task as the bomber was 65 feet long.

As the work progressed it was inspected by Evelyn Coates, she found they were not only doing the job quickly but also perfectly and she could find no faults; as they say, practice makes perfect.

Grace Walley and Hilda Dodd were busy assembling the bomber's cabin heater. Despite only having been working for one hour and 17 minutes the wooden floor had been fitted into the fuselage. On the wings testing the flaps was Eva Williams who previously had been a nurse! They were working so fast that the Chief Cameraman, Chick Fowle, was having a job keeping up with them.

The short dark-haired woman assembling the ailerons was 23-year-old Evelyn Homeward whose husband was serving in the RAF. She had been one of the first five women to work in the plant. Gerald Winney the test pilot said they looked like a lot of 'bloody ants' and he hoped they did not forget anything. In the afternoon things were developing in the stitching and doping sections. The four great sections which gave the bomber its 80-foot wing span and which had to be covered with fabric, and then sewn by hand. One false move and the needle would hit metal and the point of the needle break off. But Agatha Robson and the others knew exactly where the stitches had to go. The fabric was bonded to the metal frame by about 8,000 tiny bolts and the hand stitching cleaned up the edges, eight stitches to the inch was the order of the day.

At the back of the fuselage Vera Butler and her sister Joan were working together; Vera had been a lady's companion before starting to work at the factory in 1941. Phyllis Evans, who before the war had been a maid, was fitting the fabric covering on the frame work. When this was done nine coats of dope were put on.

A tiny brunette, Eva Powell, who ran the crane and way up under the roof girders brought the engines the length of the workshop and then gently lowered them into the nacelle, or the power egg as it was known. Ailsa Grindley was working on the engines, something she preferred to the confectionery store she had worked in previously. When it got to 23 minutes past eight in the evening the workers began to place bets as to the job being finished or not, there was still 17 hours and 20 minutes to go. One girl, Ivy Bennett, was wearing a pink chiffon blouse; she had come straight from a party to the night shift to help the record-breaking attempt. At 10.30 pm the landing wheels were installed. They were 4½ feet high and weighed 300lbs each.

At 3.30 am the aircraft was towed to the running shed. At 6.15 am on Sunday morning, and exactly 21 hours and 15 minutes from the start of its construction, the bomber was a complete fighting unit and saw the light of the first dawn of its lifetime. At 8.50 am everything had been checked. Gerald Whinney had planned to test fly the aircraft that afternoon, but it was built so fast and ahead of schedule that they had to get him out of bed. The aircraft, Wellington LN 514, took off 24 hours and 48 minutes after the first bolt had been placed. The aircraft was delivered to No 8 Maintenance Unit at 7.45 pm. It survived the war and finished its life on the 11th March 1948 when it was scrapped.

Mignon Morisat Jones worked in the drawing office of the aircraft factory at Vickers Armstrong. Here they were working on the modification to the Spitfire, extending the number of blades on the propeller from three to four, at the time a very 'hush hush' job. 'Careless Talk Costs Lives' was the motto of the day then. During the night shift they would be in a blacked out drawing office, with shaded lights and kept working throughout even when the air raid siren went and listened for the roof spotters whistle. When it came they rushed down to the shelters which in the winter were freezing, and in the summer, stifling hot. During this time, Mignon contacted TB. In those days there was no compensation, or thoughts about asking for it, and the illness was put down as to the misfortune of war.

Milly Kilbane also worked in an aircraft factory making radiator tubes to keep the water cool in the aircraft. She worked on a jig with her twin sister. Then after work they went strawberry picking until about 5pm, had a short sleep and went back to the factory for 9pm. In those days there were no stockings to be bought so it was a trip to the chemists to purchase a liquid which, when put on the legs, looked as if one had stockings on. Meals were acquired at the British Restaurant at 1/1d for a dinner including a cup of tea. Milly said she would do it all again. Her twin sister died in 1985, but her older sister, who also worked in the factory, married an American and she became a GI bride and now lives in Texas, USA.

The Lancaster became the most powerful and efficient bomber in the world and was built in several factories in the UK and Canada in terrific numbers. In all, over 40,000 women were working solely on building Lancasters. Angela Roberts was a capstan operator, Massie

Rafferty worked on the press, Joan Evans on melting, and Alice Warburton and Rachel Strong on trimming and hammering.

When the war started, Marion Tildsley was at the textile factory of Tootal working as a shorthand typist, she also undertook her share of fire watching in the factory, and twice a week helped at Manchester Royal Infirmary with general duties on the wards. In 1941, she married and, as the company policy then was not to employ married women, she had to leave Tootals. She and her new husband, who was not medically fit for military service because of a disabled shoulder, began to work at A V Roe the aircraft designers and builders at Woodford, Cheshire. It was here that the Lancaster bomber was being built. She was put on inspection at the factory and had to list all the service numbers of each part fitted, the aircraft before being assembled was split into wings, front, centre and rear sections to check the service numbers meant climbing from the rear to the front and getting over the famous main spar known so well by the Lanc's crews.

On one occasion she and another woman named Hilda, were taken out and fitted with parachutes over their boiler suits. Being too long for them they hung down below their backside. It was to be the maiden flight of the Lancaster. They were shown inside the aircraft and told if they felt sick to use the portable toilet at the back of the aircraft, known to the aircrew as the Elsan. If they did not make the toilet they would have to clean the mess up themselves. She sat on the navigator's table at the front of the aircraft; there were no seats at this stage. The test pilot was Captain Worrel. They flew over Cheshire and Derbyshire and the flight has been in her memories ever since. Every bomber that left the factory got her prayers for a safe return from operations, having flown in the aircraft she felt much closer to the crews. On one occasion Gracie Fields came to the factory and sang 'Bless This House' to a packed hangar.

On one occasion Barnes Wallis paid a visit and part of the workshop was sealed off. Marion's husband was personal secretary to the works manager and he told her that he had to stay on at the factory and work overtime because they had a special very hush-hush job to complete. It turned out to be the bomb doors being removed to accommodate the bouncing bomb for the Dambuster raid of May 1943. The saddest part of her job was going through columns of serial numbers recovered from the wreckage of the crashed aircraft from the land or sea to establish the names of the crew.

The dope used to seal joints on the aircraft was a varnish-type material, smelt of pear drops and was red in colour. The women would get the men to put a drop in a bottle for them to use as nail varnish. The smell was pungent and never went away. At a dance or in the pub, one could soon tell if the women were factory workers from A V Roe. The smell of pear drop was the giveaway. No amount of perfume would cover this up. An aircraft never lost its smell of dope, oil, and petrol etc.

Marion's brother-in-law came up to the factory to pick up a Lancaster and went on to fly 30 ops in it. The first time he did not fly in this particular aircraft it went missing. A war artist made a pencil drawing of a Lancaster and gave it to her, this coinciding with the birth of her baby on the 22nd December 1944. He gave it to her, so she could one day show her child what she did in the war. She still has this today.

Kathleen Judge worked in the brass shop at Gorton Locomotives, commonly known as Gorton Tank. During the war it was turned into a Ministry of Supply Depot. She worked on a lathe making petrol cocks for Wellington bombers. There were 18 women on the lathes working a shift of two weeks on days and two on nights and a 12-hour day. For this she was paid £3, plus one shilling per week bonus. It was a cold job, the only heating coming from a pipe coke stove, which during the lunch break they would crowd around and eat their sandwiches. The conditions generally were appalling with no washing facilities. Despite this morale was high they would sing for hours while working on the lathes. She was 17 and the youngest, as many of the other women were married and much older. Frequently a message would come through for one or another of them to say that their husbands were 'Missing presumed killed', but still they came to work and carried on. One woman working on a drill, was not alert enough and the drill went through the palm of her hand, her screams being terrible as the machine jammed. In 1940, a factory commented there was a 24% increase in fatal accidents and a 20% jump in non-fatal ones since 1939.

After a 12-hour shift and being very tired a 40-minute walk home as the factory was off the bus route, but she was young and fit. For the older women it was a hard slog each day. Her boss was a hard man who allowed no slacking at all. During the war Kathleen married a man who was in the Navy, and after a short honeymoon in Blackpool he went off to sea and she did not see him again for two years. In that time Kath had a baby, but it was 18 months old before he knew he was a father as her letters had not reached him.

Mrs. Bailey was trained at the Saunders Roe Training School at East Cowes and then worked at West Cowes on control panels for the Walrus seaplane as an electrician's mate. When the factory suffered a direct hit, they switched to the mainland at Basingstoke.

Mrs. Dyer worked at Godins factory in Newport. While there she damaged her face when a file caught her in the face while she was working on a lathe smoothing copper. The blow knocked her front teeth out but as usual there was no compensation. She then moved to Stewart & Lloyds making between six and 24 lb. shells. From there she moved to Lucas making gun turrets, her final stop was making uniforms at a stocking factory. To keep up morale, shows were put on by the women who would themselves dress up as Old Mother Riley and Flanagan and Allen. On one occasion a woman at Lucas had her clothes stripped off when they caught in the machine she was working on. Luckily, she survived. Many of the women who worked in these factories had steel cases turned into cigarette lighters, neatly packed with cotton wool and a flint mechanism. Mrs. Hayler made 25 lb. shells, six lb. tank shells, and mine fuses. This involved taking a three-month course. For tea in the factory they would have thick slices of bread filled with dripping, we all have heard of bread and dripping I am sure. For a halfpenny one could buy a bun or fairy cake. On one occasion she remembers a telegram coming from Winston Churchill. It was congratulating them on having made one million tank shells in a set time. The shells had been used at the victory at El Alamein. Her own husband was a prisoner of war for5 years, her greatest wish today is that she could spend some time with the old gang. As she said there were no medals or place for the munitions workers in the victory parade at the end of the war. Rita Pearce also worked in South Wales at the Royal Ordnance Factory. She had wanted to join the WRAF but did not want to wait until she was 17½, her father would not sign the consent needed for her to join under this age something that nearly broke her heart. Her sister was engaged to a Welshman, a soldier, and his Mother asked her to come to Wales to work in the factory her but only if Rita went as well. She was of course too young at the time, so they offered her a job in the admin side of the factory, but as she wanted to be with her sister the factory bosses relented and so began a 3Y2 year stint making shells. She often looked at the admin staff later with their nice hairstyles and nylons and then looked at herself in slacks, overalls and turban which were worn at a jaunty angle, until someone caught her hair in a machine one day and she was almost scalped, so each day they were checked to see if the turbans were on correctly. The numbers in the factory grew from 200 to 3,600. Ironically the gauging machines used in the factory were German; in typical German manner the machine made thirteen checks on each shell case and rejected any that were not perfect. Some cases would shine like gold, and others were dirty and oily. Working under artificial light, a new thing then, but a strain on the eyes, which of course even today it still is. They always knew a big push was on when the bosses came round and tipped a box of rejects into a machine and said 'Let them go if they are not bad', but the women, taking pride in their work would say "No, we are not sending out substandard work which may kill our boys" and would down tools, that is until someone came and explained that certain defective bullets were safe and that nothing that could be dangerous was sent through. Sometime one of the older women would fall asleep at their tables upon which another woman would put a small detonator on the women who were asleep metal chair and then give it a tap with a hammer; this would cause a slight bang and wake her up, all harmless fun in which no one was hurt. When she came home on leave her father, who was in the Home Guard, showed her his ammunition and she found it had been made in the factory she worked in.

Honore Todd registered for war work and was sent to a filling factory in North Kent, the Thames Ammunition Works. This factory was part of the Royal Arsenal Woolwich. Every Friday they got paid and each woman would put sixpence in one of the women's brown overall cap and the lucky one that was pulled out got the kitty.

Eileen Stokes, despite only being four feet high, worked on a huge capstan lathe which was worked by a foot pedal, to do this she had to stand on a block to reach the handle on the machine. The work was making radar equipment. Going to work was depressing some days after the bombing, jumping over hosepipes with water still gushing out, smouldering buildings and knowing someone had died, someone you may well know. Perhaps having gone back into the house for something they had forgotten, they had a direct hit and all that was left was a pile of rubble.

Beryl Hourahine worked in the Royal Naval propellant factory which came under the Admiralty and was based at Caerwent in South Wales. She worked in the laboratories where tests were made on the high explosives in shells and torpedoes used on ships and submarines. The factory had its own fire service manned by RN Personnel and a cottage type hospital run by naval nurses. The main line trains were shunted into the station, and sidings, where various explosives were loaded and transported from. The workers were brought in by a fleet of red and white buses each day. On one occasion she went to Cardiff to see Glen Miller and his Orchestra at the City Hall. At that time, they were not so well known in the UK as, say, Henry Hall. The factory was that important that the area was regularly patrolled by Spitfires and Hurricanes.

Mrs. Meredith was a 'feller' a machinist who sewed the seams and put the sleeves in the shirts. She made shirts and pyjamas for the Army. She had a good boss who had served in the WWI however he did not allow any missed stitches in the seams.

Mrs. Smith was a hurler and mender in the woollen textiles industry, helping to mend thousands of yards of army blankets; they were very heavy, and the workers worked in pairs. The reason that they were so heavy is that they were full of grease. From this job she went into munitions making shells and land mines.

Mrs. Coade worked in a tannery when the hides arrived they were in a raw state and had to be treated. The women wore clogs or wellies, canvas aprons and gloves and carried a wicked looking hook. She always wore wellies and remembers constantly falling on her backside. The lime water that the hides were soaked in went through the canvas gloves and gave them nasty sores on their fingers. A fleshing machine took all the flesh off the hides. Nothing was wasted; the hair off the hide was taken away to make army uniforms presumably battledress; the fat was turned into gelatine, and the trimmings made into glue.

Nancy Kroeger was a nursemaid when war broke out, she tried to join the ATS but was turned down because her father was German, he had been interned in WWI. As she suffered with hay fever, working on the land was out. So, she went to a clerical switchgear firm in Chester. She worked on brass castings and threading, and at night redeeming brass swarf out of her feet. The copper was the worst even with slosh on or industrial coolant it still came off in hot spirals which got down the overalls and burned one's chest, got stuck in one's hair, that is, the bit that showed from under the caps they wore. She also operated a circular saw cutting up six-foot lengths of brass. The first aid room was run by a man and he kept a supply of sanitary towels, known to the women as 'Bunnies' wrapped in newspaper and by the door of the first aid room.

Mrs. Banks worked in the South Metropolitan Gas Company in Greenwich and known as a plaster's mate. Some of the women worked in the retorts houses, dark places lined with furnaces where the coke was pushed in to extract the gas. They emerged at the end of the shift looking pale, despite the coal dust and exhausted. She helped to carry large sheets and bars of mild steel and used a41b sledge hammer and oxyacetylene burner.

Pat Scott worked in the ship yards in Scotland where the women were employed in all the trade, all manner of ships were built, trawlers for minesweeping, corvettes, and landing craft. Her own husband was in the Merchant Navy.

Hazel Doyle worked as a railway workshop labourer. On one occasion a wagon load of huge canisters of paint were shunted into the railway yard, the charge hand said to the women "Get that unloaded they're for the paint shop". The canisters were three ft tall and there was no crane to lift them off the wagon, which had a drop of four ft to the ground. Hazel had the idea of using rope and wood strips of two ft x 7, the method was as used in unloading a ship on a pulley basis. It worked, and the charge hand never did find out how they managed to do a job which he did not think they could do.

Eileen Downward worked in the Michelin tyre factory, her job being to check the tyre inner tubes on a continuous chain belt. They

216

checked 2,000 tubes every eight hours, a very hot and dirty job. After work they would go to the local dance halls. As a foundation cream they used lard in those days. When Eileen was old enough she joined the WAAFS.

Doris Knight was born with displaced hip and so was not fit for military service, so she worked kin a factory at Tower Bridge Road in London, a factory making scientific instruments, at the time exactly what they were making she never knew as careless talk cost lives was the motto in those days. The first doodle bug she saw fell on a factory and they had to get ropes and ladders from the local bus garage to help rescue the trapped people inside. The tea lady came around with baskets of sandwiches and you ate them while you worked; the finish time was 7pm with a 15-minute break at 4.30pm.

Ida Wadey used to fire watch at night and work in a factory laundry in the day, a job classed as a reserved occupation, she had wanted to go into the ATS but could not because of the job she was in. In the laundry they washed clothes for the Army, shirts, socks etc. all bound up in a towel, this was still the method used in the late 1950's one might hasten to add. The hours were 5am to 8pm.

Margaret Robbins also worked in a laundry at Tamworth taking in laundry from the camps at Nuneaton, Coventry, and later the American camps in the area. They were contracted by EWO (Essential Works Order). The temperature in the laundry would rise to 100° and the sorting out of labels, washing, packing, and pricing went on from Sam each day six days a week. She was 141/2 when she started there straight from school. The US troops would call trousers, pants, and their jockstraps, holdalls.

Marigold Miller was born in New Zealand but brought up in the UK, and here when the war broke out in 1939. In 1941, she married an airman, Hugh Miller, who was in the Royal New Zealand Air Force. The very day she was married her call up papers came for the ATS, but as she was married she elected to go to work in a munitions factory near where her husband was stationed. By this time, he had completed a tour of operations, and been awarded the DFC. She found after some while she was asked if she would like to become a welder and went on to make exhaust pipes for Hurricane fighters. She hardly ever saw her husband, only death, or pregnancy would get you out of the factory. The women whose husbands were officers were resented by the other women, but on the whole, she found the women wonderful, they worked under tremendous pressure in keeping the work up and the parts going out. It was lucky that it was spotted she was wearing the wrong goggles for the welding job, as it was she suffered blinding headaches and would have had permanent damage to eyes if the mistake had not been spotted. When she became pregnant and had miscarriage she was given a week's leave and then told in no mean terms to get back to her work. At the end of the war her gums were bleeding and malnutrition had started to creep in, only when she got back to New Zealand, and started to get tasty food did her health improve. Margaret Robbins said, "It is so hard to convey all the joys and the pain, but I surely would love to live it all over again."

Above left: Factory workers (Author). Above right: Godings factory at Newport (Mrs. Dyer).
Below: Saunders-Roe Training School at East Cowes, November 1941 (Author).

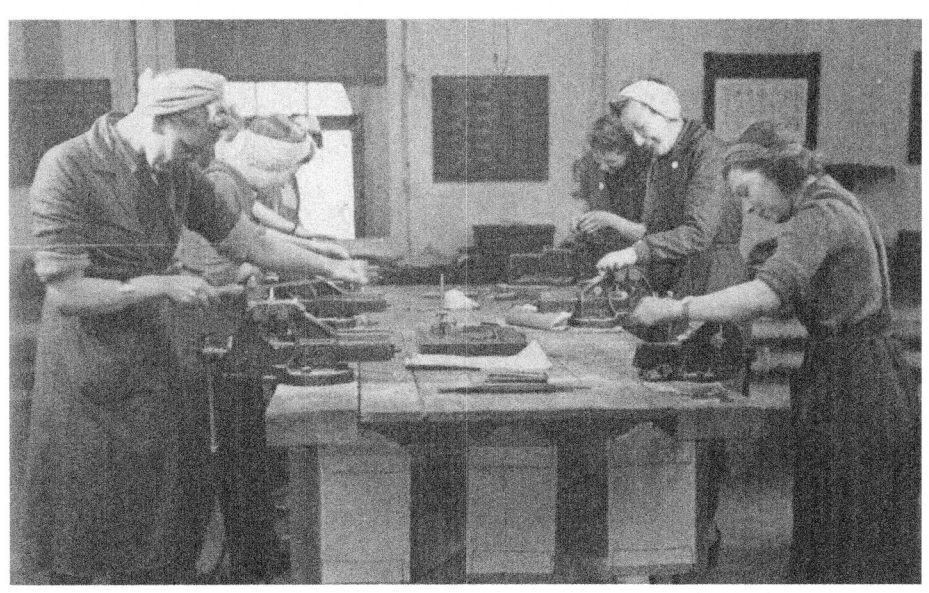

Chapter 9 FANY

The First Aid Nursing Yeomanry, or FANY as it is always affectionately known, was formed in 1907. It was the first women's volunteer organisation and went on to serve in France and Belgium in WW1, assisting in the hospitals and driving the horse drawn ambulances. When the ATS was formed in 1938, members of FANY were asked to transfer to form the Motor Driver companies and rose magnificently to meet the emergency which occurred when the Dunkirk evacuation arose.

In 1946, the Right Honourable Lord Justice Laurence wrote to the Undersecretary of State for War. He was Chairman of the Advisory Council of the Women's Transport Service (FANY) and drew to attention the work and service rendered by the members during the war, and to consider them when campaign stars and medals were awarded. The women of FANY were employed at M01(SP) under the direction of the Army Welfare Service, at the War Office. The figure given for women working with the Poles, Red Cross and under M15 and the Foreign Office was 500. In Kenya there was a FANY section who handled cyphers in code. On any day an English FANY could speak to a relative in the UK via Nairobi's Brady Street.

When An Kup, a sergeant at the time, was there, she was one of only two from the UK and the only one to travel from Mombasa and speak direct to the UK. On her return to the UK she went to the Colonial Office doing a similar job as she did in Nairobi. Dallas de Burgh Paigie went to Nairobi in 1939, her Commanding Officer was Lady Sydney Farrar. Dallas served with the signals attached to the 6th Kings African Rifles at Dar-es-Salaam with whom she spent six months. Then, volunteers were asked to go to France, this she did and sailed on the BI Ship Madura in a convoy of 38 ships, many of which were sunk by Italian submarines. When the ship arrived at Bordeaux they took on board 2,000 refugees nearly sinking the ship in the process. Finally, they sailed and arrived in Falmouth. She did not get to serve in France till later. Initially she served with four Group, American Ambulance Great Britain. She served with them through the Blitz, the Fire of London and the Chinese escape from Limehouse. In 1943, she served in Scotland and in 1944, she finally got to France with a Red Cross unit travelling through France and then into Italy. She returned in1948 when she was attached to the Royal Dorset Regiment and stayed with them until 1961. Her own mother was killed in an air raid on Blackheath. Her father was in the RN and her brother a POW.

The uniform worn by members of FANY was much alike the ATS uniform worn by the officers, khaki jacket, and skirt with a soft top peaked cap with a leather strap on top.

Pamela Blaxland in 1939 was 17 years old and found herself by chance recruited into the SOE (Special Operations Executive). She began as a secretary dealing with railway intelligence and sabotage in occupied territory. Her boss came from Austria. He decided she should undergo intensive railway training and took her on visits to railway yards and acquire sufficient knowledge in sabotage operations on trains. After training, agents were sent behind enemy lines to disrupt the railway traffic in Europe. She worked, with SOE, in Baker Street. When the war ended she went to Germany with the British Control Commission as personnel assistant to the British Military Chief of the Railways directorate. It was a case that having done one's utmost to disrupt the railways one must now do one's utmost to get them working again.

Mrs. Brinkow lived in a large house in the village of Simpson. Her husband was in the RAF, so she let out half of the house to a Captain in the Royal Signals and his wife an officer in the WRAF. The back bedroom was turned into a radio station complete with wall maps, the language used was mainly French and many high-ranking officers and people came and went, they included Dutch, Belgian and French. During the day two RAF men worked in the bedroom, and in the night the Captain and his wife. There was a lot of contact with the RAF airfield at Tempsford, it was from here that many of the SOE Agents were flown out. In the garden there were two aerials, and in the drive often stood a large black Buick car with the windows blacked out.

Mary Lindsay started work in 1937 as a telegraphist in the Post Office in Aberdeen, at the time she was 17. When the war started two years later they began to work in shifts dealing direct with Reykjavik in Iceland and Berwick in Scotland using Morse code.

Above left: Odette Hallowes (Mr. Hallowes). Above right: The Field of Remembrance, Westminster Abbey (Author). Below: The Women's Transport Service (FANY) memorial Knightsbridge, London (Author).

Above: L'Avenue Foch, Paris (Author). Below: The former SOE Headquarters, Baker Street, London, subsequently occupied by the Cheltenham & Gloucester Building Society amongst others (Author)

The method used was called 'Wheatstone' using a ticket tape with the Morse code letters as holes in the tape.

In the Spring of 1942, aged 21, along with friends Olive Hendry and Etta Mutten, she was asked to go to England on secret work. They set off and reported to the postmaster in Cheltenham, they were told they would be working with the US Service of Supply (USSoS). The signal officer was four miles from Cheltenham on the road to Gloucester, which today is Cheltenham Racecourse. Twenty-one women had been recruited for this work, but they were the only ones from over the border in Scotland. They had to send coded messages on teleprinters which arrived on the 'Wheatstone' method. They also received messages on the teleprinter which had to be put into a five-letter code, this was then sent to the code room to be deciphered. After a few months, they realised they were dealing direct with Washington. Their code or password to enter the code signals room was 'Singer of the Signals' Singer being her single name at the time. In 1944, the three women were sent to London to work with the Minster of Information. She was housed in the University of London and her job to send the news to TASS Moscow in a five-letter code. Her own brother was shot down while serving with the RAF and hidden by the resistance for 6months.

SOE during the war was a very hush hush organisation, and only mentioned in resistance circles. There were two branches, the French (F) under Colonel Maurice Buckmaster and the Republique Francaise (RF) under Colonel Devavrin whose code name was Passy. The French section was an all controlled British organisation, the RF semi-independent under the French direction but still within the framework of SOE. Having said that one found many French on the staff and working with Buckmaster and the RF had many British working with them so there were no real cut and fast rules. There was one clear thing however and that was those in the French section had all instructions given in English and in the RF in French. As well as sabotage, the role was to build up resistance groups to keep the enemy occupied. One problem for the female SOE agents was getting them into uniform for their training period, they of course did not have to stand out. The regular services could not grant them permission to wear service uniforms while undergoing agent training, but of course they were still being paid by their respective units. As the training schools were run and organised by FANY it seemed logical that they should wear their uniform, which they did for the entire period of the training, and the reason why those who died as agents are shown on more than one memorial. They all received commissions before being sent into the field as it was thought but did not work out that if they were officers they would be treated better by the enemy if captured.

The records of Noor Inyat Khan, who was in the ranks of the WAAF show that she was given a commission in the WAAF but there was nothing in her record to show she was in FANY. Her records show she was commissioned on the 16th June 1943 as an acting section officer.

The first woman sent to an enemy occupied country was Miss Mary K Herbert who was landed in a small boat off the south coast of France in late October 1942. She then made her way to Bordeaux where she stayed and operated until 1944.

Noor Inyat Khan GC (Crown Copyright).

Noor Inyat Khan was trained in Aylesbury, having already been a wireless operator in the WAAF she was of course ahead in that department of the others on her course, which included Diana Rowden, and Yvonne Commeau also from the WAAF. Of the three Yvonne was the only one to return.

Diana Rowden and Noor Cecily Lefort were dropped in France by a Lysander of 161 Squadron from Tempsford flown by Flying Officer McKern. Noor was given the code name Madeleine but after she had been there for a while she was betrayed by a Frenchman and arrested. She was taken to Paris and to L'Avenue Foch, Gestapo HQ and then Karlsruhe in Germany where she was kept with her hands and feet in chains. From there she was taken to Pforzheim 20 miles east of Karlsruhe, her hands and feet were still handcuffed, and a chain ran from the cuffs on hands to those on her feet. Her last journey was to Dachau concentration camp where on the 12th September 1944, she and three other women were executed by firing squad. On the 5th April 1949, she was awarded, posthumously, the George Cross. In July 1944, Diana Rowden, Andree Borrel, Vera Leigh and a Polish woman Sonia Olschanesky, who looked and was thought at one point to be Noor Inyat Khan, were taken to a concentration camp at Stuthof/Natzweiler and put into cells. On the night of the 6th July they were taken to the crematorium block, injected with a lethal drug, and put into the crematorium ovens for disposal. The four had been seen by Lieutenant Commander Pat O'Leary, himself, later, a holder of the George Cross and many other decorations. At the end of the war, a War Crimes tribunal was set up at Wuppertal and a number of Germans were convicted for the deaths of these four gallant women. All of them are remembered on the Runnymede memorial for airmen and airwomen who have no known grave. Their names are also recorded on the FANY Memorial in Knightsbridge, London.

Mrs. Odette Sansom was awarded the George Cross in 1946. She became a prisoner of the Gestapo in 1943 and remained one until 1945, being kept in Paris under the sentence of death and ending up in the concentration camp at Ravensbruck, an all women camp. She remained here for three months and in complete darkness. When she was in training school, MI5 men dressed as Germans would awake her in the middle of the night and interrogate her to give her and other agents some experience of what could happen to them when in the field. She was at first taken to Gibraltar and boarded a fishing boat disguised as a fisherman. The boat docked at Marseilles and she then went by train and car to Cannes, and all over France. On one occasion on a train and carrying her heavy suitcase which contained her radio transmitter a German colonel helped her put it in the rack. Her cover was betrayed by a Frenchman who was a double agent. When she arrived back in the UK and awarded the George Cross she said "What I did was nothing I feel this honour is too much for what I have done. I have never been very strong, nor very brave. I am just an ordinary sort of woman who is very pleased to be back with her children". As well as the GC she was awarded the MBE in 1945, and the Legion d'Honneur in 1950, her own mother had been awarded the Croix de Guerre and Medal Militare. Today, she is the Vice-President of FANY. In Who's Who, one of her hobbies is listed as 'Trying to Learn Patience.'

Chapter 10 Entertainment

War, entertainment, and keeping up morale go hand in hand. Many entertainers in WWII kept up the morale of the troops, in the UK and around the world. They also kept up the morale of the civilian population, in the factories with broadcasts and live concerts, and in the dance halls and cinemas. The two main organisations were the Combined Services Entertainment Unit (CSEU)and Entertainment National Service Association (ENSA) which had originally been called Actors National Service Association (ANSA). The Tommy Trinder version of ENSA was 'Every Night Something Awful' or 'Every Night Same Act'.

Christine Norden as Captain Molly Thornton, leading lady of ENSA's Column One, in 1944, when she became the first entertainer to land in Normandy after D-Day (Author).

ENSA was formed by a theatrical agent, Basil Dean, who organised a band of army entertainers together, ready to go anywhere troops were stationed. When war was declared the unit was mobilised and Drury Lane Theatre became its HQ on the 11th September 1939. The dressing rooms were turned into offices, and instead of grease paint they smelt of ink and typewriter ribbon. The finance was provided by NAAFI, assisted later by the Treasury. When the King and Queen visited Drury Lane on the 24th November 1939, they were pleased to hear that NAAFI were paying the bills. Over 14,000 auditions were made from 50,000 applications of which 500 were offered employment. Only 50 of the women employed stayed in show business after the war. The first concert was given at Pirbright Camp to the Scots Guards who were waiting to go to France. The signature tune adopted by ENSA was "Let the People Sing." Pay was £10 for a top artist, and £4 for the chorus line.

By Xmas 1939, ENSA was giving 1000 shows a week in the UK. The ENSA Film Unit played its part as well, on one occasion they went to the Shetlands to put on a film 'Roof Over Britain', the story of the early anti-aircraft defences. People came from miles, many never having seen a film show before. On the 27th May 1940, the Minister of Labour and National Services, the Rt.Hon. Ernest Bevin, wrote a letter in the Daily Telegraph outlining his interest in inaugurating a service of lunch time concerts for munitions and factory workers. The first factory concert was at Woolwich Arsenal on the 22nd July 1940, which Ernest Bevin attended. At this time Lord Haw-Haw was on one of his propaganda broadcasts saying that British Troops had to be paid to attend ENSA concerts. In July 1940, came the first RAF Gang Show. Before the war Ralph Reader, who produced the Boy Scouts Gang Show, was asked by the RAF to do a similar thing within the service, this he did using the Halton Apprentices or Halton 'Brats' as they were known.

In 1940, Gracie Fields gave the first ENSA concert, at Rheims in France to the RAF She went on to give concerts in Sicily and Italy. At first, ENSA artists wore civilian uniform but later wore an officers type uniform designed by Basil Dean and known as Basil's dress, it was mainly introduced to make sure artists came under the Geneva Convention if they were captured and made a POW. Between the 18th March 1940 and 7th May 1945 no less than 940 live broadcasts were made by ENSA. In October 1941, came 'Stars in Battledress' or to give it its official title 'The Central Pool of Artists'.

One man in show business who was in this organisation was Charlie Chester, whose Radio Soapbox programme on a Sunday was very popular. An early ATS member was actor Wilfred Hyde White's daughter Faith Brook. In June 1944, came the WAAF Gang Show. Ralph Reader selected eleven women and less than two months after D-Day they set off for France and within 30 minutes of landing were giving their first concert. This was followed by a tour of France and Belgium. The sing song parties were known as 'Ensatainments'.

Many well-known artists such as Beatrice Lilley, Bebe Daniels, Josephine Baker, Vivian Leigh, Margaret Rutherford, Anna Neagle, later Dame Anna, Dame Myra Hess, and Dame Edith Evans to name but a few. Eighty percent of the artists in the entertainment world gave their services to ENSA. The cost of upkeep was £17,000,000 and between September 1939 and March 1946, 2,656,565 performances of one kind or another were given to 300,000,000 troops and civilians. In June 1942, the Bengal Entertainment Service Association was formed to entertain the troops of Eastern Command and the 14th Army, known always as the Forgotten Army. In 1943, ENSA arrived in the Far East and within a year had taken over from BESA.

Elsie and Doris Waters were the first entertainers to arrive in India with ENSA. On the 6th November 1943, 123 ENSA artists were on their way to the Middle East, via the Straits of Gibraltar aboard the SS *Marnix van St Aldegonre* when the ship was torpedoed. They managed to get into the ship's lifeboats and eventually were picked up and arrived in Egypt, minus all their props, instruments, and equipment, which was sitting at the bottom of the Mediterranean.

Nellie Wallace was with ENSA in Hamburg in 1945. When she felt her performance was below par she would rush outside at the end and ask the troops who of course did not recognise off stage what they thought of the performance the usual reply was "Bloody awful."

Molly Thornton was the first ENSA entertainer to arrive in France after the Normandy landings. "I had only been married a couple of weeks and had just discovered I was pregnant when I was informed that Basil Dean the head of ENSA had chosen me as the leading lady of Column One. I told no one about the pregnancy because I knew they would never let me go if I did.

"I was given the rank of Captain and we set out in convoy from Hindhead in Surrey at five am. At Weymouth, where we embarked I suddenly realised what an invasion was all. about. Thousands and thousands of British and Canadian soldiers were slowly boarding ships, many of them were hurriedly handing written notes to passersby to post. The crossing that night is something I will never forget, pitch black, absolute silence, no smoking and moving at a snail's pace. We were all ordered to eat with our fingers in case the smallest sound alerted a U Boat. We landed in Normandy at a place

Above: Two views of the stage, Drury Lane (Drury Lane Archives).

Above:Nellie Wallace (right) in Venice (Mrs. Neilly). Below: Two photos of the Mack Sisters, Margaret and Frances McFarlane. Margaret is the blonde woman (Mrs. Scott)

Above: Christine Norden in 1947 and the Eighties. Below: Two ENSA posters c. 1944 (Author)

Ivy Benson and her band in the wartime years and, above right, Ivy in the 1990s (Author).

232

we called St. Aubin-sur-Mer. As I stepped ashore great cheers and whistles went up. One Canadian soldier yelled 'Brother have we been starved of something good to look at, and lady you're it.' The Canadian C in C told me I was the first entertainer of any nationality, male or female, to land in Normandy after D-Day. The next entertainer to arrive was George Formby three days later on 26th July. I gave four shows a day on a makeshift portable stage, in fields, caves, in fact anywhere. Sometimes less than three miles from the front line.

"I remember playing a town called La Deliverance with a German gun at Le Havre firing towards Bayeux, I sang that night with German shells whistling over my head. I was 19, and fanatically patriotic; like an idiot I went around shouting 'I want to see dead Germans.' A Canadian Officer looked at me and said, 'So you want to see dead Germans, do you? Right, jump in the jeep.' We drove to the Falaise Gap, it was a very hot day and we began to smell it from thirteen miles away. When we got there, German bodies and dead horses were piled six feet high. Some of the horses were still alive and a man was going around with a gun putting them out of their misery. The image of that place has never left me, nor the smell. I never again said I wanted to see dead Germans, or anyone dead. There was one very young German boy slumped over the wheel of a jeep, I counted 16 machine gun bullet holes in his back. We turned him over, he still had a letter with a picture of himself clutched in his hand, I took it and after the war sent it to his girlfriend in Germany.

"At one camp I asked for the women's room the officer in charge went rather pink and said, 'That does present a bit of a problem, old girl.' he yelled for two orderlies and we all marched past yards of barbed wire and German prisoners into an open field, the men put up three sticks covered with tarpaulin another Major yelled, 'Ten paces forward, eyes straight ahead,' and that was the women's room."

After more than 200 shows in Normandy, and when her pregnancy began to show Molly was flown home from Le Havre to the UK. She gave birth to a son Michael Glenn Cole, named after American band leader Glenn Miller, in Sunderland Infirmary Molls home town 'on the 4th March 1945. In all Molly gave over 500 shows in her time with 'Stars in Battledress.

On the 5th August 1945, she was standing in a cinema queue outside the Royal Cinema in Edgware Road when she was approached by three Hungarian film people who invited her to meet their boss, film magnet Sir Alexander Korda. He gave her a screen test, and then a seven-year contract with London Films and Metro Goldwyn Mayer. He told her that her name Molly was no good and with her cheek bones she looked Nordic, so she became Christine Norden, the name she kept to the end of her days. Her first film was 'Night Beat' in 1947in which she played a ruthless night club singer. This film put her into the list of Britain's top ten box office stars. At her peak she received 12,000 fan letters a week. In 1950, she topped the bill at the London Palladium as a singer, and in 1951 as Prince Charming in a West End production of Cinderella. In the1960's she starred on Broadway in Harold Princes' musical 'Tenderloin' in which she stopped the show on the opening night. Korda had asked her to marry him in the fifties but she declined. Her last show business appearance was in June 1988, when she played with Simon Callow in the Thames TV series 'Chance in a Million'. On 10th July 1988, she entered hospital and four days later underwent a four-hour double bypass heart operation. That very afternoon 'Night Beat' her first film was shown for the first time on British TV. Another popular series in the fifties was PC 49, and it was with Brian Reece who played PC 49 that she starred in the first 1951 TV film 'A Case for PC 49.'

In June 1984, the 40th anniversary of the D-Day landings at Normandy, the girl who had been the first ENSA entertainer to land after the invasion was not accorded an official invitation to the celebrations yet there were entertainers there who in fact were nowhere near Normandy at the time. In May 1984, when interviewed she said "D-Day, of course, is something immensely important, it liberated Europe from evil and ensured the freedom of all of us in the western world. But this was achieved at the cost of so many young lives. For them it was the end, for me, the beginning of everything. It was in Normandy that I first realised fragility and transience of life. The things I saw there brought home to me that you must make the utmost of every second you live, I have never forgot the lesson. I have consciously tried to do that ever since." On 21st September 1988, Christine died in the West Middlesex Hospital very close to Worton Hall Studios, where in 1947 she made her first film 'Night Beat'.

In 1939, Joan Hammond, later Dame Hammond, put her name down to join the WRAF but owing to a disabled arm from falling off her bike as a child, she was found unfit for military service. She had in fact nearly lost her arm in the accident. So, she turned to entertaining and her first concert was given at Chelsea Barracks. She went on to sing in most of the barracks and camps around London. In 1940, she went to Milan to give three performances at La Scala, but before leaving she gave a concert to the RAF at Pembroke Dock in a freezing hangar. In June 1940, when France fell she went to see Lady Colmondely at the Admiralty, in the hope of joining the WRNS but she was told she would be of far greater use and value as a singer than a Wren. At the end of 1940, she began to sing with ENSA, and later CMA. In London she attended lectures on fire fighting and first aid. Her ENSA concerts began with a concert in Bangor, North Wales. Her brother Tony was in the UK with the RAAF and ended the war as a Pathfinder pilot on Lancasters, having been awarded the DFC and bar. During the war she gave 455 performances of which 71 were for charity. In 1942, she served with the LCC Ambulance service at first in the East End Ambulance Station and then Clerkenwell Ambulance Station and finally Cannon Street Row, Stepney.

Subsequently Dame Joan became the head of vocal studies at the Victorian College of the Arts, in Victoria, Australia. In the days working with the ambulance service she would ride to the station on a grocer's bike with her pet dog Pippo in the basket in the front. On one occasion her photograph was taken and used in a daily paper.

Jesse Matthews set off on the 19th August 1944, for an eight-week ENSA tour of Normandy, giving three shows a day to the troops. She set off in a giant convoy of 50 trucks and jeeps, and 110 performers, including Gertrude Lawrence, Ivor Novello and Margaret Rutherford. Jesse was going against all doctor's orders having had a severe bout of flu, but it was a case of the show must go on. Within 24 hours of landing in France she had given three concerts, and gave herself a nervous breakdown trying to sing until four am. She had to be flown home on a stretcher suffering hallucinations. It was not until the 20th November that she began to perform once again, she opened at the Lewisham Hippodrome in a variety tour for Bernard Delfont. Gertrude Lawrence used to go to bed early every night in complete exhaustion.

Isabel McGraghan, who had been in the Women's Home Guard in Newport, Monmouthshire, was also in a concert party called the "Flashlight" which used to entertain troops at the 'Little Théâtre' a chapel near the docks in Newport, where so many British and American troops disembarked, including the famous American boxer Joe Louis. Emily Perry spent several years in ENSA and remembers there were happy and sad experiences. On one occasion while playing the camps around Wales she bought a tiny duckling in the market at Tenby and every evening when setting off in the coach for the concert 'Donald' as she had named him, accompanied her complete with food and water. He travelled in her knitting bag. After the show in the officers' mess he would entertain the officers; a bath was sent for and "Donald" would have a swim entertaining everyone as he did. When she played the RAF camps she remembered how sad it was when the aircrew would creep out during the show to fly on operations; she often wondered how many lived to return.

Ruth Colyer, who had also been in the Women's Home Guard and while there learned to shoot despite being pregnant was also a member of a concert party known as the Cambridge Progressive Players. Driving to the concert venues in the blackout and then driving back at the end was quite a headache. When she arrived back to where she was picked up she then had to cycle two miles back home in the dark and late at night.

Mayette Rowe performed with her sister under the name of 'Sally & Duval', her sister was seven years older than she and was not only a sister but partner, friend, and stand-in mother. In 1939, they were at the Bolton Theatre Royal when her sister became ill and died at the tender age of thirty. Mayette then became known as Miss Duval and worked for ENSA. During her time, she went to Malta and ended the war in Calais. In the concert there were six performers on a makeshift stage made from six old barrels and planks of wood. Two army blankets were used as a curtain and an old upright piano provided the music. On one occasion, when performing, a bomb came down and the pianist made a grab for the piano. Mayette then must have blacked out because the next thing she knew was when someone touched her shoe with his feet, from then on, she believed she had a 'Guardian Angel.'

Margaret Scott was born in Scotland, when the war started she was thirteen and began work by sewing pyjamas at school for the troops. She oversaw the electric sewing machines whereas the others had the manual hand machines with a foot treadle. She and her sister Frances were dancers and began to take part in concerts and dinner dances. They then began to work for Scottish Command, the officer in charge was a Captain Archie M'Culloch. His wife was Kathy Kay who later sang with the Billy Cotton band. The compere was Janet Brown a very young and lively impressionist. Margaret was still in school in the day wearing her school uniform and in the evenings in her dance dresses etc. and looking much older. She would often see a young man she had met the night before, hoping he would not recognise her in her school uniform. When she left school, she worked in the office of the Embroidery Department in a Thread Mill. However, eventually she passed an audition for ENSA and was taken to see the boss of the Scottish ENSA, Horace Collins, also a Theatrical Agent.

The two women were paid £10 for a doubt act, which wasn't bad as the average wage then was £3/10s. Of the £10, £1/10s was paid back for board and lodging, the standard rate whether you were staying in a hotel or digs. Her mother made most of her dresses being a seamstress by profession. Here they spent the next five years along with a comedian, pianist, and a young man who played musical instruments. They were known as the Mac Sisters. Frances did the tapping and Margaret sang and danced. They took lessons from a Buddy Bradley who is mentioned in a book on his life written by Lionel Blair. The transport they used was known as the 'Black Maria.' The three men sat in the front and they in the back looking out of small windows one-foot square. Later they went into a large show with twelve in the cast, but when the show went to North Africa they were left behind as they were, at sixteen, too young to go abroad although they did on one occasion fly to the Shetland Isles in a Harrow aircraft, quite a thrill for a 16-year-old.

On another occasion they played on an RAF station in Lincoln and met a few South African airmen who said they liked the show so much they would see them again the next night. But when the next night came, they did not turn up; like many air crew they had been posted missing.

Between ENSA shows they performed on the Theatre Circuit playing in the Theatre Royal, Glasgow, the Dundee Palace, and Tivoli Gardens. What a joy it was to have a full orchestra and stage with lighting. On one occasion she wrote a letter to Lew Grade for a part in 'Babes in The Wood' but somehow never got around to posting it. While in London she visited the Drury Lane ENSA HQ.

In August 1945, Margaret married a Fleet Air Arm pilot and while playing a concert in Gourock for the Navy the spotlight went along trying to pick up her new husband Taylor, at the time she was singing 'It Had to Be You.' When he left the Navy her showbiz career ended, but for her and her sister it was the most enjoyable period in their lives. Sadly, Frances was fated to die after falling down a flight of steps. Margaret was born on the same day as the Queen and, out of 500 people, three including Margaret were chosen by the BBC to appear on a show that day. They were given a 1920's style breakfast and a birthday cake.

Ivy Benson was born in 1913 in Leeds, Yorkshire, her father played the trumpet, cello, and tenor sax. She began playing the piano when she was three years old. When she joined her first band she was by now playing the clarinet and had bought an alto saxophone for 2/6d a week. In 1939, she formed a nine-piece band and performed in a revue with Hylda Baker. Most of her woman musicians came from Scotland or the North of England, particularly the brass players. She then got a 22-week stint at the London Palladium with Max Miller and became resident band with Henry Hall and Billy Cotton. Her signature tune became 'Lady Be Good' and all she wished for was to have a lovely band. She then got a call from ENSA to say the troops were waiting to see the band and so began a tour of the Middle East, Europe, including Cyprus and Egypt, in fact wherever there were troops she went with the band. It was on these tours that she lost most of her girls, particularly at the end of the war, many marrying US Servicemen and going back to the USA to live. Ivy kept many memories of having to push the land bus on an icy road to Tripoli, living in tents in Egypt and playing on an isolated gunsight. On one occasion they were required to play a fanfare. When they did all the bats hidden in the roof of the building began to fly through the women's hair.

In Austria at the end of the war she smuggled two Italian children out, they had been part of an Italian circus act and whereas their parents had managed to get back to Italy they had not. They were hidden in the army trucks by the wardrobe mistress, Kitty, and the driver. When the truck reached a checkpoint, Ivy made the girls give up all the booze they had collected at the NAAFI stores and after a little get-together with the frontier guards they were waved through. A whip round was made for lira and the children were put on a train for Italy.

It was 1945 when Ivy's band got the name 'Ivy Benson and Her Girl Band'. They were booked into the Ritz in Manchester and were paid six guineas a week each. Because of the Discrimination Act the name of the band had to be changed later to 'Ivy Benson Showband'. One thing she always remembers is when the band was booked being asked what they look like and not how do they sound. Her band went on through the 1940's, 50's, and 60's and to the end of 1970 before Ivy decided to call it a day. Over 300 women made up the band over that period including trombone player Sheila Tracey who later presented 'Big Band Special' for the BBC each week. When they were performing with Jack Hylton with the BBC in Bristol they had to do their share of fire watching at the studios.

At the end of the war when they entered Berlin they found it in ruins and were told not to drink anything but bottled water as there were 30,000 bodies buried in the sewers. The troops broke the doors down to see the band there. No smutty jokes, just good music, singing and pretty dresses. After the war in the 1960's they gave a performance for 600 ardent Commandos and there was not a dry eye in the house. She occupied her time entertaining the elderly at homes around her house, apply called 'Harmony'. Then she only played the piano having sold her clarinet and sax; she could not bear to have them around her unless she could play them and not just to look at them. Sadly, in May 1993, at the age of 79 Ivy died. She was at the time organizing a charity sale for the old and needy in Clacton.

Chapter 11 Women's Land Army / Timber Corps

On 1ˢᵗ June 1939, the Women's Land Army was formed and by 1ˢᵗ September had 900 recruits ready to take to harvesting the fields. By December 1939 this had risen to 4,544 and by September 1940, to 9,000. The largest group was 262 in Kent. In July 1941 the Queen, became the WLA Patron. It came under the Ministry of Agriculture and Fisheries Minister Robert Hudson. The Honorary Director of the WLA was Lady Denman who was also in charge of the Federation of Women's Institute. She gave her home at Balcombe Place over to the national cause.

The house became a quartermaster's store for the WLA, having a room stacked with the familiar green jerseys. The women were advised to wash them like stockings but instead of hanging them up to dry, to spread them out on a piece of newspaper and dry them slowly, this way they kept their shape and size. The jersey was worn with brown breeches, or jodhpurs. The boots were brown and laced up at the front, if the work involved wet conditions there were wellington boots. The shirts were airtex and pale in colour with long sleeves, the short sleeve shirts were cellular. Thick long woollen stockings were worn over the breeches. Lastly a short fawn overcoat rather like a British Warm, and slouch type hat with a metal cap badge, if the hat got wet you were well advised to stuff it with newspaper to keep its shape and size.

Each county in the UK had its own organising committee and the women had to be mobile and go wherever they were sent. The jobs they did were varied; ploughing, milking, even getting rid of rats on the farm, all came under their range of jobs. A quarter of the WLA women overall were employed in milking. Many of the women had never even seen a cow, let alone milked one. Most had lived in cities and towns and knew little about the countryside, but they soon found out. The training came with free board and lodging and a small allowance. After training a minimum wage of 38 shillings for a 48-hour week or 18 shillings with board and lodging taken out.

A special WLA Auxiliary Force was recruited to undertake temporary seasonal work for a minimum of four weeks at a time, with was known as the Emergency Land Corps.

In 1938, Phyllis Batty received through the post a booklet which outlined the women's services in the event of war. Having spent a great deal of her youth on a farm in Cambridgeshire she plumped for the Women's Land Army. At the time, she was working in a solicitor's office in London. She began voluntary work on a farm being taught how to milk cows. On 21 September 1939, she went on a course to Midland Agricultural College at Loughborough. Here she found girls from all walks of life and that the arduous work soon sorted out the wood from the chaff. At college they learned to look after pigs, cattle, and horses. At 6am each morning they would have to go into an uninviting pig sty and muck out the pigs; the smell was appalling. When the pigs were wormed they had the unenviable job of picking up the discarded worms by hand and putting them outside the pens.

In July 1940, Phyllis was called up for full time service and was sent to a farm which was run by a man whose son had been called up for military service. He disliked women, and especially WLA women. Consequently, he gave them all the worse jobs and took out of their pay fourteen shillings for their board and lodging. Their only means of washing at night was by boiling a kettle of hot water. On one occasion when working in a field in the boiling hot sun, the women suffered sunstroke. In the winter he made the women hack grubs out of a tree with an axe. In the miserable conditions they got colds and flu.

On no less than three occasions the were strafed by German aircraft while working in the fields. On one of these occasions the German fighters then machine-gunned a party of school children at Odiham. Eventually her friend asked for a transfer owing to the behaviour of the farmer and Phyllis went with her to a nursery farm at New Milton. It was here that she spent the rest of the war.

Another duty which seems to be common wherever one worked was fire watching, which was done at night after an exhausting day on the farm. But on this farm, she did enjoy herself and learned so much from the owners, both being men who had been gassed in WWI. She learned all there was to know about flowers and crops and even how to make wreaths and bouquets.

The women of the WLA always seemed to be out on a limb. Phyllis remembers they were not allowed to use the NAAFI canteen unlike the servicewomen and they received no issue of underwear, just the basic uniform. Their pay, 38 shillings a week, did not alter for the whole of the war. When Phyllis and the other girls left the WLA there was no gratuity such as the servicewomen got, somehow it was not thought that their efforts on the land and in helping to keep the country fed warranted any reward. Yet on one occasion, when a farmer was taken to hospital, the farm of 150 acres and a herd of 20 cows and 35 ewes about to lamb was left to two WLA girls to run on their own. For five seven-day weeks they worked and did not lose one lamb. The age for joining the WLA was 17, younger than the age for compulsory national service. They were known as 'Poor Cinderellas' because of their uniforms.

Joyce Jarman still had a year to go to finish a three-year hairdressing apprenticeship in London. However, she felt perhaps she should be doing a little more towards the war effort and at 16 she was too young for the services. And so, when she reached the age of 17 she went for an interview, was accepted, and sent to a farm for training. Here she learned sheep dipping, a quite heavy and dirty job, and helping the foreman to put number tags on the ears of the young bull calves. When delivering milk on a horse and cart, the horse knew the way, which helped as she did not; he even knew when to turn and come back.

When her training was over Joyce was sent to a farm outside Chesham in Bucks. Here she lodged in a cottage with the farmer, his wife and four sons. There was no bathroom and the toilet was across the yard. To wash meant a jug of icy water. Before breakfast she would milk four cows. In summer they had to work until 11 pm as then it was Double British Summer Time.

When the hay was opened the women had to watch for mice and tie up the bottoms of their trousers to make sure they did not go up their legs. Her training in the WLA gave her confidence and broadened her mind.

Dorothy Watson spent three years in the WLA. She also worked with cattle and on one occasion when she saw an Army truck coming over the hill she could not resist letting the cattle fill up the road, so they could not get back. One can imagine the comments that came from the soldiers. On another occasion, on seeing a bike by the side of the road, she hid it as a joke. It turned out to belong to the local policeman and he viewed this not as a joke but as the 'crime of the century'. Dorothy remained friendly with the farmers she was with during her time in the WLA and spent holidays with them in Somerset. Other WLA girls married farmers in Somerset.

Molly Butcher enrolled prewar in the WLA and spent a month training at the Hertfordshire Institute of Agriculture, near St Albans. She was at the time also working in London as a ledger clerk in Wimpole Street. Her WLA number was 450. At the institute there were refugees from Austria and Holland. Here she learned how to handle horses and drive a tractor. When her training finished she was sent to a farm in Norfolk. The bailiff of the estate sent her out with a double barrelled shotgun to scare off the pigeons, as far as Molly was concerned the pigeons were quite safe. When her father died she came back to Ealing and worked in the gardens of a private mental home, but she did not like this, so she joined the WRAF and served with Bomber Command in the Norfolk area.

Mrs. Winterbottom tried to join one of the Services, but her father refused to let her go and so the WLA was her last hope. When she and a friend went to volunteer they were told they had to get a doctor's certificate and two references. She was 23 at the time and engaged to a soldier, so she quickly sent off her papers to join the WLA before her father could change his mind. In February 1941, she was told to report to Carmarthen in South Wales. Then came another letter cancelling the previous letter, this was followed by a further letter on 2nd March telling her to report to Bletchley in Bucks.

She was issued with a uniform but no overcoat, to get this you had to have been in six months. At the hostel they slept in bunk beds with a two-inch-thick mattress of straw, two pillows, one pillow case, one sheet, two army grey blankets and a quilt. The breakfast consisted of porridge, which was thick and dark in colour, and was so revolting she could not touch it. Even the resident dog would not eat it.

After the first day working behind a thresher and using a pitch fork, her back felt like it was nearly broken, and her hands were covered in blisters. Despite not being able to drive she volunteered for tractor work. The tractors mainly being used were Fordsons and Caterpillars, but they were relieved to learn that they were not expected to drive these but the new Ford Ferguson from the USA.

A few days later she was taken out for the first time on the open road to learn to drive. She took part in a film compiled by the Ministry of Information called 'Reseeding'. As she drove her tractor downhill it slipped a gear but somehow managed to turn it at the bottom which the film director liked and asked her to do again, which she refused.

Iris Walters worked on a farm in Surrey which is her home today. The WLA representative was Lady Dorothy MacMillan, wife of Harold MacMillan later to be Prime Minister. She came to see them in all weathers walking across the fields in her wellington boots. She was always there when a shoulder was needed to cry on. Iris remembers working in the fields with German and Italian POWs, and only being able to communicate by sign language. The farm she was on belonged to the Hayward brothers of 'Military Pickle' fame.

Kathleen Coombs left her job in the record department of a Brighton store to join the WLA. She was unable to work with cattle, as she was prone to throat infections possibly brought on by animals, she was sent to a horticulture nursery looking after no fewer than twelve greenhouses. In the summer they were full of tomatoes and in the winter lettuces. All the produce was sent to Covent Garden Market, London. Out of her pay she paid 27/6d for her board and lodging. Although food was on ration the WLA women got two pounds of cheese instead of the two ounces allowed to others. After the war had ended the same greenhouses had carnations instead of tomatoes. Kathleen liked to say that her romance 'started in the greenhouse' when her naval husband came to work at the nursery and they later married.

Dorothy Barton became a milk maid in the WLA. After four weeks training she was awarded a certificate as a competent milker. The farmer took one look at her when she turned up on his door and said she was not tough enough for the job; at the time she was eight stone. She stayed the night and before she left the next day he sent her out to bring in the cows for milking. She squelched through the mud to the cows, but they did not know her and ran off. As she turned to go after them she fell head first in the liquid mud and cow manure. She returned to the farm without one boot and without the cows. She smelt from head to toe so much that the farmer's wife refused to allow her into the house. She had to go to the chicken shed to change. After eighteen months and work at another farm she decided to move on and went to a farm in Lenham, Kent living in a hostel. She reported to the farmer's field and came upon a large shire horse, the largest horse she had seen in her life. She was shown how to lead him around the field and to walk him between the cabbages pulling a hoe to break up the soil and weeds. She was 5' 6" tall and the horse's nose was level with the top of her head whilst his feet were the size of a dinner plate. The horse soon realised she could not control him and suddenly broke off in a fast trot with Dorothy hanging on to the bridle. When the horse suddenly stopped, he had walked over the cabbages instead of between them. Having been taught to turn the horse, which was aptly named Tinker, she decided she could do it on her own and was so engaged in watching the horse when suddenly it stepped sideways and put one of his hoofs on her foot which fortunately sank into the soft ground. Even so her leather lace-up boot had to be cut off and her foot strapped up. She ended her WLA service looking after sick horses as the farm became mechanised and the horses became redundant.

Mrs. Wheeler worked in pest control, killing off rats, rabbits, and moles. For her efforts she got a policeman's badge for pest control and received an extra five shillings every fortnight.

Joyce Koski joined the WLA in 1942. In March 1944, while planting potatoes by hand she was given a telegram which just said, 'Come at once today'. There had been a bombing raid in her home town of London. She arrived home to find a 500 lb. bomb had dropped in her street destroying all the houses and killing 22 people including her parents. In 1945, she went to work in a convalescent home for Land Army women in Torquay. It was here that she met her future husband, who was in another home nearby for wounded Polish soldiers.

Dora Myers joined the WLA in 1944 at the age of 18. She was only 5'1" and her uniform had to be made for her. The men on the farm in Somerset where she was sent resented the women workers and one put a mouse down the front of her jumper. Her friend chased the man into a field with a pitch fork. She went from threshing in the fields to milking. On one occasion one of the cows butted her and knocked her over, at the time she was carrying the cow's calf which the cow seemed to resent. The cow never forgot her and would take any opportunity to try to knock her down. They say the elephant never forgets; in the case of Dora it was a cow. Another time she was knocked over by a charging sow, at the time she had on her best uniform and she fell face first in the mud. The sow was not content to just knock her down but kept on barging at her head and back which by now were ripped and bleeding. It took her three weeks to get over it.

At the end of the war and victory in Europe she drank Somerset cider to celebrate and woke the next day with a terrible headache and nausea. Her days in the WLA came to an end when she contracted ringworm, for which she had to go to Bath every week for treatment. This meant she could not work with animals, and if she stayed on she could only work on the land, so she took her release and went back to city life.

Elizabeth Leak was asked by a farmer to get a mangle off the farm while he took the cows into the cow shed. Off she went and found the mangle, but it was very heavy, and she could not get it across the yard and into the farmhouse where the farmer was. When she asked him for help he came to look and laughed when he saw the washing mangle, what he wanted was mangelwurzel, a cow food which was a substitute for proper food during the war.

The WLA girls worked in terrible conditions, particularly in the winter. The snow ploughs would have to clear the yard before they could get out and then they would struggle across fields to pull up turnips and feed the sheep. The icy winds and snow drifts in Yorkshire were almost unbearable. Joan Thompson did not fancy the services and liked to work outdoors. The WLA had to be volunteered for, there was no conscription. To get her uniform she had to give up most of her ration coupons. It arrived in a kitbag. After eighteen months she got 'Industrial Ten Clothing Coupons' given to those who needed heavy duty clothing. If one was lucky one got issued a second pair of gabardine breeches. The warden of the hostel took their ration books and gave back two ounces of sugar every week to use on porridge or another cereal at breakfast time.

Threshing (top) and tractor driving were just two of the many tasks which woemen undertook on the farms of Britain (Author)

Above: Gwynneth Patterson (on far right) with fellow members of the Women's Timber Corps (G. Patterson). Below: Time for a brew. Members of the Women's Timber Corps enjoy a hard-earned cup of tea (Author).

Above: Loading a trailer with cut logs. Below: Tree-felling by hand (Author).

Above left: Queen Elizabeth inspects the Land Army women (Author).

Above right: Land Army women Dorothy and Valerie Watson at Manor Farm, Haslebury Plucknett, Somerset (Mrs. Watson

They worked from 8am to 12pm, 1pm to 5pm Monday to Friday, and eight to twelve on Saturday.

On 3rd July 1940, Her Royal Highness the Duchess of Gloucester watched a parade of WLA led by the Home Guard band to the Guildhall in Cambridge. It was a recruiting drive and over 300 women took part. Molly Rogers remembers 17 high-ranking German officers, sent from Featherstone Camp near Haltwhistle, for work in the fields.

When the girls treated cattle for ringworm, they also caught it and had to go for ultraviolet treatment, this at first had beneficial effects but then it came back about a month later, twice as bad. The ringworm did eventually disappear, but it did take a long time. They would go to the local dances wearing long sleeved blouses to cover up the rings. When Molly ended her WLA service she returned to her former job in a solicitors' office.

In 1944, there were 80,000 WLA women working on the land. One former WLA woman said 'The war was the best thing that ever happened to me. The war made us stand on our own two feet.'

The Women's Timber Corps (WTC) was a special section of the WLA. The lighter side of their role was forestry commission work such as planting and the cultivation of young trees. The heavy side was cutting down and transporting trees for wood. The WTC wore the same uniform as the WLA, except for the headdress, which for the WTC was a green beret instead of the WLA's bush hat. They also had their own cap badge, a fir tree, surrounded by the royal crown with the words 'Timber Corps Women's Land Army' around it. They were sent to camps established by the Home Timber Production Department of the Ministry of Supply. There were 4,000 in England and Wales, and in Scotland 2,000.

The work of felling trees was very heavy and the sawing up of the felled trees one that called for extreme care, precision, and concentration. The trees were then selected for telegraph poles, pit props and poles for ladders. The pit props were 9 feet long and there were no cranes or any mechanical devices to help load them on to the lorries which were then driven away by a WTC girl. A lorry load could easily weigh six tons when loaded. The trees that were felled could reach anything up to 150 feet high.

Jessie MacLean was all set to join the WRNS when suddenly she got hooked on the WTC. At first, she had not even heard of them, as many today have not. Her training was done in Scotland, PT classes were laid on to make the women fit enough to cope with the job of felling trees.

One of her friends tripped over a log stump or 'stool' as it was known; as she did she put her arm out in front of her to help her fall. As she did a man was going about the action of cutting down a tree with an axe and was unable to stop the swing of the axe and her hand was nearly severed. The surgeon who treated her performed a miracle and managed to save her hand. On another occasion three women were killed in an accident with a lorry.

Jessie was often asked what regiment she was serving in. When she replied, 'The Timber Corps' she was usually then asked, 'What are you making, watches?' No one seemed to believe they felled trees. The axes they used for the tree-felling weighed three pounds, but some were even heavier, and the mallets weighed the same.

There were, as there are everywhere, instances of bravery in the WLA. Mary Baker was a dairy girl. On one occasion a bull attacked a cowman and Mary ran to his assistance with a pitchfork, as she did the bull turned on her, tossing her over a hedge. She was taken to hospital with bruises and broken ribs. For her bravery she was awarded a 'Certificate for Courage'. There were other stories of land women who dragged airmen from crashed aircraft, and dousing hayricks set on fire by incendiary bombs, and bringing out blazing oil drums from burning barns. A Timber Corps woman who helped to get a blazing railway truck under control. At the time she was barelegged with her hair still prettily decorated with wild flowers picked during her lunch break.

Chapter 12 The Civilian Services

The largest voluntary service in Great Britain was the Women's Volunteer Service, or WVS as it was known and now the Women's Royal Volunteer Service. It had during the war over one million members giving important services in many fields in the war effort. Though run on a voluntary basis, the WVS was officially recognised by the Ministry of Home Security.

On 16th June 1938 Sir Samuel Hoare, then Home Secretary, launched the WVS and asked the Dowager Marchioness of Reading to be its first Chairman. At first it was known as the Women's Volunteer Service for Air Raid Precautions. At the outbreak of war, it had 336,000 members which increased to one million in 1942. During the Munich Crisis of 1938 the WVS began to prepare for war. In a letter dated 24th June 1938, it was proposed to appoint regional representatives in each of the thirteen regions around the country. Their main role at this time was to help householders prepare themselves for air attacks. At the outbreak of war their title was changed to 'WVS for Civil Defence'.

Peggy Norden joined the Personnel Service League undertaking part-time work with Lady Reading. In 1939, she joined the WVS serving meals to Civil Defence workers in North Kensington and she also became Secretary of the WVS Centre there. In 1940, she became Joint Head of the Services Welfare Depot and in charge of buying for the 700 WVS service canteens. When she retired in 1965 she was in charge of 1,737 canteens, clubs and hostels.

Much of the WVS funds were made from selling tea at one penny per cup and sandwiches at 3d. Only the bookkeeper and two secretaries were paid in the whole of the WVS organisation, everyone else volunteered and was unpaid. The WVS provided wedding dresses for the ATS women when they got married. They started the magazine adoption scheme and despatched 200 bundles per week to units and ships all over the world. In 1940, at the time of Dunkirk, a canteen was set up on the East Coast of Kent. The people in the area were very generous and even gave the washing off their washing lines to help clothe the returning soldiers. The trains were coming through at the rate of six or more per hour. 180 helpers worked in shifts serving tea and food to starving troops.

The Queen's Messenger companies were started with six mobile canteens in 18 convoys. They were ready to go within minutes notice and went to many bombed areas and were capable of serving 30,000 people with a hot meal if necessary.

The raid on Coventry on 14th November 1940, is a prime example of how well the WVS coped with adversity. The centre of the city lay in ruins and had been brought to a complete standstill. The public services were put out of action after an attack which lasted eleven hours. Only the outer shell of the WVS offices survived. At 3am, the Regional Administration was asked by the Regional Commissioner to arrange for as many mobile canteens as possible to go to the city. At 8am, they began to arrive and up to 15,000 snack type meals per day were provided for over a week. The Regional Organiser mentioned to Lady Reading that she had been cutting bread and putting margarine on sandwiches from 4.30pm to 9.30am with only a 30-minute break while she got supplies. A fireman said, "I guess the WVS have won the Battle of Coventry, but if there had been any water the AFS would have done so". The women slept where and when they could, working 16-hour shifts.

The first two companies of the Queen's Messenger were inspected by Her Majesty, being her own personal gift. Later there were eighteen of these companies all over the country. Each consisted of twelve vehicles, one water tank lorry, two food storage lorries, two equipment lorries, three mobile canteens, and four motor cycles. They were all painted blue and silver and had a pennant on the front. Each convoy was staffed entirely by WVS women, 50 in each convoy. They wore on their uniform the Queen's Messenger badge.

Mrs. Elizabeth Sworder was sent from Brigg in Lincoln to Coventry, and after the raid she worked on the Glandford Brigg WVS Mobile Canteen. They had two private cars and a large furniture van which was stocked with everything from tin hats to a 700-gallon water tank. When they arrived, the raid was still taking place. On one occasion a piece of shrapnel hit the tin hat she was wearing. For her efforts she was awarded a commendation.

Mrs. Pearl Marguerite Hyde was the Chief Officer of the WVS in Coventry and she shepherded people to the shelters and then continued to visit them throughout the night. When the raid was over she helped to feed the homeless who for many had only what they stood up in. Despite many unexploded bombs, she went out and organised refreshments for the homeless and rescue workers. For her efforts and bravery, she was awarded the George Medal.

Evelina Miller served in the WVS from February 1940 to August 1959, shortly before her death. She began in Glasgow helping to find accommodation for men waiting to join their ships. Also helping to comfort women whose husbands had been lost at sea.

One of the very first Germans shot down in WWII was captured by a WVS lady, Mrs. Cardwell, the WVS representative for Holderness in Yorkshire. From her kitchen window she saw the German plane shot down on 8th July 1940. It was shot down by a Sgt. Allinson whose combat report gave the time at 11.30am, and SE of Scarborough. He also mentioned one of the crew being taken prisoner. Mrs. Cardwell tried to phone the police but failed as the phone was out of order, things don't change. So, she sent a boy to take a message to summon help while she, armed with a pitchfork, ordered the German to surrender. He put up his hands and surrendered promptly. In his fall he had twisted his ankle but was able to hobble to her home where she made him a cup of tea. By this time the Local Defence Volunteers, later the Home Guard, turned up and tried to pull rank saying he was their prisoner. The German gave her one of his uniform buttons as a souvenir.

Mrs. Grace Rattenbury was awarded the George Medal in 1941, for her actions on 7th September 1940, when she volunteered to assist in the evacuation of people from the docklands area of Rotherhithe. It was after the first heavy raid on London. She began at 5.30pm, a shuttle service, and continued until 1am, by when every man, woman and child had been evacuated from the area. She was thrown down by blast and her van blistered by flares. At the end of the night her van was full of steel helmets, blood-soaked badges and all manner of things that were signs of a very bad night.

Ena Bowen was in the WVS (India) and based in Rawalpindi from 1940 to 1948. At the start she was working with the Camel Corps Regiment which, to say the least, was different. From there she went to setting up Rawalpindi Railway Station which was known as the 'Royes Canteen' as it had been opened by General Royes. She also took over, as superintendent, the Rawalpindi Soldier, Sailors, Airmen's, and WAC Club for Corporals and below, which for short was known as the SAW Club. This provided wholesome meals for the troops and every Thursday a dance was held, as well as ENSA concerts. For her efforts Ena was awarded the Kaiser I Hind decoration.

On 9th December 1940, Dorothy Cook was driving a canteen vehicle around the Bristol Docks and in the blackout when her vehicle fell over the quayside. Dorothy was trapped and drowned.

Emily Holthouse was killed by a shell fired from a long-range gun in France and across the Channel, her mother was killed at the same time.

Just after Dunkirk Erica Whittaker received a phone call telling her to report to the town wharf in Newport, South Wales. She disobeyed orders by not telling anyone where she was going. When she arrived the door to the wharf was closed so she knocked and said 'WVS here', the door opened and to her surprise she found the area covered by weary young soldiers, many were lying down covered in blankets. They had escaped from France and were exhausted. The WVS went in amongst them to see how they could help and she stayed until 11pm. As she left a soldier asked her to post a letter for him, which of course she did in the main post office in the High Street. At the time her own husband was serving in the Middle East with the RAF. In all there were some 148 mobile canteens and one 'Dock Rat' as the embarking and disembarking soldiers were known. A note was left on the driver's seat of the mobile canteen saying, "To the women who feed the inner man, thanks a lot".

Noel Streatfield who wrote 80 children's books including 'Ballet Shoes', served in the WVS on a mobile canteen. In May 1941, her own flat in Deptford was destroyed by bombing and she continued to live in a disused coal cellar.

During the flying bomb period the Regional Mobile Canteens in the South East served 43,770 snack meals. On one occasion, when asked to send a contingent to march in a parade, they were described as the 'Marching Mothers'.

By May 1941, some 25 WVS offices had been destroyed by enemy bombing of which nine were in the London area, and 102 women had become war casualties. on the happier side, five George

Medals and two British Empire Medals had been awarded to them, and, by 1943, this had risen to 78 BEMs.

On 14th August 1940, a Whitley Bomber P4965 of 10 Sqn, coming back from a raid to Turin, ditched in the sea off Dymchurch Redoubt in Kent. The pilot, Plt Off Parsons and the second pilot Sgt. Champion, were both lost with the aircraft. Mrs. Pegg Prince went out in a canoe and picked up the wireless operator, Sgt. Marshall, who was clinging to a buoy. She got him back into the canoe and paddled back to shore, thus saving his life. For her efforts she was awarded the BEM on 20th August 1940.

The choice of uniform for the WVS was interesting. Several leading London dressmakers were invited to produce designs for a tweed jacket and skirt, a top coat, jumper, hat, and frock. The choice of colour was important. Black had been used by the St John's Ambulance, brown by the Land Army, Khaki by the ATS and light blue by the WAAF. The only colour left was green, but as it was a superstitious colour, grey was woven into the green. It was also a serviceable colour and would not show the dust. The beetroot red colour used in the jumper and the hat trimmings avoided the uniform looking too drab. The top coat was so designed that one could sleep in it if required and yet it would still look presentable. The first time the Prime Minister Winston Churchill reviewed a march past by the WVS he said to Lady Reading "Look at your girls, each hat is worn at a different angle". She replied, "Here is a case of individuality of operation but uniformity of pattern". It meant the WVS women could do the same job but in different ways. The uniforms had to be bought by the women themselves using valuable clothing coupons to do so.

On 3rd June1943 Admiral Sir Edward Evans said that the WVS were the army Hitler forgot. His pet name for them was 'Women's Victory Services'. The WVS also undertook the organisation and administration of the volunteer pool scheme. By 1943, there were 570 car pools and nearly 18,000 cars, th organisation of this massive transport empire was entirely due to the WVS. Some facts are worthy of mention: 1,000,000 pies and snacks were supplied to agricultural workers in some 2,750 villages in WWII. 38,000 pairs of socks were darned for the Army. 65,000 WVS women were working in canteens and British restaurants. Over 350 depots were making camouflage nets for the Army, at a rate of 3,500 nets per week. In October 1943, the WVS was extended to the combat zones. They served in North Africa and Italy, landing in Algiers and Naples. WVS Clubs were later setup in Paris and Brussels.

At home the WVS assisted with evacuation of mothers and children from areas likely to be bombed. In 1945, the words 'for civil defence' were deleted from their title. The Home Office decided that they should continue tending the sick and other such roles.

In 1966 Her Majesty the Queen bestowed her approval on the organisation, which accordingly became the Women's Royal Volunteer Service. Her Majesty, Queen Elizabeth the Queen Mother, said at the time of the dedication of the WVS Roll of Honour in 1951, "When future generations look back on this most terrible war they will recognise as one of the chief features the degree to which women were actually engaged in it. In the community at any rate, the war could not have been won without their help". The dedication at Westminster Abbey was attended by some 2,000 people. Lady Reading always said, "Never let your feet get off the ground".

The YMCA or Young Women's Christian Organisation gave invaluable service to the workers on airfields. During this time, they lived in Nissen Huts which were very damp and cold. Gwen Shoesmith, whose father ran such a canteen, on one occasion put tea in the cocoa giving it an unusual flavour, but the Irish workers who were building the airfields liked it and came back for more.

It was Lady Blane who in 1939 took over the running of the YWCA mobile tea car canteens, all manned by women and in the London area. Their centre was at King George Hall and their work went on night and day and throughout the bombing in London. The national Women's Auxiliary of the YMCA was responsible for women's work and help in the YMCA canteens and hostels for HM Forces throughout the country. They were established in camps, dockyards, towns, and railway stations. A round of toast and a mug of steaming hot tea, not cups, cost one penny. There were 250 mobile tea vans in all. Before France fell in May 1940, 37 centres and 44 mobile canteens were serving with the BEF in many parts of France. The number of provisions provided is interesting, 1,200 cakes on trays, eight tea urns, three crates of milk per day, cigarettes, chocolate writing paper and envelopes and many other things. A cup of tea and a cake cost three pence.

Lt Col Edith Kirk was in the Salvation Army during the war, as was her husband. In March 1940, they set off on a ship from Folkestone bound for France, they arrived six hours later and were suffering from sea sickness due to gales in the channel. They stayed the night in Paris and then set off for Brittany where they set up a mobile canteen known as the 'Red Shield' for the troops. In May1940, they were sent for by the officer commanding and were told to evacuate as the German advance was only five miles away. They set off for St Nazaire with the roads choked with refugees and several times were stopped by attacks from German aircraft. At St Nazaire they boarded a ship and after three days landed in Devonport. The journey had been packed with incidents, one being the SS *Lancastria*, a troop ship sunk with many casualties.

Their next stop was an RAF airfield in Yorkshire and then to Farnborough serving with a Tank Regiment. Here they opened 18 mobile canteens and a static club. Her husband ended up as Director of the Red Shield Clubs in the Ukraine.

Lorraine Bladon also went to France with the Salvation Army. Lorraine came from Bridgend in South Wales and went to France after volunteers were asked for. They also spent three days getting out of France, via Brest.

In 1938, the Salvation Army were approached by the council in Brixton asking if they would distribute gas masks in the area. They had to be properly fitted on each person. The test was when a piece of paper was put in front of the nozzle of the gas mask and the person asked to breath. If the paper adhered to the nozzle it fitted correctly, if not another was tried until it did. There were in fact three sizes of gas mask. Children were fitted with the 'Mickey Mouse' type gasmasks and babies in large incubator type gas masks which had to be hand pumped. When the bombing started in 1940 many people were evacuated in the area because of a time bomb that had been dropped.

One memory of Brigadier Eva Rowland was of 29 men travelling to join HMS *Hood* all full of life and energy. They helped with the washing up. When they reached the docks at Thurso they marched down to the quay and embarked for Scapa Flow. As the ship left they shouted 'We'll see you when we come back'. Within days came the sad news that the Hood had sunk with all but three hands. She felt terrible and so helpless.

On another occasion, on an airfield in Lincoln she preached the sermon and you could hear a pin drop; the men had never heard a woman preach a sermon before. On one occasion it was German POWs that they met and one, on seeing Eva's husband's epaulettes, opened his tunic to reveal a Salvation Army jersey. He was himself an officer in the Salvation Army who had been conscripted into the German Army, and subsequently was captured.

One must not forget NAAFI, or to give it is official title Navy, Army and Air Force Institute. Some 35,000 women worked in NAAFI. They started work at 27/6d a week, plus board, lodging, laundry, and uniform. Serving the troops with food was important. They were also the only females that the men were likely to see for some time which had a beneficial psychological effect. But it was demanding work peeling potatoes, scrubbing floors, and cooking meals for hungry troops, serving several million cups of tea and mugs of beer. At its peak NAAFI had reached 60,000.

Annie (Nancy) Keen was so tired on one occasion that when she went home for the weekend with a friend all they did was sleep. Her living memory is the soldiers saying to her 'Got any fags, Nancy?'

Agnes Higson started her NAAFI service on gun sites, then after D-Day she went with others on a troop train between Victoria, Dover and Folkestone. A NAAFI woman was never short of an escort, but one rule did prevail, the soldier had to give a receipt for the woman and deliver her back on time.

In June 1941 a scheme of awards to NAAFI personnel was instituted. The men were awarded an inscribed clock and the women a gold bracelet bearing the NAAFI crest. During WWII 550 men and women of NAAFI died or were killed, including some 300 on the troop ship *Lancastria* which was sunk at St Nazaire in 1940.

Miss Gallagher was in a canteen at Tilbury Docks just before D-Day. They were living under canvas at the time. She volunteered for overseas duties which meant coming under the wing of the ATS and wearing uniform. This became known as the ATS/EFI (Expeditionary Force Institution). She set off in a convoy along with the Duke and Duchess of Gloucester and landed in Naples on Christmas Eve 1944. She then proceeded to follow the 8th Army for which she and the others got five shillings a week extra, danger money as it was known, and could wear the 8th Army flash on their uniforms. She went on to run the Ridatto Cafe in Rome for a year.

Moira Platts did her initial ATS training at Queen Camp, Guildford. She remembers everything having to be done at the double. From there she went on an officers' course at Windsor.

Mary Churchill had been commissioned on the previous course. Eventually she left the ATS/EFI Depot in Dulwich for Liverpool Docks and then by ship to Algiers in North Africa, and then Italy. By the time 1943 came, 85% of the NAAFI staff were women, they came from school, shops, factories, some had even been models and typists. The Empire Tea Bureau helped many of them to make a good cup of 'char' that was fit to drink, bearing in mind the quality of the tea available at that time.

When Grace Hector began to march and salute she began to regret volunteering for overseas duties. But after six weeks and making the best of it she boarded the SS *Scythia* at Liverpool and began deck drill and coping with the rough sea in the Bay of Biscay. The Med and Gibraltar brought calm seas, blue skies and flying fish, and she felt that this, indeed, was the life. When she spotted Vesuvius, she knew she was in the Bay of Naples, in Italy. As she crossed the temporary pier she dropped her tin hat in the water and hopes today it is covered in coral and has a tinge of beauty as she hated it at the time. They were taken to the Red Shield Club in Naples, it was Christmas Eve and she saw oranges on the trees which, after the rationing in the UK, was a shock. The level of the care and respect from the soldiers who invited them to parties was remarkable, no bad language in their company in which they felt safe. She was posted to the NAAFI at Pontecagnano in the province of Salerno. It had previously been the HQ of the Fascists who administered the province.

Only weeks later she was told she had been posted to take charge of the huge Club, Salerno Arms. There were 131 women and 250 Italians working in the club. Her office was a huge marble lined building, just across the road from her bedroom was the sea. The club had everything, laundry, barbers shop, music and games rooms, bikes could be hired out, ice cream and tea rooms and a wine bar. The troops could have a full meal or a snack in the club. She learned to speak Italian very well and when the beach area became a hive for pickpockets she was able to go down to the market and retrieve many of the stolen goods. From there she went onto Athens in Greece, flying in a Dakota; she took over the Phoenix club and had a holiday villa for use on local leave. At the end of the war NAAFI had 23 resident and 35 non-resident officer clubs, 19 for SNCOs and 66 for other ranks.

Above left: NAAFI recruitment poster. Above right: NAAFI women, 1942 (G. Watson). Below: Mobile canteen staffed by a WVS party (Author). Bottom: Members of the Salvation Army back from Dunkirk in 1940 (L. Loveless)

Above: A very familiar sight to all ex-service personnel (Author).

Below left: NAAFI uniform (Author).

Below right: Grace Hectopr, NAAFI, 1942 (G. Hector).

Chapter 13 Prisoners of War

When the Far East fell in 1941/42 to the Japanese invasion, men, women, and children were interned, or made prisoner. The official Japanese policy, thinking the war would not last long was that all Westerners in Asia were to be interned for the length of the war. There were Australian nurses and Dutch nuns of which a number were nursing nuns. People of mixed races, some of which offered their freedom refused as the only people they knew had been interned in the camps set up by the Japanese. Many of the women were wives and families of planters working in the Far East, missionaries, or nurses, or as in the case of the armed services Australian or British Army nurses. The camps were set up in Java, Sumatra, and Borneo. The women and children were separated from the men. One of the camps was on Bangka Island, and later Palembang, in Sumatra. In this camp there were Australian Army Nursing sisters, Dutch nuns, and civilians, Dutch and British Eurasians, one Chinese, and one lady from New Zealand.

Nell Hannah, or Mavis or as she was known to some, was born in Australia in1910. Her uncle had served in Gallipoli with the Australian Forces in WW1. She was the apple of her father's eye, who was medically unfit for war service having ear trouble. In her childhood Australia was still a pioneering country, without all the mod cons that they have today. She became a nurse in the 1930s and in the late 1930s, she was a sister in charge of a blood transfusion unit. When war was declared and within hours in Australia, recruiting stations had been opened, the 'Old Country Needed Help' was the theme. within hours she had enlisted but it was February before she was called up, besides being a fully qualified nurse, she was also a pharmacist. Nobody, she remembers, quibbled about joining up; it had to be done and 'let's get on with it' was the way the people thought. She became a nursing sister with the rank of first lieutenant and was sent to 2/4 Casualty Clearing Station, it was here that the front-line troops were sent to be patched up before being sent on to the main hospitals, many of course died here.

Prewar, Nell had paid £40 for a course on midwifery at Queen Charlottes hospital in London. This she lost and never did get her course. With the 2/4th she embarked with other sisters on the liner Queen Mary, then a troop ship, for Singapore. One of her sister colleagues was Elaine known as Laine Balfour Ogilvy. She trained at the children's hospital in Adelaide before the war. She was a cheerful laughing girl. During the journey on the Queen Mary, concerts were organised in the music room and Laine, having a fine voice, would sing. When they arrived in Singapore the 2/4th settled down to battlefield casualties, thousands of troops were brought for first aid treatment and then passed on. Many a time Laine and Nell stood shoulder to shoulder attending to badly wounded troops.

On the 13th February 1942, with the invasion of Singapore imminent, Nell and 64 other Nursing sisters were ordered to board the ship *Vyner Brooke*, great reservations were held by more than one officer on the shore that this ship would not make it, but they had to go. They set sail for Australia, on the 14th February. On board were 200 passengers and 47 crew. The ship was bombed by Japanese aircraft and sunk in Bangka Straits, 15 miles north of Sumatra. Nell got off the ship by climbing down a rope as the ship heeled over. A Mrs. Brown was calling for her daughter as she came down the rope and rather holding up proceedings, so Nell shouted at her to get a move on, her daughter was in fact already in the water below her.

The Japanese planes were continuing to attack the ship and survivors with machine gun fire. Many of the lifeboats had been holed or destroyed in the attack on the ship. One sister who was a Roman Catholic was covered in oil and proceeded to pray, Nell once again feeling on this occasion something more positive was need told her to shut up and to do something constructive and get rowing. She had in fact got on a raft as she could not swim and make the only surviving lifeboat that the other sisters had manned. She had pinned her pay book and two Australian dollars inside her uniform pocket. The raft was a yard wide with wooden slats edged with wood and held together with rope. Her last memory of Laine was in the water. She was clinging to a rope on the side of the lifeboat and calling to Nell to swim to the boat, but as she could not swim she stayed where she was. Gradually the raft drifted away from the lifeboat, something that in the long term was to save her life. Nell said of Laine 'She was second to none'. The raft over the next three days kept drifting in and out with the tide towards the island of Bangka, they were unable to land as the rocks were too slippery to grasp.

After three days afloat and near exhaustion they decided to leave the raft and try and get ashore. The sea was like glass and as the sun came up the sky a lavender colour and the flying fish were performing. The non-swimmers were at first escorted by those that could. Nell set off in a form of breaststroke. When about a mile from the shore she suddenly felt the presence of her mother who was in Australia. She was urging her on and saying, 'Don't give up, don't give up'. A fisherman came out in his boat and told her to hang on to the side of his boat. This she did, and he brought her ashore. He left her there and said he would be back with food. When he came back some while later he brought cold black coffee and tapioca roots with a string in the centre. It was nectar to her after three days without a drink or food. In return she gave him her two Australian dollars.

The Japanese came to the island in large ships and then landed small assault landing craft to get the troops ashore. As one of them returned to his ship he saw one of the rafts, on it was Mrs. Brown, they came over and picked her up and took her ashore. On board as well as the Australian Sisters were 21 sisters from the QAs and TANS under the leadership of Principle Matron Violet Jones. None of them survived and today they are remembered on the Singapore Memorial as having no known grave but the sea.

Out of the 200 passengers 125 were missing and 35 interned. As Mrs. Brown landed she suddenly realised she had left her handbag on the raft and hailed to the boat to take her back but of course they just ignored her, and she never saw her handbag again. On the shore Nell argued with the others about what they should do next, she then decided that in the position they were in, and hearing about women who had roamed around outside the camps and were raped to give herself up, but of course she had no idea then how the Japanese would treat her.

The first Japanese she saw was a little, as she described him as 'a bandy-legged rabbit', with a great big pith helmet on his head and a long rifle and bayonet. He beckoned her to cross the bridge to the HQ where they were then put in the old Dutch Customs House packed in like sardines on the floor, here they stayed for about three to four days and without any food. The sisters in the lifeboat had reached the shore and lit a fire, which those on the raft could see but not reach. The wounded were put in the fisherman's huts on the beach.

On the 16th February, the civilians decided to walk along the beach where as the sisters stayed with the wounded. When the Japanese arrived they promptly shot the wounded in the huts and bayoneted the men who were not wounded. The 22 sisters on the beach were lined up and told to walk into the water which they did, it was then that the Japanese opened with machine guns and killed all but one. The sister who survived was Vivian Bulwinkle who had been with the 2/13 AGH. She had been shot through the fleshy part of her side, the bullet passing straight through. She pretended to be dead until the Japanese had left and then put a water bottle on each side of her wound to stem the bleeding. The matron in charge Sister Drummond was very short sighted and lost her glasses in the water, as she tried to find them she was shot and killed. The other 20 sisters were all dead and today have no known grave.

When she got back to the huts she found a British sailor Stoker Ernest Lloyd still alive despite having a bayonet wound through his lower buttock. Together they set off and for ten days wandered about the jungle until one day they were picked up by a Japanese Staff car. The officers were in the Japanese Navy and in most cases more humane than the Army, having been trained by the Royal Navy. They gave them a drink of milk and took them to the POW camp.

The camp on Bangka Island had sisters from 2/4 CCS, 2/10 AGH, 2/13 AGH and two Queen's Alexander Sisters. There were also nurses from the 3/4 Malayan Civilian Service and some 1700 civilian women and children. Each person was allocated a space of 21inches on a bamboo platform. In the wet season this became muddy. There was no soap and very little food. The toilets were virtually nonexistent, just a hole in the ground, which frequently overflowed. No one had any shoes, having kicked them off in the water as they were told. This was substituted with wooden 'trumpers', a form of sandal with rubber tyre strips for holding straps. Once a week a local Indian man would come in on his bullock cart to sell them the trumpers. For Mrs. Brown this was of no use as she took size 10. Her salvation was a pair of men's sand shoes that had been found.

After the massacre of the sisters the policy in Australia was changed and all sisters were given officer status in the hope that the Japanese would treat them as such. However, it meant nothing, the treatment was exactly the same. The Japanese gave them nothing in the way to cook or eat with. Their daily diet consisted of 2 ounces of dry rice which they cooked in a bully beef tin. After it had been cooked there was just enough to half fill a coconut shell. This came with a green spinach-like vegetable called Cancon. For breakfast they had a mixture of starch and rice which they called Boo Boo, when mixed it came out something like a wall-paper paste and tasted just as revolting. The sweet potatoes were left in sacks until they had nearly gone rotten, and only then were they issued. The Japanese would say to them 'There is plenty of room in the cemetery' and their attitude was, 'you should not have let yourself become a prisoner'. They were inconsistent and unpredictable.

Any meat was thrown on the ground as if they were dogs. Cooking was later done with the use of latex cups from the rubber trees. Coconuts and bamboo was very useful for all manner of things. The women and children talked and dreamt about food as there was never enough. They sometimes had a limed rice which was yellow in colour. In four years as a prisoner Nell had only half a pound of meat or proteins. When the Red Cross parcels came in the Japanese stole all the cigarettes and chocolate and stored away the medicine that was so urgently needed. When the sisters asked for extra medicines the Japanese would make them stand in the sun or slap them about the head or neck, or as in the case in the sun or slap them about the head or neck, or as in the case of Nell hit with a rifle butt which cracked her shoulder blade and today still effects the use of her left arm.

The hospital was a farce, by the time 1944 came the only treatment available was hot water and rest. For such diseases as Beriberi, Malaria, Dangy Fever, Dysentery and diarrhoea this was useless. Salt and sugar was urgently needed but none was forthcoming. The supplies were there but not distributed. Nell today is convinced her

Australian upbringing, healthy heritage, military, and nursing training is what saved her. One lady was punished for daring to pick up an apple box which had dropped off a lorry and use it as a seat.

The steel tin helmets that had been found on the beach and other places was of the greatest use. The Japanese would tell them that all the bamboo castles in London had been burnt and the rice crops in the Strand. Whenever a Japanese solider passed them they had to bow; if they did not they were beaten up. They got some consolation out of it; as they bowed calling the Japanese all the names they could think of. He, of course would not know what they were saying, and if you smiled he was not worried. Nell made a pact with herself, that after the war the only person she would bow to would be herself. On one occasion she saw an Indonesian have his head cut off which was a favourite Japanese method of execution. They treated children reasonably and occasionally gave them sweets, but, having said that they never gave any extra food for them.

As well as Japanese there were Indonesian and Korean guards; by far the worst, in Nell's estimation, were the Koreans. She only met one Japanese who recognised the Red Cross badge and he was a doctor. Apart from this any Red Cross badges were ripped off saying they did not recognise them. The Dutch nuns were very tough and would do anything for their patients.

Nell made hats out of grass matting. To do this she hired from a Dutch lady a sewing machine, the few cents she made from this was pooled and used where and wherever it could be. The Dutch were very good to them without them they would have not had any clothes, or money. They did the chores and the Dutch paid them. Each time they moved camp the Japanese would say "We are going to a better Camp", but, of course it never was better, often it was worse. For the journey from Bangka Island to Palembang they were put in the hold of the ship in a blazing sun. During the journey 50 people died, their bodies simply thrown over the side of the ship or left at the railway sidings in Palembang.

The pride and humour of British and Commonwealth could not be crushed and was always there. The nurses were allowed outside the camp to visit the hospital, the Dutch made a form of money belt which was meant for messages to be carried to the men in the hospital, but this was soon discovered by the Japanese so Nell, with the use of an unused sanitary towel, carried messages back and forth and was never detected.

Helen Bull, a civilian, had a little girl with her but when the ship had been sunk she told her other two children to swim away from the ship as it went down. An Australian boy picked them up in a sampan and took them to Java. When Nell visited the hospital on one occasion a man said to her 'Do you have a Mrs. Bull in the camp?' When she replied 'Yes,' he said, 'Tell her that her children have reached Australia'. Her husband had been a judge in Singapore and interned.

The Australian nursing sisters would not nurse outside the camp, however, Margo Turner and Mary Cooper, both Queen's Alexander Nursing Corps did, but only for a short while. Then they were accused of giving away information and put in solitary confinement. One of the great salvations in the camp which broke the frustration and boredom was singing. Mary Dryburgh, who wrote poems and Nora Chambers who had studied music at the Royal Academy organised and rehearsed the singing. The voices became an orchestra and were arranged for voices in four parts. The women sat on boxes at night and rehearsed with Nora conducting. Some two dozen well-orchestrated pieces were arranged for the four-part voices. One piece that Mary wrote, and Nora put the music to was 'The Captive Hymn 'which was sung at each Sunday service in the camp, she wrote this in 1942. On the lighter side one Dutch lady sang 'Land of Hope and Glory' and not being able to pronounce her Ws they came over as Vs much to the enjoyment of the other prisoners who kept asking her to keep on singing. Finally, the orchestra had to stop as the women were too weak to rehearse, and fifteen of the members had died. Between October 1944, and April 1945, 44 died on Bangka Island. In all, 76 women and children had died during the time they were prisoners. The camp in Palembang was a placed called Belalak, a former rubber plant. It was here on the 23rd April 1945, that Mary Dryburgh died and was buried.

A Japanese civilian called Miarck who had run a curio shop in Singapore, and whom many of the women knew was now working for the Japanese Military running their officers' club. He also set up brothels and found women for these brothels. The sisters were told they were to attend the officers club to entertain them and they knew what that meant but they at first refused, saying they were army officers and should not be treated this way. He told them if they refused he would starve the children. So along they went, looking quite a sight having cut their hair short with a pair of scissors that Nell had somehow managed to acquire. They all sat around glass top tables with the officers in their immaculate green uniforms, long swords, and beautiful high leather boots. They could not speak English and the women could not speak Japanese. After a while they said they wanted to leave but Miarck said that four had to stay or the children would be starved. Nell made up her mind if she was to be raped then so be it, but they were not going to have the satisfaction of killing her. While they were in the club and keeping the attention of the officers one of the sisters was able to go in the back of the club and get sugar and tea. Only Nell went outside with one of the officers but when they got outside she said she was leaving but he followed her and put his arms around kissing her on the cheek saying he loved her. She pushed him back and he fell over losing his cap and glasses. She ran back into the club and he followed her but did not say anything as he would have lost face. The outcome was it did not happen again, and the repercussions were faces being slapped and doors banged. One thing is certain; none of the women would or did go with a Japanese soldier.

The experience had affected Nell as her heart had palpitations which left her unable to do many of the chores that she had previously done. Even much later her heart did a repeat of what it did all those years ago. Also, she suffers from a shrunken throat and has had to have it dilated to be able to eat meat etc. She also had a lot of bowel trouble, all attributed to her days in the camps. Nell, who moved to the UK in 1952, kept all her teeth. Being a pharmacist, she had thought of a remedy that would compensate for the lack of toothpaste. She would grind up egg shells into pulp and take one spoonful a day. She is convinced today that having had a stable diet as a child with plenty of eggs and butter saved her in the camps.

In the middle of August 1945, two Africans were parachuted in to tell them the war was over, they had thought that this would be a time for great celebration but instead they were just stunned into silence. In 1945, they had lost no less than eight sisters who had died from one disease or another. The Japanese Commandant stood on a table and said if they had done anything to harm them over the last four years, he hoped they would forgive them. One night about midnight they were told to get ready and at three am they set off in lorries and then by train to a Dutch Military Camp at Libut Lingawand from there to an airfield to be flown to Singapore. Out of 65 sisters when they started, only 24 were still alive. Thinking they were all alive two planes were sent so they took out as well as the 24 wounded and sick British prisoners. When they arrived in Singapore they were met by sisters they had known in 1941, and who had managed to get back to Australia. It was a joyful reunion.

Nell married in 1946, her husband was in the Royal Artillery and had also been a prisoner. They stayed out in Malaya as planters and got caught up in the terrorist actions of 1947/48. She never went anywhere without a Sten gun or revolver, her husband having taught her to shoot. In 1980, on a visit to Los Angeles she went aboard the Queen Mary which is now permanently berthed there. As she walked along the corridors and the music room, she could hear the laughter and talking, and Laine singing. Today she remembers the sisters who did not return but did not grow old and stayed eternally young. She cannot forgive the Japanese for what they did, not only to her but to the others, mentally and physically. When a television engineer told her to buy a Japanese TV set because her British one had gone wrong and she told him of her experiences in their hands he told her she should forgive and forget. In 1985, in Amsterdam a reunion was held, and an all lady choir sang the songs that they sang back in the camps, including the Captive Hymn.

Margery Jennings was a nursing sister in the Medical Auxiliary Services, her husband had escaped from Singapore in 1941, but was later recaptured and sent to the men's camp at Palembang. Mary was herself taken prisoner and sent to the same camp as Nell on Bangka Island. When she arrived, she was 11 stone. At 9.25 am on the 12th May 1942, at the age of 37 she died, and her name was inscribed with a hot wire on a wooden cross. At the time of her death, she weighed just six stone. She had been moved to a camp at Loebok Lingham, on the mainland of Sumatra, south of Palembang.

Angela Templar was interned in a camp at Santo Tomas University in March 1942. Before the war she had been stationed with her husband and two children in Hong Kong. Their life style had been very good despite the rumblings of a future war in Europe. Suddenly, in 1942 they were told they were being evacuated to the Philippines, a two-day journey away. They were only allowed to take what they could carry; having two young children this was very little. They boarded a ship and set sail for Manilla, when they arrived they were taken to a Hill Station. Here she lived with her children which had now grown to three as she had been pregnant at the time of the move.

In 1942, news came that the Japanese had landed close by and that a car was coming to take them away. When it arrived, it was a small saloon but somehow, she, the three children, the nanny, and three others besides the driver got in. Off they set on a black night and along a mountain road. The children were singing 'Away in a Manger' which they had learned at school for Christmas. They next went to an internment camp at Santa Thomas University which was now a POW camp for civilians. They were all worried about any jewellery they had and so stitched them inside the children's pyjamas thinking the Japanese would not search them.

At the camp they lived sixteen in a room, eight of which were children. The food was not suitable for the hot climate consisting of a thick stew which had been cooked in a can along with rice. At the beginning things were bearable but as time went on it got worse. If you were able to support yourself, you could live in the town. Angela was keen to do this and heard that some Spanish friends were lending money to people outside the camp. One still had to report each day to the camp and wear a red arm band, so everyone knew who you were and where you had come from. But, after 3months the living out privilege stopped, and she had to go back to the camp.

The food by now was mush, rice mixed with corn meal, boiled over and over until it was like porridge. There were 2,500 people in the camp. The next camp they were moved to was 60 miles away at Los Banos, south of Manilla. Here they lived in large barracks made of bamboo each person having a little cubicle each. In 1944, the food had become very bad and Angela was down to seven stone, she and many of the mothers were giving their share of the food to the children.

Above: Nell (Mavis) Hannah, seated front row, right, was the only member of this group to survive captivity by the Japanese. Below: Nell with fellow survivors, after liberation and a month of recuperation in 1945 (M. Hannah).

In 1945, suddenly came a message from a man shouting that the staff had left, and there were no guards. A week went by and then a setback as the staff returned and they were told to stay away from the fence around the camp. When they returned they found that all the rice, ham and any other food had been taken. As a punishment they were only given rice and hush to eat, which if mixed was in fact dangerous, the hush had to be got off which was not easy without the right tools, which of course they did not have. Eventually, the Americans sent in paratroopers and the camp was finally liberated. Their stomachs had shrunk, and they were unable to eat very much, but this did not stop the children coming back from the US troops with chocolate and sweets. A month was spent in a base hospital and then home by hospital ship to Liverpool.

In 1941, Miss P M Briggs was a civilian nurse based in a hospital in Northern Malaya. On 8th December 1941 Japanese planes came over and dropped bombs. On 13th February 1942 they were taken to the docks and put on a ship, the *Mata Hari*, which had a maximum speed of thirteen knots. Out at sea a Japanese destroyer came alongside, boarded the ship, and ran up the Japanese flag. They were taken off by launch and taken to a POW camp. On 21st February, while operating on an RAF officer and amputating his foot with a saw made from a knife, another man nearby who had been trying to get a drink of water was bayoneted in the stomach as he lay on the ground waiting for attention and another Japanese came along and ground his heel in the man's wound. Within a few days a Sister Turner turned up, she had survived her ship being sunk by collecting rain water in the lid of her powder compact. On 4th April 1942, they were sent by ship to Palembang and on 29th, in honour of the Emperor's birthday, they were given one piece of pineapple to share between 15 people. On his next birthday they got nothing.

On 4th March 1944, Mary Anderson, once a large lady with booming voice and a keen golfer died. She lay dead in the tropical heat until finally she was taken away by the Japanese. In April 1945, they were moved in a train which had been used to carry coal and the doors were kept closed throughout the journey, no facilities for ablutions. On 24th August 1945, rations were increased including tinned milk and butter, even a lipstick. A plane flew over and dropped supplies and South East Asia Command newspapers. They ate their first bread in 3'/2 years. She left the camp on 16 September dressed in a Japanese uniform with yellow leather boots and was flown to Singapore and the Alexandria Hospital. She was now down to six stone and had scabies. After ten days on a diet of bacon, eggs, and ice cream she was moved to the Raffles Hotel. On 30th September, she boarded a plane for New Zealand, via Darwin, Brisbane and then Auckland.

Timah Sigurdson was born in Banka. Her father was a headmaster of the local grammar school. He was made a prisoner on 8th March 1942 and had been a captain in the Red Cross, her mother had the rank of Sister. Her brothers were taken away to a separate camp. She stayed with her mother, they did not have any contact with her father or brothers. In 1943, they were taken by train to Batavia. On arrival they were hit and kicked off the train and pushed into open lorries and taken to a camp called "Tjideng". On arrival they were made to stand in the sun from mid-day until 4pm. Several died in that time. The size of the room allocated was nine metres by three metres and shared by thirteen women and children. The house itself had five rooms, a garage, and a bathroom which 124 people shared. There was no furniture and one had to live on the floor. The two mattresses they had were folded up in the day and used as a seat. The toilets did not work, so 5lb butter tins were used and emptied into the gully outside when full. They were overrun with bedbugs and headlice, but everybody was in the same boat, so no one needed to feel ashamed.

Twice a day they had 'Tenko' which meant a head count or roll call. The sick and infirm also had to attend and were not allowed to be helped, if they fell they stayed there until the roll call was over. The food was the usual rice which had been boiled and a piece of bread which they used to put in their rice ration in the sun to make it swell and look more. Once a week came a water cabbage leaf soup, the stock being drawn from unwashed beast intestines, or unwashed beast intestines which volunteers scraped clean before boiling for soup. The camp commander was called Sonai, a brute of a man. As with Nell there was a hospital but no medical supplies and so many of the 10,000 women and children who were interned died.

Nell's two brothers found each other in a camp at Bandoeng. They also learned that their sister had been transported to Karees, Batavia and followed on lorries, buses, and trains. They were repatriated to Holland having been got to an area protected by Gurkha patrols. From the Red Cross she learned that her father had been working on the Burma Railway and his homecoming would be delayed as he was in charge of the repatriation of POWs from Saigon. He arrived back in 1946 and they were repatriated to Holland on a troopship in September 1946.

In Jersey, Channel Islands, Joan Coles was being removed to Germany. This was after two years of occupation by the Germans and then a rule that all British-born subjects would be deported to Germany. A local policeman and a German NCO turned up and they were told to take enough clothes and food for a two-day journey. On 18th September 1942, 300 people left on a ship, as the islanders gathered and sang "There'll always be an England" which resulted in reprisals by the Germans. On the ship they were taken to St Malo and then on a train with six to a compartment. The train went north of Paris and into Luxembourg, then into the Ruhr and on to Saarbrücken. From there it was a day's journey across the Mossell Valley.

On 21st September, the men were separated from the women and children at Biberach Riss. The women and children were taken to a POW camp in Bavaria. This had concrete huts surrounded by wire. In each but 25 to 30 people slept on double decker beds with straw palliases, only one blanket and their own clothes to keep out the cold. The food was two slices of rye bread and some ersatz margarine with a little honey, and once a day, weak vegetable soup.

On 30th October, they were taken by train to the village of Balwiz Ach, 30 kilometres from the Swiss border, and near to Lake Constance. Their home was a former Bavarian Schloss, once the home of a prince and princess. It was 400 years old and had steep stairs and the rooms were filthy and damp[14]. On 3rd January 1944, they had their sixth death since arriving, when a little boy named Richard Gould died of meningitis.

On 28th April, the castle was repatriated and on 7 July 1945 they left by air from Mengen airfield. As they landed at Hendon a tyre burst on the aircraft. A large bus marked ambulance took them to

---

[14] In 1971, they had a reunion there and were welcomed by the Mayor, Herr Mirth.

Victoria Station and then by train to Sutton, Surrey. They had been behind the wire for two years nine months and had travelled 590 miles from Mengen to Sutton, a journey of 9'/2 hours but now at last they were home.

Chapter 14 Casualties and Awards

On Saturday 28th September 1940, a young lady finished her morning's work as a nursery hand at George Sapsford & Co Market Garden, Hankam. Peggy Rosemary Harland was only 17 and was looking forward on her half-day to visit her friend, Myrtle Wilkinson, in Eastbourne, and buying a new winter coat. She lived at Peelings Cottages, Milton Street, Hankam with her parents.

Prior to starting work she had left Hankam Primary School at the age of 14. Her brother Robert was reported missing at Dunkirk, aged of 21, whilst serving with the 7th Battalion, Royal Sussex Regiment. He is commemorated on the Dunkirk War Memorial.

Before marrying her husband Karl, Myrtle, who was aged 32, had lived at 5, Hankam Street, Pevensey with her parents William and Olive Reed who ran the post office in Hankam. Karl's father owned Wilkinson Limited, Electrical Engineers in Eastbourne.

At 5.38pm that day, Eastbourne was attacked by two German bombers, this being the town's 20th raid of the war. The first aircraft was dealt with by two Spitfires but the second got through and dropped six bombs, one landing on the junction of 69/71 Cavendish

Peggy Harland (back row, second from left) with her Girl Guide troop (Author).

Rescuers search for survivors in the rubble of the Eastbourne house where Peggy and Myrtle were taking tea (Author).

Peggy Harland's grave in St. Mary's Churchyard, East Sussex (Author).

Place and 127 Tideswell Road. The bomb exploded directly on the three-storey house where Peggy and Myrtle were having tea. Myrtle was killed outright but Peggy had dropped into the cellar, where she was trapped by a steel girder on her ankles. She lay there for 36 hours until Dr Roy Barron, the First Aid Commander, and surgeon Dr Laurence Snowball from Princess Alice Hospital reached her. They found it impossible to extract her and had no alternative but to amputate her legs. The situation was critical as another H.E bomb, dropped 200 yards away, had not exploded and the water mains had burst, so pumping operations had to be put in place by the Fire Brigade.

Throughout all this Peggy's demeanour was remarkable despite great pain and stress. One of the doctors tending her at the time later told an Eastbourne Gazette reporter "She had more pluck than any person I have ever known."

When, eventually, she was freed and brought out of the cellar she was taken to Prince Alice Hospital where it was found she had also suffered a broken back and, despite a great fight for life, she died on the morning of 30th September and is now buried in St Mary's Churchyard, Westham.

Her headstone also commemorates her brother Robert and has the insignia of the Girl Guides Gold Cross for Fortitude, the highest award to the Guides for Gallantry. In 1941 Peggy was recommended for the award by Dame Alice Godman, the County Commissioner for Sussex and in June 1941 the awards committee put forward a request that it be awarded posthumously. The medal had been instituted in March 1941 and Peggy was the third person to be recommended but the first posthumously. Her citation read, "Gallantry in face of danger and great suffering before her death after an air raid."

On top of the medal with its green ribbon are the immortal words 'For Gallantry', and the award is thought of as the Guides' Victoria Cross.

Two others also died before being rescued; Stanley and Olive Giles aged 33 and 28. Both were air raid wardens but at the time of the surprise attack were off duty. Their funeral was on 9th October 1940. Karl Wilkinson age 35 survived but was also injured and trapped in the cellar. He had seen the German bomber overhead and, when the bomb hit, lapsed into an unconscious state and woke up holding the hand of his aunt who was close by. He called out to the others who were trapped and they all replied except his wife. By now the water was rising in the cellar and up to their chins. Having his hands free, Karl was able to hit the turncock with a piece of masonry and turn the water off. The water was pumped out of the cellar by means of a tube. The rescue squad was able to break through the kitchen on the corner of the house and level with the cellar break intervening wall and get to the trapped people. Karl gave them valuable assistance as to the lay out of the cellar. They had cut through twelve inches of concrete and a matchwood refrigerator lined with cork, in very confined conditions. During the rescue Blackmer, who was also a member of the 21st Sussex (Eastbourne) Home Guard, and Turney, who had served in the Army Service Corps in WWI, were overcome with cold and escaping gas and had to be taken back to their depot for a spell. They later came back to continue the rescue. Despite the many problems five of the seven people trapped were rescued alive.

While the rescue was going on, two H.E. bombs with delayed action fuses went off injuring some of the rescue squad. The other main problems were gas, cold and the water level.

Many of the rescue squad were builders, or labourers some working for the corporation answering every air raid siren since the war had begun. Some were WW1 veterans who had experience of such conditions. The rescue was described as the largest and most difficult rescue in Eastbourne during WWII.

For the rescue no fewer than four men were awarded the George Medal: Alfred Ernest Blackmer, Edwin Humphrey May, Francis Charles Frederick Stevens, and Ernest Lawson Turney who had served in the Army Service Corps in WWI. Medals are now on display at the Redoubt Museum, Eastbourne. Alfred Blackmer, aged 35, was later called up for military service and had on his uniform the ribbon of the GM. The awards were London Gazetted in March 1941.

Also decorated was Chief Fire Officer Phillips, who was awarded the M.B.E. He had already been awarded the Military Medal in WWI for taking messages under fire when with the Royal West Kent Regiment. There were commendations to: Dr John Fenton, The

Medical Officer of Health for Eastbourne, Dr Roy MacGregor Barron, Dr Laurence Snowball and the leader of the rescue quad Roland Victor Harvey, Sub Officer Sidney Nelson Waymark of Eastbourne Fire Brigade, Police Constable R.T. Jeffrey, Senior Air Raid Warden H.M. Barnes and Air Raid Warden A.J. Barkham. In addition to the four who died, a further fourteen people were injured.

In any war there are casualties and awards for gallantry. The first woman killed in action serving in the Services in WWII was Aircraftwoman Second Class Marguerite Hester Hudson of the Women's Auxiliary Air Force, from Sheffield. At the time of her death on 15th August 1940 she was aged 19. Her death came at the height of the Battle of Britain while she was serving on a bomber station at RAF Driffield. The station was attacked by a formation of 30 aircraft for 45 minutes dropping 100lb bombs in that time. The casualties were thirteen killed and 21 injured. It was 1pm when the first place to be hit was the Motor Transport Yard. It was here that Marguerite had just stopped her lorry. As she did a bomb blew her and her lorry against the yard wall, she was killed instantly. She was a very popular young lady and the previous night she had danced the dance of the seven veils in the airmen's mess, she was also knitting a pullover for a member of 77 Squadron. Marguerite was later buried near her home town of Bradfield, Sheffield. Before the war she had been well known in the Operatic Societies and she and her sister were members of the Sheffield Teachers Operatic Society. Her father was a doctor, and a wing commander in the RAF and her sister Helen drove an ambulance during the war. Both Dr Hudson and Mrs. Hudson are now buried in the same grave with Marguerite. Private

Nora Caveney was only 18 when she died on 17th April 1942. At the time she was serving as a predictor with the ATS in 529 Battery 148 Medium Heavy Anti-Aircraft Regiment of the Royal Artillery at Beaulieu Heath, Netley, near Southampton. The guns on the 17th had been firing nonstop and straight up into the air to stop the German aircraft flying to London. The firing was so intense that shrapnel was dropping back down on the battery. One or two of the women had fainted in the attack, but, one by one, they came round, except for Nora, who had been hit in the back by a piece of shrapnel and was pronounced 'killed in action' at the hospital where she was taken. Her place was taken by Pte Gladys Keel, who was a spotter but took over as predictor. Lord Nuffield of Nuffield Centre fame came down to start a memorial to the memory of Nora, which was a hut normally used as a rest room. In the room was a large picture of Nora which was unveiled at this ceremony, below the picture was a plaque with the details of Nora's death. This hut was meant to be kept for all time in her memory. Her body was taken back to the camp at Netley and all available personnel were instructed to wear best uniform and follow the coffin procession on its way from the camp to Southampton Railway Station. Her body was then taken to Hound in Hampshire for burial, although she came from Walsden, near Rochdale, and had worked in a silk factory before joining the ATS in December 1942. Her parents and sister attended her funeral.

On 8/9th September 1943, at RAF Mepal, a Stirling Bomber flown by Fg Off Ian Menzies, prepared to take off with a full bomb load. Suddenly, it swung to starboard. In an attempt to miss the houses alongside the airfield, the pilot opened the throttles but failed to avoid two of the houses and the aircraft burst into flames. Section Officer Joan Easton was watching the takeoff as Ian was her fiancée. She and a Flight Sergeant Dobson, a navigator not flying that day, rushed over to try and evacuate civilians from the houses but as they did the bomb load onboard BK809 exploded and they were both killed. Ian, who was aged 21, came from Auckland, in New Zealand, and two other members of his crew were killed and are now buried in the Cambridge City Cemetery. The other members of the crew survived but were injured. Joan came from Welling in Kent and was taken back to Charlton Cemetery for burial. For her bravery she was awarded a Mention in Despatches posthumously. Her brother Eric, a sergeant pilot, had been killed in April 1941 and they are now both buried in the same grave along with other members of the family.

Philomena Tibbenham served with 630 Battery, 188 Heavy Anti-aircraft Mixed Regiment at Camber Sands near Rye in Sussex. They were under canvas and it was the flying bomb era, during the day the beds had to be covered with groundsheets, and at night the puddles drained off. Water was on ration and the toilet consisted of a large creosote oil drum resting on a length of wood and divided by a canvas curtain. The washing up was done in lukewarm water without any form of soap or detergent and lumps of turf substituted for brillo pads. They were on call for eight hours every other day and eight hours in the space of 24 hours. When the call came they would run to their guns often in their blue and white striped pyjamas pulling on boots and trousers as they ran and at the same time trying to keep their tin helmets on with curlers underneath. On 17th August 1944, at the height of the flying bomb era, and on a very hot day, Philomena was wearing her battledress jacket over her underwear as it was so hot and made her way to the canteen which was in the local pub, the Royal William. The canteen was run by the Duchess of Bedford. On this day the Duchess was off duty and her daughter Daphne was in charge. She had two other women helping her and all four of them began to roll up their sleeves when suddenly there was a flash, a huge explosion and then a cloud of dust. One of the women who had been at the sink had metal embedded in her back and her shoulder blade broken. The other woman had been lifted off her feet and hit her head on the gas stove. Philomena seemed to come off worse as she was left holding her left eye with one hand and the other over a cut eyelid. They were able to get out of what was left of the pub and were put on a lorry which took them to a Royal Navy first aid post and then by ambulance to a hospital at Hastings. The two women who had been hurt were soon repaired and discharged from hospital. But for Philomena she spent the next five years in hospital undergoing plastic surgery on her badly scarred face which had 93 stitches put in. She had also been cut in the throat by a flying plate and had cuts to her arms and scalp. While she was in hospital three men were killed and another three wounded after crossing the sands to take a dip in the sea, the only means of bathing. She had lost her left eye and her eye socket had to be rebuilt. The flying bomb had landed only 25 yards away. Lady Daphne was wounded in the leg by the explosion. The Duchess came to the hospital to visit Philomena. Although not admitted to St Dunstans, that wonderful organisation set up to look after service people who had been totally blinded, she did go for a checkup with them a few years ago. She was thankful to still have her sight in her right eye.

The Air Transport Auxiliary had 166 women serving, of which 17 were killed. One of course which comes instantly to mind is Amy Johnson who crashed and drowned in the Thames Estuary. Of the 17 killed 15 were British, one from the USA and one from New Zealand. All but two were pilots, one a flight engineer and the other a nursing sister. First Officer Dora Lang was flying a Hudson on 2nd March 1944. As she landed at Cosford she hit a cross wind and the port wing hit the ground. If she had had a medical check it may have meant a 24 hour stay at Cosford, but instead she flew from Cosford to Lasham in a Mosquito. As she approached the airfield she undershot and climbed up to 150 feet, then stalled. She opened the throttle and up went the nose of the aircraft; as it did the aircraft went into a snap roll to the left. The result was that the aircraft crashed and was burnt out. Grace Stevenson from the USA had flown in another aircraft to Cosford and then to Lasham with Dora. She had already landed when Dora crashed. She said that Dora was one of the most experienced pilots in the ATA. She thought Dora had turned the tail-plane aircraft heavy which made a three-wheel landing easier. A down drop would cause a sudden loss of altitude and instinctively she would have opened the throttle. This sudden burst of power could have made the tail-plane heavy causing the snap roll. Dora's engineer was Janice Harrington who was also killed in the crash.

Two female ATA pilots were killed on 15th March 1942, when approaching White Waltham airfield. Their aircraft hit a bungalow on the outskirts of the field and the two, Bridget Hill and Betty Sayer, were killed outright, another girl suffered cuts and burns but survived. In the crash the petrol tanks exploded, and several people were hurt. Lesley Murray crashed on 20th April 1945 at Taplow. She went into a spin flying a Hudson and lost control. Her 'stooge' on this trip was an Air Training Corps cadet Geoffrey Regan whose father was also an ATA pilot. Second Officer Tanya Whittall was not actually flying the aircraft when she was killed. She managed to get a lift on 8 April in a Lancaster flown by Wg Cdr Eric Campling. All the others aboard were groundcrew as the aircraft was being tested. She had been due to go on leave the next day. The Lancaster R5672 had previously been with 97 Squadron and had 695 hours on the clock. It went into a steep dive from 1700 feet, a fire broke out and the aircraft stalled and crashed into the ground.

On 3rd April 1944, Douglas Fairweather, head of movements flight, took off on a flight of mercy in an Anson. Aboard he had Mrs. Kathleen Kershaw, a nursing sister in the AFA. The aircraft came down in the North Sea and she was never found, she is remembered on the Runnymede Memorial, Panel 287. Douglas's body was later washed up at Thornhouse Foreshore, Girvan on 22nd April 1944. His wife Margaret was also an ATA pilot and she was killed on 4th August 1944 when flying a Proctor aircraft; she ran out of petrol and attempting a crash landing. She later died in hospital.

Kathleen Wainwright joined the Wrens in 1941 and became a writer. She came from Hull and had joined the services to get away from home. She had been taken out of school at the age of fourteen and worked long and hard in her father's grocery business. When she could get away at night she went ballroom dancing. Her parents were against her joining to the extent neither said goodbye to her when she left. She set off by ferry across the Humber to Lincolnshire and then by train to Skegness. From there she was taken by Navy bus to a camp known as HMS Royal Arthur. Before the war it had been a Butlin's Holiday Camp but now had been taken over by the Admiralty as a training establishment. She enjoyed her new-found freedom and went dancing, roller skating and played tennis. She began to work in the clothing store and very soon could estimate a person's size just by looking at them. Her 21st birthday came and went as it did for many in the war. Her best friend Yvonne Capon came from New Malden in Surrey and used to take Kathleen home for the weekend. They would go ice-skating at Richmond and to the Cafe Royal in Regent Street. Her brother Cardale had been a fighter pilot and was killed on 1st January 1941, aged 21. His aircraft had crashed in a snowstorm on the airfield at Coltishall. At the time his CO was the famous Wing Commander Bob Stanford-Tuck, who had distinguished himself in the Battle of Britain. It was he who arranged a memorial service in a hangar on 5th January 1941.

On Easter Sunday, 5th April 1942 a lovely spring day, a day Kathleen would remember all her life for the events that lay ahead. They had both been to church and decided to walk the three miles back to camp. It was in fact the last comfortable walk that Kathleen would have. They decided to go on to the beach which was crowded with service people and to walk back through the sand dunes. The tide was out at the time and as they turned to walk back she found herself on the ground. There had been no bang or flash, but she did have a loud noise in her ears and a white fog ahead. Her hands groped the sand, which felt wet and cold. She tried to sit up but could not, she then felt the side of her head. It felt like pulp and she could not feel her ear. She thought there must have been an air raid. Kathleen heard someone say, 'Oh my God' and she found she could feel her left leg and shoe but not the right. It was then she realised she had lost part of her right leg. She began to pray. There was a roaring in her head and she was gasping for breath, and two women were cutting off her clothing and found she was a Wren by her ID discs.

For a week she was near to death. Surgeon Lt Commander Campbell saved her life, she now says. He had to amputate her right leg above the knee and repair what he could of her scalp and ear. She knew somehow that Yvonne was dead although no one had told her. Over the next three days her jaws were pinned and wired together as she had multiple fractures of the jaw and had lost some teeth. She had to be fed with a straw and the handle of a spoon through an opening in her teeth. She dared not look at her legs. When she first looked into a mirror she found she was disfigured and above all else she would never walk properly again.

One day a sister brought her in a string of pearls, thinking they were hers. When she looked at them she said to the sister, 'They are not mine but belonged to my friend Yvonne who never took them off. She used to say pearls were tears'. Very soon after the accident, Kathleen was wheeled into a room where three army officers were present. They began by asking her to swear on a bible and to tell the truth. They told her she had walked into a minefield. She replied that she did not know it was a minefield although she had been there for over a year. They asked if she had been any sign, she said there was one as she looked from the sea towards the beach, but it was a long way off. An RAF sergeant had also been killed on the beach as he tried to go for help. Her father fainted when he heard the news of her injuries. In June, she was moved to a Ministry of Pensions Hospital in Leeds, her companions were two sisters aged 20 and 22 who had both lost a leg below the knee because of air raids. Here in Leeds she got the first sight of her artificial leg. It repulsed her to the extent she said 'I will stay on crutches', on which she at least could run. The section for artificial limbs was a wooden but manned by a 1914/18 veteran who had also lost a leg. At first it was a slow process with her leg.

In July 1943, she was transferred to Queen Mary's Hospital at Roehampton where she underwent a long operation on her ear and face. It took 51/2 hours; a section of skin was taken off her thigh and grafted through the ear to make a new passage. The skin was pulled up almost like a pleat to make the scar smaller, but nothing could be done to build up that side of her face owing to so much tissue being lost. The stitches she described as being like a railway line. The worst problem of all was this continuing noise in her ear which had been there ever since the accident. The whole side of her face was paralysed and she could not even blink, her eye would remain open even when she slept. She lost so much weight that her artificial leg would not fit, so it was back to the crutches.

While she was there two twelve-year-old women were brought in from a school which had been bombed, they had lost both their legs. In the next bed was a German Jewess who had fled prewar Germany from the Hitler tyranny only to be knocked down by a car in the UK and lost both her legs. The ATS women were suffering from a rheumatic condition, one causing her arm to be twisted so she could not even comb her own hair or sit down even in a wheelchair. Her condition was caused by living in damp conditions.

While in hospital Kathleen was paid seven shillings a week and given one soap coupon. The pay parade to get it was the same as for those who had both limbs. Your name was called, and you walked forward and saluted. The first time she did this she was so nervous her right-hand crutch dropped on the floor. She would go and stay for the weekend with Yvonne's parents at New Malden. She wanted to stay in the Navy but on 10th December1943 she was discharged as medically unfit. She was told that further work would be done on her face, but it never was. She was sent a metal badge from the Ministry of Pensions, known as the King's Badge for Invalided Persons of the Forces and Merchant Navy. She returned to Yorkshire to try and begin a new life, to help her do this she was given an 80% pension, of which 60% was for her leg and 20% for her facial injuries. In plain money this amounted to £1/4 shillings. Only a matter of weeks later this was reduced by 20% because it was felt her injuries were caused by, or contributed to, by her own serious negligence or misconduct. She was offered an appeal but told that the outcome could mean an increase or decrease in her pension. She decided to appeal but came out of the tribunal in tears, the board having decided that a degree of negligence was accountable to her, and so at the end she still only got 60% of her agreed 80%. In the 1960s, she was given a 10% increase to her pension, but still with 20% deducted for her negligence.

Over the years, having been on her feet longer than she should, her leg became very sore and she asked for an appointment at her old hospital in Leeds. There she found the very same doctor who had looked after her all those years ago in the 1940s. He took one look and said she must have an operation, which she did in 1977. She was in hospital for five weeks and unable to wear her artificial leg for six months. In 1978, she went through all the original paper work connected with the appeal in 1944. In this and now being much wiser, she found many loop holes. 'Who in their right senses would walk into a minefield if it had been clearly sign posted?' she asked. The result was the pension was raised to what it should have been, 90%, and is now 100% on the grounds of her accident being attributed to war service. She has been a member of that wonderful organisation BLESMA (British Limbless Ex-service Men's Association) since 1943. In 1986, she decided to visit Yvonne's grave in Surbiton, she and her brother were buried together. When she saw the grave, she remembered the beauty of her youth.

Miss Monk was Captain of the 2nd Rotherhithe Girl Guides and awarded the Bronze Cross, the Guides' VC, on 29th August 1941. Several children were sleeping on sawdust in an air raid shelter when it was hit by incendiaries and set alight. Captain Monk and Mr. Burgess, a Scout leader, forced their way in and brought four children out. Miss Monk also opened the first aid post and treated many minor casualties herself. Heather Barnes was the Captain of the 1st Colegate, Sussex, Company. She rescued the local district nurse from a house which had been hit and took her to the village hall where her injuries were attended to. As they did the hall was hit and heather received fatal injuries. She was in great pain but never once grumbled or cried. She was also awarded the Bronze Cross.

Dorothy May, a former nanny, now a Red Cross nurse said that Heather was one of her 'Babes'. Dorothy was awarded the George Medal but always felt it should have gone to Heather who died at her post. On Sunday 7th February 1943, four German aircraft FW

190s dropped 500lb bombs on the town of Eastbourne. They scored a direct hit on the Central Fire Station and among the six National Fire Service people killed was firewoman Pearl Chitty. Earlier in the war, on 1st August 1940, two houses in Cavendish Road, Eastbourne, were destroyed.

The one person trapped was Peggy Harland who was only 17. She was trapped by her legs and the only way of getting her out was by amputating her legs. Throughout this tremendous ordeal she remained cheerful, raising the morale of the rescuers. However, sadly, she died two days later in hospital. She had been trapped for 24 hours and it was discovered in hospital that she had also broken her back. As a tribute to her bravery in what was for anyone, leave along a17 year old, a frightening situation. She as a girl guide was awarded the gilt cross for gallantry three of her rescuers were awarded the George Medal.

Thelma Finch became a nursing orderly in the WAAF in March 1942. After training she was sent to the officers' convalescent home which originally had been the Palace Hotel, in Torquay. Most of the patients were Battle of Britain pilots recovering from a variety of injuries. On 25th October 1942, a Sunday, at11.05am the home was attacked by four German FW 190s dropping 500lb bombs on the east wing of the home. There were 19 casualties and 45 seriously injured. Of the killed five were WAAFs and of the injured seven were WAAFs and two VAD nurses. One WAAF died three days later from chest injuries. One of the men killed was Staff Sgt. Pickering, a PTI, whose job it was to rehabilitate patients with damaged limbs. He was only standing in for the regular RAF officer who was on a weekend leave. This was Squadron Leader Dan Maskell later to become the famous tennis commentator. With others, Thelma was taken by hospital train to RAF Wroughton. She went on to train in the Air Ambulance Service and made her first flight in a Dakota. After one operation to Novelles she was posted to Palestine in the Middle East.

On 7th March 1943, the Mostyn Hotel in Eastbourne was bombed, five airmen were killed and one WAAF was seriously injured in the blast. All were members of the Equipment Training School. Joan Clarke had been posted to Eastbourne in 1943 as clerk general duties. She reported to the Mostyn Hotel and was promptly told that clerks were being billeted in the Cumberland Hotel along the sea front. On 7th March 1943, a Sunday, the dining room of the Cumberland was full for Sunday Lunch, suddenly there was a shout 'Get Down', then came the all clear and they all went back to their lunch. Afterwards they made their way to the Mostyn and found it in ruins. One WAAF was coming out shaken and covered in dust but unhurt. Her main worry was for her friend who had been in the kitchen at the time. At night time whenever the air raid warning known as 'Cuckoo' came, they had to run some 500 yards to the pier and huddle underneath until the 'All Clear' came. The Cumberland Hotel is there today but the Mostyn was pulled down and never rebuilt. The German aircraft had flown at 20 feet from the ground to be below the radar which was situated on top of Beachy Head. The bomb that hit the Mostyn was a 250-kilogram bomb. On 3rd April 1943, the Park Gate Hotel received a direct hit and five WAAFs were injured.

On the 13th November 1943, Flight Officer Pam Barton was killed flying as a passenger in a Tiger Moth, RM 902. While taking off from Detling airfield. a10.50am it collided with a petrol bowser. The pilot, Flight Lieutenant Angus Ruffhead, was slightly injured in the crash. Pam was buried in Margate Cemetery, Kent. From 1936 to 1939, she was the British Open Amateur Ladies golf champion, and in 1936 the US Ladies Open Champion.

On 13th August 1941, the SS *Aguila* set sail for Lisbon from Liverpool via Gibraltar. On 18 April, the convoy OG71 was attacked by German He-IIIs which dropped several bombs but did not hit the ship. Three hours later the *Aguila* was hit by two torpedoes. The ship broke in half immediately and sank in less than a minute. So quickly it was impossible to lower the boats. Onboard were 21 Wrens and a Naval Nursing Sister, all killed immediately by the explosion. They were cipher officers and wireless operator Wrens. The ship had been attacked by U-boat 201. The reason they attacked the *Aguila* was because it was the convoy commander, Vice Admiral Parker's ship. They were all first-class operators. On 28th June 1952, a lifeboat was launched at Aberystwyth, it was named the '*Aguila Wren*' in memory of the 22 Wrens lost on the ship, a memorial fund had been set up to pay for the boat. The parents of 2nd Officer Ogle conceived the idea. Canon Ogle sadly did not live to see the fruits of his work.

On board the 21,000 tons *Empress of Canada* were six chief petty officers of the Wrens bound for leave in the UK. They joined the ship at Durban having got there from Ceylon when the Japanese had invaded. On board were 340 passengers and 44 crew. On 13th March 1943, having left Durban ten days before and about 400 miles south of Cape Palms, the ship was struck by a torpedo and sank in 16 minutes flat. In that time nine of the ten boats aboard had been launched, the 10th had come adrift and fallen in the water. The ship had been attacked by an Italian submarine '*Leonardo Di Vinci*'. Also onboard the ship were 300 Italian prisoners. CPO Bonner who later became a doctor was chatting to Lt Cdr Kenneth Firman who had not been home for six years. When the ship was struck he waited at the boat station for the Wrens to arrive, but he never did get home on leave.

The submarine surfaced and came alongside one of the lifeboats. Aboard was a prisoner, an Italian officer who was also a doctor, and they took him aboard. They then fired a salvo of torpedoes into the ship to finish it off. Freda was two hours later picked up by a rescue ship, HMS *Boreas*, who in all picked up 200 survivors. They were all taken to Freetown. All the Wrens had survived and ten women refugees, but 200 were missing. Freda was so impressed by the gallantry of the naval officers who had stayed behind to the last helping the Italian prisoners to get away. For her own efforts she received a commendation, her conduct was described as exemplary and deserving the highest praise. Some of the passengers in the water were bitten by sharks and barracudas. She succeeded in later becoming a doctor and becoming the head of Public Health in the West Indies and in charge of a hospital in Sydney. After the war she could still see in her mind officers swimming back and for to the rafts checking if people were all right. CPO, later Dr, Bonner died in 1986.

Another Wren on the *Empress of Canada*, Betty Kopson, had sailed around the world before the war aboard the sailing ship '*Viking*'. Pamela Gray was the last to be picked up from a raft and taken to Freetown. Lillie Keeney was on board with her husband, an RN Telegraphic. They both burned their hands on the ropes as they slid into the water. Margaret Hall had gone over the side and down a rope. She found a small float in the water and sat on it until the sun came up the next day. As she sat there a ship's ladder came floating by with a rather rotund officer sat on it, he had a bald head which by now was getting rather sun burned. She took off the white top of her cap and handed it to him. He took it and bound it around his head, then floated away. She later saw him at Freetown. She herself was picked up by a large raft and taken into Freetown. When put in a hospital to recover she asked if she could go for a walk in the grounds of the hospital but was told promptly 'but there are men out there'. She replied, 'But I have just spent two days on a raft alone with four men.

Having taken off 258 hospital patients from the Normandy beaches, SS *Amsterdam* left Juno Beach on 7th August 1944 with orders to return to Southampton. At 7.04am the ship was rocked with two explosions, the result was30 of the crew as well as ten RAMC Staff including two nursing sisters, and 55patients of which 15 were German prisoners of war, were lost. The two sisters were Senior Matron Dorothy Field and Sister Mollie Evershed, their names are today recorded on the Bayeux Memorial as having no known grave. Both were given mention in despatches for brave conduct. They with the crew and RAMC staff were able to get many of the worst cases away. Miss Field was last seen going from deck to deck assisting the wounded and remaining with them until it was too late to save herself and she was not seen again.

The *Centaur* was also a hospital ship, had a red cross on her funnel and her bridge was fully illuminated at all times. On 13th May 1943 she was torpedoed by Japanese submarine 50 miles east of Brisbane. About 200 people were in the water when the ship sank, among the killed were 18 Army doctors, Matron Jewell, and ten nursing sisters of the Australian Army Nursing Service. One sister, Edna Savage, survived when the ship sank in three minutes. She was later awarded the George Medal. The SS *Ceramic* was an 18,000ton ship and bound for Sydney via St Helena when she was sunk on 25th November 1944. On board were 650 men, women and children. All but one man, Sapper A E Munday of the Royal Engineers, were lost. He survived because the U-boat U515 surfaced and picked him up as proof that the ship was carrying troops, and in their eyes a legitimate target. There were 26 nursing sisters from the QANs and three nurses from the TANs on the casualty list. Although many lifeboats got away the sea was very rough and huge waves were breaking over the boats. Many were capsized, and the people thrown into the water. The captain of the U-boat was a Lt Cdr Henke whose submarine was later sunk by a US destroyer and he was taken prisoner. He was later reported as having been killed while trying to escape. Sapper Munday spent the rest of the war in a prisoner of war camp in Germany.

On 5th February 1944, the SS *Khedive Ismail* left Mombasa in convoy KR8. On 12th February the ship was hit by two torpedoes in the area of the Maldive Islands. At the time she was carrying 1,390 troops and 183 crew. The ship sank in 1 hour 40 minutes. The submarine had been Japanese and depth charges forced it to the surface where it was attacked by HMS *Pitard* and later sank. Of the 138 crew, 137 were lost and of the passengers 1,134. Many, when the ship rolled over, were in the water when the lifeboats slid off the deck and fell on top of them; others died when the troop deck and accommodation ladders collapsed. Many of the troops were in the saloon listening to a concert given by the nursing sisters who were aboard. The grand piano slid over the floor and trapped many people against the ship's side. Some 200 survivors were picked up by HMS *Pitard*. In the sinking there were 51 nursing sisters all from 150 General Hospital lost and three officers and 17 other ranks from the Wrens lost.

When the SS *Stenton* was sunk on 27th October 1942, some 200 miles off the Canary Islands four nurses were lost, one from the QANs and three from the TANs.

On 10th July 1943, HM Hospital Ship *Talamba* was sunk three miles off Avola in Sicily. Maud Johnson of the TANs, was the only nursing sister lost. Another hospital ship sunk was the former Western Railway Packet St. David. She was sunk on 24th January 1944, 25 miles south west of Anzio. On this occasion the ship was dive bombed and suffered a direct hit. three nursing sisters were lost.

The SS *Newfoundland* was another converted hospital ship on its way to Bizerta and Salerno with a crew and medical staff aboard, but only two patients. Six nursing sisters and five RAMC doctors were lost on 8th September 1943, the hit on the ship was below the bridge and funnel, it was felt all the missing people must have been killed outright by the bomb. The six missing sisters are today recorded on the Cassino Memorial. Sister Kathleen Neilson was saved by Sister Pat Jenkins who pulled her clear of her burning bunk. The US nurses aboard were unhurt.

The SS *Avila Star* was torpedoed on 5th July 1942, at the time she was heading for the UK from Freetown. She had a refrigerated cargo. There were 30 passengers of which three were from the previously torpedoed SS *Lyle Park*. With the crew the ship's complement was 196 of which 84 were lost and three died later in a lifeboat. The ship, which had left Freetown on 28th June, was hit by two torpedoes. One passenger, Marie Elizabeth Ferguson, aged 18 or 19, was in number seven lifeboat. She spent the night helping those who had been injured, one with a broken leg, another with broken ribs, two of the four that she looked after later died. When a motor boat turned up at sunrise she dived overboard and swam to it, she was covered in engine oil from head to foot. She was later transferred to number two lifeboat. At the time Marie was on her way to the UK to join the WRNS and, in all, she spent 20 days in the lifeboat. During that time eleven of the 27 men died. When she arrived home in the UK her first question was 'Have I been accepted?' She had been. Although named Marie she was known as 'Johnnie' and on 24th November was awarded the British Empire Medal and the coveted Lloyds Medal for Bravery at Sea. When she joined the WRNS, she had two medal ribbons to sew on before she had even donned her uniform.

The SS *Strathallen* was bound for Algiers from Clyde when on 21st December1942 she was struck by a torpedo. On board at the time was a crew of 466, over 5,000 officers and 4,000 other ranks plus 248 nurses. The ship's boats were launched but with the sea calm there was still a danger of further attack. The ship was hit at 10.25pm on the 21st but was still afloat at 4am when HMS *Laforey* came alongside to take her in tow. At 10.20am 1,200 troops were taken off the ship, and at 1115am a further 1,179 were taken off. The ship finally sank on the 22nd but not before 4,600 of the troops and 420 of the crew had been rescued. Sister Janet Davidson was killed and later buried in Oran, Algeria and another four sisters lost are remembered on the Brookwood Memorial as having no known grave.

Out of the 188 Queen Alexander Nursing sisters, and nurses killed or died, 110 were lost at sea, of which 83 are remembered on the Brookwood Memorial. And in the TANs, 33 were killed of which 16 were at sea.

In 1940, the Government sponsored a scheme to send a limited number of children, many in the areas liable to be attacked in air raids and who could not afford the fares, to the USA, Canada, Australia, New Zealand, and South Africa. The Children's Overseas Reception Board (CORB) was founded under the chairmanship of Mr. Geoffrey Shakespeare MP. The task of the Board was to select children and when selected to organise their passage overseas and to arrange for their care and education. At the end of the war, it had to arrange for their return. Over 100,000 names were submitted. As no parent or guardians could accompany them, escorts were arranged on the ratio of 15 children per escort. A nationwide appeal was put out for escorts and as with the children submissions were far greater than required. When the big raids started in London on 7th September 1940, ten escorts were sent on the 9th to Liverpool to prepare for a voyage to Canada.

Among the ten were seven women, Dr Beth Zeal who specialised in medical care for children, Sybil Gilliat Smith an artist, Nurse Smith, Mrs. Lillian Towns aged 30 from New Zealand, an LCC Infants Schoolteacher and an ARP Ambulance Driver. She had been a replacement taken on at the last moment. The senior escort was Miss Marjorie Day aged 53, who was house mistress at Wycombe Abbey women School. Mrs. Hillman was also a teacher, and lastly Mary Cornish aged 41, a music teacher whose address was Baker Street, London.

On 30th August 1940, the SS *Vollendam* had been sunk. On board were 321 children, all of whom were picked up within a few hours of taking to the boats. On 13th September 1940, the ten escorts and 90 CORB children set sail on the 11,000-ton *City of Benares*. The youngest children were five and the oldest fifteen. On 17th, at about 10pm, a torpedo struck the ship on the port side, below where the children were sleeping. At the time Mary Cornish was on her way back to the children when suddenly everything was plunged into darkness and her way was blocked by debris. The hole in the centre of the ship was by now filling up with water rapidly. On the other side of the debris was Lillian Towns and the children who had not been killed by the explosion. Mary began to pull them through a gap in the debris and get them up on to the deck. The boat she was ordered into had several small boys and some Lascar seamen who had formed part of the crew. The nearest ship to the *Benares* at the time was the SS *Marion*, this was also torpedoed and sunk. The five-day journey out from Liverpool had been rough with a heavy swell and a wind of 60 to 70 miles an hour. It was also raining. Many of the boats were overcrowded and people were hanging on to the floats on the sides of the boats. One escort hung on all night with three children before being picked up. The destroyer HMS *Hurricane* arrived at 11.15pm on 18th, by now only a handful of survivors were in each boat. The last survivors were picked up at 6.40pm. In this boat were Lillian Day and Marjorie Towns. The *Hurricane* landed eighteen women, thirteen children, 46 men and 36 Lascars. Of the thirteen children only seven were from the original 90CORB children. The only other surviving escort was Mary Cornish. It was 4.30pm on 23rd, when HMS *Anthony*, also a destroyer, was seen coming towards the boat she was in. They had travelled 200 miles but were still 400 miles from landfall. They were landed on 26th. For her bravery and efforts in the boat, Mary was awarded the BEM, which was gazetted on 7th January 1941. The seven children that survived were: Rex Therne aged 13, Jack Keeley aged 8, John Baker aged 7, Louise Walder aged ten and his sister Bessie aged 15, Eleanor Wright aged thirteen and Elizabeth Cummings aged 14. Five of the children were from London, one from Sunderland and one from Liverpool. On 2nd October 1940, the scheme was scrapped.

On 13th October, Princess Elizabeth, now Queen Elizabeth, and her sister Princess Margaret, broadcast to all children of the Empire and overseas. It was particularly intended for children who had been evacuated overseas to Canada and the USA.

On the SS *Talabot*, the stewardess and only woman on board, Margaret Johnson, was awarded the British Empire Medal. The ship, in convoy with two other ships, attempted the dangerous passage from Alexandria to Malta in March 1942, to bring relief to the garrison. Two reached the island including the *Talabot* but were bombed while discharging cargo in Valetta. The third ship was sunk in an air attack. Overall in the convoy 42 ships were sunk trying to bring relief to the besieged island. Included in the many that lost their lives, there were some particularly worthy of mention. Emi Hothorne was in the WVS and was killed on 3rd November 1943, by a shell fired from across the Channel in France which hit her house in Ramsgate, her mother was also killed. Marjorie Brookham, also in the WVS, was killed by falling masonry on 11th September 1940, while directing a rescue worker. Another WVS woman was killed on 9th December 1940, when the YMCA canteen she was driving fell over the quay and into Bristol Docks.

Sister Ellen Davidson from New Zealand died on Christmas Day 1939. At the time she was at Le Treport in France with No 56 General Hospital. She contacted pneumonia after a bout of flu and in freezing conditions. She had left for France on 11th November 1939. Marjorie was buried at Le Tre Port on 27th December 1939.

In Algiers on 23rd October 1943, Sister Gertrude Toon of No 96 General Hospital was killed in a motor accident and buried on 25th at El Alia.

In the ATS, 950 women were killed by direct enemy attack or in accidents. In the WRNS 329 officers and ratings are recorded on the book of remembrance at the Royal Naval College, Greenwich. In the WAAF 724 women made the supreme sacrifice, the ATA 17 and VAD two, making a total of 2,229. The 3,076 military and civilian nurses lost in the war are recorded on a Roll of Honour in the Nurses' Chapel at Westminster Abbey.

Many of these women or young women were only in their teens or early twenties when they lost their lives. A considerable number were far from home at the time and now lie alongside the men whom with whom they ably and willingly served. When men are remembered in the years to come, let us also remember these gallant women.

Above: WAAF Christian Cox, Nurse Brown and Wren Kathleen Wainwright at Roehampton, 1943 (Mrs. K. Williams). Below: Kathleen Wainwright, below left with Nurse Jordan at Cary House, Skegness, on 7th June 1942 and, below right, at HMS Arthur in 1942 (K. Wainwright).

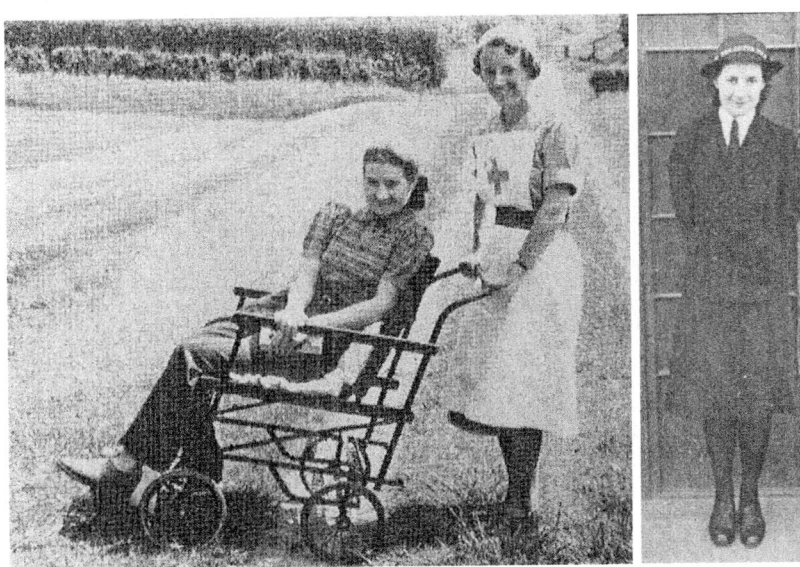

Above: The Mostyn Hotel, Eastbourne (Michael Ockenden). Below: The ceremony to mark the unveiling a seat near Scarborough lighthouse, in commemoration of the loss of twelve Scarborough-based members of the WRNS when the SS Aguila was torpedoed en route to Gibraltar on 19th August 1941. The ceremony was on the thirtieth anniversary of the sinking (Author).

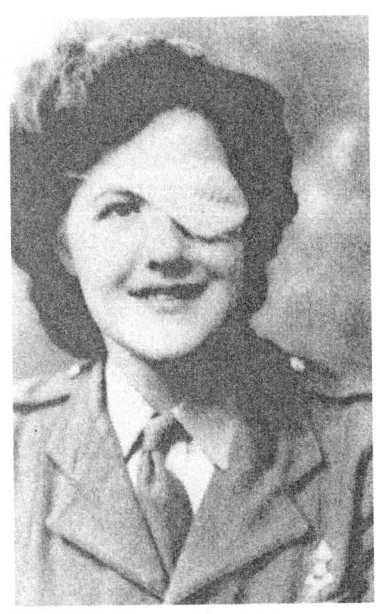

Above left: Pat Tibbenham (P.Tibbenham). Above right: Yvonne Capon, HMS Arthur, 1942. Left: Section Officer Joan Easton's grave. Below left: A ride round the walls of Jerusalem. Below: ACW MH Hudson's grave (Author).

Above: A beautiful memorial in Upavon Village Cemetery, inscribed: 'In gratitude for the work of British women in two world wars'. The inscription around the base reads: 'A Maiden Knight, To me is given such hope. I know not fear. I am the door'. In the same cemetery is the grave of Squadron Leader AP Cranswick, 35 Sqn., Bomber Command, who completed over 100 ops before being posted missing in July 1944 (Norman Ling).

Chapter 15 They Were Also There

Isabel McGraghan who had formed the Women's Home Guard in Newport bought a house in Newport for £200, it had fourteen layers of wall paper on the walls and the ceiling was coming down when they moved in. After getting off all the old paper from the walls, the only thing left to repaper the walls with, was newspaper. Most of their vegetables were grown in the back garden, parcels were received from a relative in Canada, sweets were home made from syrup and dried milk with a dash of peppermint and formed into a ball. It was a terrible time but for those who survived, it was a remarkable time of unity and mutual support.

Olive Rutherford was a projectionist, another job giving great service as many of the cinemas would have had to close without people to operate the projectors. Sitting in the projection box during the bombing outside is something she will never forget.

Edith Rowbotham in 1939, had her husband called up for service with the army, at the time she had a six-month-old baby. She took in as lodgers a couple who were working in Ford's factory at Trafford Park, and ended the war with three women from Newcastle who were also working at the factory.

Margie Ebbutt began working as a secretary with the BBC in April 1939. She had tried to join the WRNS but at the time they were only recruiting in naval areas of the UK. When the London Blitz began they went to the basement of Sleaford House which was the block of flats they were staying in. There they had camp beds and slept fully clothed in trousers and jerseys under eiderdowns, there was no such thing as duvets in those days. A large open fire was kept going by the caretaker. They played chess, and one of the women became the ladies champion of England. They also knitted for the forces. When they went to the toilet they wore their tin hats because the roof of the toilet was open to the elements. On one occasion when Margie forgot to wear her helmet a piece of steel casing came down and fell about a foot away from her. She remembered reading in the 'Punch' magazine one day, a joke a man was saying goodbye to his hostess 'Well, I must go, or I'll be caught in the street by the 'All Clear' and then the buses will be full! She joined the BBC Auxiliary Fire Service manning the pumps and fire watching on the roof. There was also a BBC Home Guard commandeered by the editor of the Radio Times. The BBC's instruction in those days probably in view at one time the UK would be invaded was 'The last stand will be made in the control room'. She learned to shoot in the BBC Rifle Club which was in Marylebone Road, and to take a Sten gun to pieces and reassemble it again. However, when the word got about that they were learning to shoot and use arms it was quickly stopped. She moved to an intelligence unit and spent most of her time on the roof of Broadcasting House taking bearings with a pair of field glasses.

Her next stop was the ground floor of number 200 Oxford Street. This was the home of the Overseas programmes during the war. Margie would often travel on the underground after midnight from Oxford Circus and then walk home to her flat in Regents Park. It was this area that many RAF aircrew were under training. When Italy surrendered in 1943, and she got the news flash, she went tearing down the stairs to the studio where Jean Metcalfe was waiting to broadcast. Jean, calmly put the mike key down and broadcast the news to the world.

When war broke out in September 1939, Gisele Delbourgo was in Cairo, Egypt, with her parents and four sisters. The British Headquarters of the Allied Forces was being set up. In 1940 recruitment for civilian personnel became intense and she applied for a job. As a Free French subject her application was considered and then accepted. She was given a job in the Salvage Department of the Royal Ordnance her job consisted of typing figures all day, and every day. In her spare time, she practiced typing and learning English. As this improved so did her position and she was moved to the main building of the headquarters and given the task of typing highly confidential material. She finally went to Aden to be with her fiancé to be married. He was working in the Royal Navy as a sort of customs officer stopping Arab boats as they entered the harbour in Aden. She was flown to Aden by the RAF in a Dakota it had two bench seats and a curtain between the crew and passengers. Her companions were four generals and their aides. On 24th September 1942, she was married.

Evacuees (Mrs A Keen).

On 10th May 1940, Eliene d'Ildekem d'Acoz was living in Belgium and awoke to the sounds of German Stuka aircraft attacking. Her husband was an officer in the Belgium army and somewhere in the Antwerp area at the time. She was alone, except for a child's nurse, and her two children. She dreaded the thought of living under German as occupation which she had sampled in WWI as a child. She decided to make for the coast and so with the children and nurse paid for a ride on an open lorry. The destination was La Panne.

When they arrived, she bought a contraption which had four wheels and four seats. And so, they set off pedalling towards the French coast. At one point she was turned back by the French police but found a gap in the sand dunes at La Panne and entered France. A lorry hit their bike and tore a wheel off but eventually stopped and gave them a lift but only a few miles when they had to get off. They were at the side of the road when along came a British ambulance which stopped to ask them the way to Dunkirk, she suggested that she became his guide in exchange for a lift for the four of them. When they reached the camp to which the ambulance belonged they had to get out as no civilians were allowed in. They went to the shelters in which were British and French soldiers.

Eliene approached the commanding officer in charge of embarking the troops on the ships and told him she had English relations in the UK, her husband had married an English woman whose father had been the Lord Mayor of London. He seemed happy that she was not a spy and gave her a permit to embark. She, the nurse and two children embarked on a destroyer HMS *Wild Swan* who delivered them to Dover. On landing, the authorities did not know what to do with them so put them in a local police station and a nice clean cell. As soon as her relatives were contacted she was released and got on a train for London, or trains as she changed no fewer than seven times before arriving in London. Here she stayed with her in-laws for a while but not wishing to be a burden to them she decided to look for a job, at first sewing which was the only thing she could do.

The family lived in a house in North London and the smaller boy went to a convent to be taught by nuns and the older one to a boy's school. Later the children were evacuated to the Lake District, she soon followed them and stayed a while in Carlisle before deciding to join one of the services, however, the WRNS were only recruiting in naval areas and the WAAF could only offer positions as balloon operators. So Eliene applied and joined the ATS becoming known as Pte d'Acoz. After her initial training she became a mechanic/driver, driving all manner of vehicles. She became a staff car driver in Glasgow. On her upper arm she could wear flashes with 'Telguiem' on them, and, having passed her mechanics course a trade badge which was a wheel.

From Glasgow she was posted to Edinburgh and then south to West Wickham near RAF Biggin Hill. On one occasion when it was her night off she decided to wash her hair, put it in curlers and then settle down with a book for the evening. Suddenly, the door opened, and a voice called her telling her to 'hurry up' as she was wanted to replace a woman who had been taken ill. She put on her slacks, which only staff car drivers could wear, and only then in the evenings, her battledress jacket and shoved the curlers under her tin helmet. An officer was waiting for her and off they drove to his appointment. The return was very late, and the officer asked her in for a drink, at first, she refused when he asked why, and she showed him the curlers under her helmet, they both laughed, and she then accepted his offer of a night cap.

Shortly after the war and having been discharged from the ATS she worked for a time at the Belgium Embassy, which was in Canterbury at the time. On one occasion she travelled back with the diplomatic bag to the continent and met her husband. After the war she went with her husband and family to South Africa. Her sons are now married, and she has seven grandchildren and one great grandchild. One of many memories she has of her time in the ATS was when driving the head of the ATS, who always had a plaid travelling rug over her knees and when she sat in the front with Eliene insisted that she share the rug with her, not practical when driving. On another occasion when she had run over a man's foot while driving around a shipping yard. When she signalled her unit about the accident the only thing they asked her was the car okay.

On 9ᵗʰ April 1942, the Women's Auxiliary Corps (India) was formed. Their duties were much the same as the ATS clerks, cyphers, typists, drivers, and stenographers. They came under the same ruling as British servicemen and women.

Laura de Silva, aged 20, and born in Singapore enlisted at Bareilly on 15th June 1943, having got out of Singapore when it fell in 1942. She became a stenographer in the Garrison Engineers office. When this moved to Burma her future looked in doubt that is until she got an interview at HQ Bareilly. She was asked if she did shorthand when she said she did she got the job. She was told to report to the tailors and get three stripes sewn on her sleeve, it appeared that when you worked at HQ you became a sergeant. After taking a speed test in shorthand and typing she was promoted to staff sergeant. There were many frustrating times on one occasion she had gone on leave to Kashmir hundreds of miles away when upon arrival she was immediately ordered back because someone could not find a file. And time and time again called away from dances and social events for the call of duty.

In August 1945, came the Victory parade which took place around the town in Bareilly led by the pipes and drums of the Iv Regiment. When she arrived back in Singapore her home had been looted and her father had died through lack of medical treatment. By July 1945, the strength of the WAC (India) had risen to 1,178 officers and 10,288 other ranks. The uniform was like the ATS but in khaki drill women who wore their saris were not permitted to wear a cap but did wear for parades and other outdoor purposes a uniform jacket over the sari. There was an equivalent WRNS (India) and they had a privilege which was perhaps unknown to women serving in other theatres this was to have a ration of alcoholic drinks which could be acquired to reach respective mess as and when required.

The Women's Legion was formed in December 1914. When WWII started in September 1939, among its members in the Women's Legion Air Section were Miss Pauline Gower and Amy Johnson, both later to serve in the ATA. The President, Lady Londonderry, in the best interests of the nation advised the younger members of the Legion to join one of the armed services. This however meant the Legion being drained of its resources and at one time it looked as if it would not be able to continue in its original form. However, it was found to be an admiral outlet for older women at first on a part-time basis but as it progressed both part and full-time members had been enrolled and it once again built itself up to strength. The owner driver section of the Legion was important in that it assisted the WVS in the first big evacuation of mothers and children. They also assisted the Ministry of Food and Eastern Command welfare officers.

The mobile canteen service was their main function during the blitz of 1940/41 when they fed hundreds of bombed out persons and the NFS where their own catering service had not gone under way and it was the mobile canteen of the WI which brought the much-needed food and drink. On one occasion tea was carried up eight stories to tired firemen who had been working all night to quell the flames. By this time, it was 11 o'clock in the morning the firemen's lips were swollen and blistered and their hands sore so much so that they could not even hold the cups and hardly swallow. The Women's Legion held the cups for them to drink and stayed with them until it became too dangerous when the fire could not be kept under control. Shortly after the mobile canteen had left, the whole place collapsed.

On 15th September 1940, and during the Battle of Britain the Acting Commandant Mrs. Noel, her second in command and two senior officers were killed 'while on duty' when Bermondsey Town Hall was bombed. Shelter feeding was first introduced by the Women's Legion. During the Blitz and on their way to feed the NFS the canteen was forced to take cover in a shelter. Here they found many welcome customers and as they did not think they could go on any further began to distribute tea and food. The tea was in large urns and the experience became known as the Miracle of the Urns. The supplies they carried were sufficient for 150 people, but the urns did not run dry until 300 people in the shelter had been given a cup of tea. The pay was ten shillings a day for full and part-time workers. The ranks very similar to the ATS.

UNITED KINGDOM WOMENS' SERVICES
1939-1945 WAR CASUALTIES

The memorial in Whitehall, London, to all the women who helped the cause of freedom in the Second World War, 1939 -45 (Author).

Auxiliary Territorial Service	950
Queen Alexandria's Imperial Military Nursing Service	203
Territorial Army Nursing Service	33
Women's Transport Service (FANY)	19
Women's Royal Naval Service	329
Queen Alexandria's Royal Naval Nursing Service	9
Women's' Auxiliary Air Force	724
Air Transport Auxiliary	17
Volunteer Aid Detachment	2
Princess Mary's Royal Air Force Nursing Service	7
Total	2,293

OUR ADIEU

Never have women been given a chance to take their stand besides men in the costly excitement of war; and few even in this generation have been partners in as noble a tradition as that of five Group.

We have been proud to have had our small share in the achievements that have made the name of this Group famous.

As we go, either direct to civilian life or to live out the rest of our service career with other formations, we shall still feel that we have a little of the glory reflected from that great name.

A TRIBUTE

Compiled with much sentiment and more difficulty by
P Prune PIO, A. Binde, Sgt; And S. Plonk, A.C.

The War is over gentlemen,
And, let it now be said,
Of all the Wars that ever were
Where Hun and Briton bled,
This is the only one of all
Where, thronging to their country's call,
Come not alone her boys, but all
Here single women — and wed.
They've plotted us across the deep,
And dosed us up (M And B):
They've called us from our morning sleep
And called us on R/T.
They've posted us to Burma's sun,
They've driven many a ration's run,
And even when the rations' done
They've wangled cups of tea.
They've paid such credits as we've had,
They've greased our wagon wheels,
They've cooked our bomb plots (if too bad),
And cooked our countless meals:
They've given us the weather gen
They've got us calls to Fu Chow Chen
And often (Oh, you helpless men),
They've darned our gaping heels.
So sing ye, all ye warriors,
How dull this ward has been
Without her flowers about the place,
Without her stitching bits of lace,
Without her nicely made up face,
The W.A.A.F. The Air Force Queen!

Printed in Great Britain
by Amazon